SERENGETI SHALL NOT DIE
Bernhard and Michael Grzimek
With an Introduction by
Alan Moorehead
Translated from the German by
E.L. and D. Rewald

BALLANTINE BOOKS • NEW YORK

BALLANTINE BOOKS, INC.
201 East 50th Street, New York, N.Y. 10022

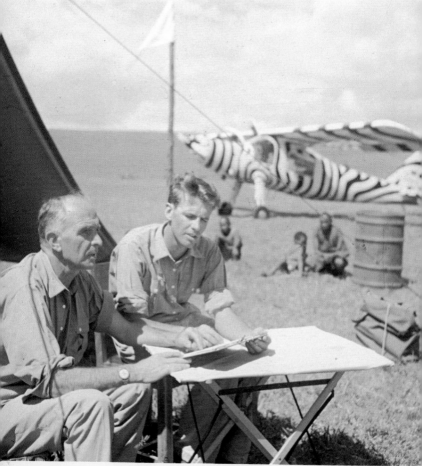

Bernhard and Michael Grzimek at their camp in the Serengeti plains.

Dedicated to the children of
Michael Grzimek
Stephan Michael *and* Christian Bernhard

For that which befalleth the sons of men befalleth beasts; even one thing befalleth them: as the one dieth, so dieth the other; yes, they have all one breath; so that a man hath no pre-eminence above a beast: for all is vanity.

All go unto one place; all are of the dust, and all turn to dust again.

Who knoweth the spirit of man that goeth upward, and the spirit of the beast that goeth downward to the earth?

ECCLESIASTES III, 19–21

Layout of illustrations by Frank Curcio. Drawings of grasses by Mrs. D. Napper, East African Herbarium, Nairobi.

The author's photographs were taken with a *Praktisix* 6 x 6 cm. camera, on *Ektachrome* color film and *Adox R* 25 film with the help of a *Sixtomat* exposure meter and on occasions a *Braun* "Hobby" flashgun.

The following photographs are not by B. Grzimek: p. 42—*East African Standard;* p. 124—W. Petana, Kaduna, Nigeria; pp. 178 and 202—A. Root; p. 189— Dr. P. D. Swanepoel, Barberton, Transvaal.

Contents

Michael Grzimek

Preface

"A school outing can be marvellous, but having to write an essay about it afterwards can ruin it in retrospect. Now my father demands that I should describe personally how I brought animals from Central Africa to the Frankfurt Zoo. . . ." That is how my son began the last chapter in my book, *Dr. Grzimek, I Presume?*[*] In this chapter he tells how I had to leave him, a sixteen-year-old lad, with only a native boy for company, in the interior of the Ivory Coast among people speaking a strange language, and how he brought the many animals to Hamburg on a tiny French cargo boat.

Michael is the co-author of this book, a project we discussed during his last days. He did not live to write one sentence of it— but he helped to create the contents of this book, which is the most important thing, in fact he created the major portion. That is why both our names are on the title page.

We both hope that the book will help to save and protect the things for which we worked so hard.

I wish that all fathers could have such a son, a son who is their comrade and friend and who understands them—even though it be for only a few years.

Bernhard Grzimek

Honorary trustee of Tanganyika National Parks,
Professor at the University of Giessen, Honorary
Game Warden of Tanganyika, Director of the
Zoological Gardens of Frankfurt.

[*] London, 1955

Serengeti National Park

Introduction

I REMEMBER years ago having a conversation with Sir Osbert Sitwell in Italy, and in the course of it I mentioned that I was considering a journey to the temples of Angkor-Wat in Indo-China but was finding some difficulty in making up my mind; for one thing the expense of the trip was very great. Sir Osbert made the lapidary remark, "Anyone who *can* go to Angkor-Wat and does not is mad." I went. I was captivated.

My feelings about the Serengeti Reserve in Tanganyika are somewhat similar to Sir Osbert's about Angkor-Wat. If you have the money to spare go there, and do not delay too long, for this spectacle may not be as enduring as stone temples. From year to year the threat of extermination hangs over these wild animals, and it is very unlikely that our children will ever see them as we can see them now — the vast procession of zebras, gazelles and wildebeest moving across the open plains, the lions lying like cats in the sun with hyenas and jackals circling nervously about them, the vultures hovering in the immense sky and the blue hills in the distance. The Serengeti is the home of nearly all the best-known African species, from the very large animals like elephant, rhinoceros and giraffe to the tiny mongoose and the tortoise. But year by year the numbers of the herds grow less as the poachers and tribesmen attack them and make inroads upon their waterholes and grazing grounds. The Serengeti is supposed to be a reserve where no wild animals can be killed, but there is insufficient money to police it properly, and the demand for the land for agricultural purposes is steadily increasing everywhere in Africa.

One can argue that the tourist trade attracted to Tanganyika by the Serengeti produces much more money than the land itself could ever yield.   One can protest that there is a moral duty to preserve this last of the great natural congregations of wild animals left in existence.   One can point out that once these beasts are killed they can never be replaced; already mankind has exterminated for ever over a hundred different species of birds and beasts throughout the world.

But none of this seems to make any difference.   The African authorities, both black and white, are decided that the interests of human beings are paramount, and that wherever human beings are in conflict with wild life it is the wild life that must go.

There is just one gleam of hope in this dismal story.   All over the world, and indeed in Africa itself, there exist small groups of men, naturalists, zoologists and others, who are determined to make one final outcry before the Serengeti is irrevocably lost.   If they can raise sufficient money for the proper policing of the reserve, for the digging of waterholes and other vital works, there is still a chance that they can persuade the political authorities to take action.   In order to do this they must first arouse not only the interest but the conscience of those of us who are not as yet absolutely committed to the idea that human beings are the only living creatures who have rights upon this earth.   They must also have the power of evoking and of communicating something of the great beauty and the excitement of the Serengeti plains themselves, so that we will wish to preserve them as an aesthetic object for the generations that lie ahead.

Foremost among these men, these crusaders for the dying wild life of the world, must be placed Dr. Grzimek, the author of this book.   Dr. Grzimek is no hidden persuader: he is an avowed and passionate believer in the cause.   To rescue these wild animals from extinction he and his son Michael were obliged to give up everything they had: their savings, their homes and families, and finally, in the case of the son, life itself.   Michael Grzimek's accidental death in Africa was the kind of tragedy that leaves its own eloquent epitaph behind.

Never for an instant in the pages of this book will you doubt the sincerity or the courage of these two men; and those who are apt to dismiss such extreme enthusiasms as fanatical and to treat the whole problem as hardly serious would do well to read here Dr. Grzimek's simple and dignified statement of his faith.

"Men," he says, "have other ideals for which they are willing to die: freedom, glory, politics, religion, the rulership of their class or the expansion of national borders. But in the long run Michael and I will be proved right.

"Millions feared Hitler and millions were enthralled by him. Millions laid down their lives for him and other millions died fighting against him. To-day when German school children are asked questions about Hitler most of them know very little about him and cannot even name his henchmen. . . . Men are easily inspired by human ideas, but they forget them just as quickly. Only Nature is eternal, unless we senselessly destroy it. In fifty years' time nobody will be interested in the results of the conferences which fill to-day's headlines.

"But when fifty years from now a lion walks into the red dawn and roars resoundingly, it will mean something to people and quicken their hearts whether they are bolsheviks or democrats, or whether they speak English, German, Russian or Swahili. They will stand in quiet awe as, for the first time in their lives, they watch twenty thousand zebras wander across the endless plains.

"Is it really so stupid to work for the zebras, lions and men who will walk the earth fifty years from now? And for those in a hundred or two hundred years' time?"

Had Dr. Grzimek nothing more to contribute than these emotions he might indeed have been dismissed by some people as another wild-life crank. But he is very far from being that. As Director of the Frankfurt Zoo he is a scholar and a naturalist of distinction, and both he and his son went about their self-appointed task in an extremely practical way. They saw that if the Serengeti Reserve was to be saved the first thing to do was to know it properly—to take, as it were, an inventory of the country and the animals in it. The land was imperfectly mapped, no adequate study had ever been made of the soil, the vegetation or the climate. It was generally thought that there were about a million animals in the reserve but nobody had ever counted them. More important still, no one could say with any finality just what their migratory habits were: just why they moved off in certain directions at certain times of the year, or how far they went, or where.

There was only one way to seek an answer to these questions: that was to fly over the reserve at low altitudes and study every detail of the ground. The Grzimeks bought a 'plane and learned to fly. Then with a mass of cameras and scientific equipment they crossed the Mediterranean and flew down to Tanganyika in Central Africa. This book is the story of their adventures and of the successful accomplishment of their mission.

It is very far from being a heavy and solemn tract; one glance at the pictures and ten minutes' perusal of the text will amply re-assure the reader on that score. Dr. Grzimek has the gift of trans-mitting his own enthusiasm as well as his knowledge, and his stories of the animals are every bit as lively and as moving as his photographs. He is a professional who works with the inspiration of an amateur.

English readers will be struck by the fact that the Grzimeks could never have been anything but Germans. They were extremely foolhardy in a tough, boyish and sentimental kind of way, and yet at the same time what other men in the world could have been so painstaking, so practical, so absolutely thorough? The thousands of little packets of soil and plants sent back to Germany for analysis, the precise criss-crossing of the ground that went on until every yard was photographed from the air and every head of game was counted, the improvisations, the dangerous experiments, the careful notetaking, the endless checking of repetitive facts and figures—who but a German could throw himself into this work with such untiring gusto?

But in the end they got it all down, and their splendid record of the reserve contains at least one major discovery about the numbers and the migratory habits of the animals. It is a remarkable achievement. The struggle to save the Serengeti makes a great bound forward with this book.

ALAN   MOOREHEAD

SERENGETI SHALL NOT DIE

CHAPTER 1

Preparations

Have the hens been fed?
BISMARCK, on his deathbed

It was the 11th December 1957, a dull morning, and I was sitting in our single-motored aeroplane flying up the Rhine towards Switzerland. The yellow tips of the propeller painted a faint, transparent circle over the grey-green landscape in front of the curved wind-screen. The famous mountain road below us glided past at 120 m.p.h. It looked empty, cold and miserable.

My son Michael and I each had a joy-stick between our knees. A slight pressure on the knob dipped the right wing downwards, the earth curved towards us and we slipped a little closer to the Rhine. As long as we followed the river we could not lose our way, so that we had time to think about other things.

I felt a trifle anxious, for this was the beginning of a 6,000 mile journey across the Mediterranean, the desert, Egypt, Central Africa and right across the equator.

I was forty-eight years old, had never been particularly venturesome and had no interest in any sport but riding. It seemed incredible to me that I should be co-pilot in a little aeroplane on its way to Lake Victoria.

I married when I was only twenty-one, and now my sons had grown up. Michael, sitting next to me wearing a sheepskin jacket, was twenty-three. He was not only my son, but my only real friend.

Even when he was a little boy he helped me with my experiments on wolves and dogs. Later on he soon surpassed me in animal photography and graduated to a cine-camera. At seventeen his documentary film got an "honourable mention" and after that he was determined to make a colour film of my book, *No Room for Wild Animals.**

Books, even best-sellers, are only read by a few thousand, and at best by a hundred thousand people. We wanted to impress millions in Europe and America with the fact that lions, elephants, rhinoceroses and giraffes are steadily dying out, and that their refuges—the National Parks—are constantly growing smaller. The only way to get in touch with millions of people is by films, television or the illustrated weekly papers.

A government agency guaranteed half the expenses of the film. On our return from Africa we learned to our horror that Walt Disney, a great artist and a very rich man, had made a film about Africa, *The African Lion,* which was to be shown at the same time. The first distributing agency we went to refused to handle our film. Finally Michael had to write cheques for about £ 50,000 to have it edited, copied in colour and provided with a sound track.

The film experts complained that our wild animals were too peaceful. Previous African films had accustomed them to constant shots of predators killing their prey, giant snakes squashing men and charging elephants being shot in the nick of time. As scientists we could only show how these animals lived in reality, not how they are supposed to behave in order to titillate the public palate. With sinking hearts we sent our film to the Berlin Festival.

No Room for Wild Animals was shown on the last day of the festival. We had invited the press to a breakfast in the Berlin Zoo, but at exactly ten o'clock there was a cloudburst and nobody ventured as far as the restaurant. We were left sitting beside a pile of sandwiches.

During the premiere of the film we felt like schoolboys on speech-day, waiting for the prize-giving. When three giraffes moved as silhouettes across the red evening sky there was spontaneous applause in the middle of the film. Michael gripped my knee. Finally he stood in the spotlight in his best suit; he hardly

*London 1956, New York 1957.

knew how to bow to the audience or even what to do with the bouquets of lilacs pressed into his arms.

In a haze we walked into the hall where the prizes were to be distributed. The auditorium was already half empty. The journalists were angry because they had been kept waiting. The film won one "gold bear" for getting the most public votes, another "gold bear" from the jury of international experts, and a prize from the government.

Everything to do with it went extremely well. In one cinema in Munich the film ran for twelve weeks. It was shown in sixty-three countries, including Eastern Europe, China and Japan. The South African censor wanted to cut it, but the press protested and the Minister of the Interior decided it should not be shortened by a single foot.

We felt that all the millions of people who were paying for their tickets wanted to help the wild animals with their price of admission. Our film protests against the British Government in Tanganyika's* proposed decision to cut by one-third the area of the Serengeti National Park, one of the last places thickly populated with wild animals. Michael offered that part of the revenues of the film which was given to us as producers, to the British Administration in order to buy land and incorporate it in the game preserve. Colonel Peter Molloy, director of the Tanganyika National Parks, came to Frankfurt and suggested that we should use the money for a much more important purpose.

The plains of Serengeti are said to harbour more than a million large animals, and these are constantly roaming in large herds. Sometimes there is one wildebeest (gnu) beside the other as far as the eye can see; at others the same area is completely devoid of animals for months on end. There are many hypotheses about this migration, and the proposed new borders of the park are based on some of these theories. Up to now nobody has found how to follow the wandering animals. During the rainy season one often cannot drive even a station wagon over the few existing "roads," let alone across swamped plains, mountains and ravines. The government has no funds to spare for such research — but what government on

* Tanganyika is now joined with Zanzibar as 'Tanzania'.

earth ever had money to spare for lions, giraffes, zebras and wilde-beest?

As we talked over this problem, we were lying on the balcony of our house, with our legs up on the railing, when Michael ex-claimed suddenly, "We'll have to learn to fly." I was thunder-struck, but had to admit that he was right; over ten years earlier he had forced me to learn to drive in just the same way. We had to fight with our wives for weeks, but finally, one fine Sunday morn-ing, I stood on the civil aerodrome at Engelsbach, outside Frank-furt. The runway consisted of a green meadow, not particularly level and without even a fence around it. The tiny pub at the periphery had dozens of ties dangling from the ceiling in the bar, for every pupil's tie is cut off after his first solo.

I had expected to be taught in an indoor trainer, but before I could blink my eyes I was sitting in a small Piper Cub in front of the instructor, while we rose gently into the air. A Piper Cub looks as if it came from Woolworth's, all thin struts and canvas. On the other hand it has delightfully few levers, dials and instruments, so it is harder to make mistakes.

Flying itself is childishly easy, one hardly has to learn it, but taking off is difficult and landing even more so. It took me nearly twice as many hours as Michael to satisfy the official examiner that I could fly the prescribed curves and land the plane at exactly the indicated spot with the motor cut.

Then there is one's first flight away from the aerodrome, where the hangars, houses and woods are so familiar. One feels certain that one will lose the way, like a fledgling first leaving its nest. As all villages and roads looked alike I clung to the autobahn along which one can feel one's way home. While landing on the high plateau at Koblenz the wind gripped the machine and I found my-self on the runway with the nose pointing the wrong way. A few days later I had to stay for 30 minutes at exactly 10,000 feet. I had to look out for commercial air-liners on their way to and from Frankfurt aerodrome. The sealed instrument behind me kept a constant watch on my altitude.

It is really not difficult to fly a Piper Cub, but the theory is another matter.

I sat in the examination room in Darmstadt from 8 a.m. to 6 p.m., ten feet away from other students to avoid cheating, and answered questions. Four weeks ago I had not even known the minor mountain ranges in Germany; now I could give the height of their main peaks. I had to fill in the names of all towns, rivers, canals and mountains on a large, unlabelled map. I had even learned the tributaries of obscure East Prussian rivers because one of the examiners came from that region. Armed with compasses, ruler and squared paper, I could calculate how long it would take me, theoretically, to fly from Frankfurt to Hamburg assuming a 63° North-east diagonal headwind, and how much petrol I would need to get there. I knew who has to give way to whom should I encounter a balloon, a glider, another aeroplane or a dirigible. I could explain the terms *local misdirection, drift indicator, vector triangle, deviation,* and *inclination,* and knew the length of a sea mile and a knot. I carried the cross-section of the motor and the carburetter in my head. I had learned to read rate-of-climb indicators as well as turn-and-bank indicators, altimeters and cylinder temperatures. I knew the names of all types of clouds and aerodrome signals. Weather charts were no longer mysterious, I could explain what happens when a cold front or a warm front passes, how a *Fohn* wind is formed, what a typical cyclone is and the meaning of the terms all-up weight, under-carriage, flaps and leading-edge slots.

At that time I knew all these things and hundreds of others and passed my exams with flying colours. Two experienced old pilots, who only wanted to renew their licences, failed, although they knew more than I did about practical flying. I simply had to work hard and pass, for otherwise it might have got into the newspapers and I would have been mercilessly teased.

You finally get a bit of brown-yellow paper to put into your wallet. You are a tested pilot now, but nobody knows the difference or asks you about it.

Private flying can affect your personal habits in the most roundabout way. I have, for instance, learned never to drink more than one modest cup of coffee at breakfast. A little aeroplane has no special arrangements—neither for ladies nor gentlemen. I once almost made an emergency landing in the open country in a desperate situation of this kind, and that would not have been a simple matter. Even if you do make a decent landing on a meadow you must at once run to the nearest village and telephone flight head-quarters in Brunswick. Then you have to await the arrival of the police and official permission to take off again. It is much easier to forgo your second cup of coffee.

I made a special flight to see my old instructor, because some-thing had been bothering me for weeks. "Please tell me honestly whether you would let Michael fly to Africa if he were your own son," I asked. The reason why I had also learned to fly was partly that I could not have slept, imagining him by himself in an aero-plane over the desert, and partly because fathers don't like being outdone by their sons. The journey could not be postponed, for the work in Serengeti had to be done *at once*, otherwise final decisions would be made before our job was done. We could not hire or buy a 'plane in Africa since we needed a machine that could fly very slowly if necessary, and land on a pocket handkerchief.

"Would it not be better to ship the 'plane out there?" I asked.

"In that case you would do your first serious flying over deserts where there is no help available," he replied. "Michael is one of my best pupils. Flying is in his blood. It makes no difference whether you keep on flying over Germany or whether you get your practice over the Mediterranean countries."

We could no longer avoid the flight. We had, after all, run big-ger risks before in a less important cause. It was well worth taking a sporting chance in order to do research in the wilderness, and the prospect was both enticing and a little frightening.

Our aeroplane, *D-ENTE*, was painted with broad zebra stripes so as to be easily visible from the air in case of an emergency landing.

CHAPTER 2

The Flight to Africa

As WE droned up the Rhine in our nice new machine, we had only one other passenger, our pet bushbaby. Beneath us I noticed a huge square building with the letter GEIGY painted on the roof, the famous Swiss pharmaceutical firm in Basle. One of the part-owners of this concern is a University professor, a medical man, a zoologist and an African explorer—all in one. Not long ago he wrote to me that he was cutting up hundreds of tsetse flies daily and carefully dissecting their intestines, stomachs and other organs.

There was no difficulty in reaching Geneva from here, since we had a radio compass. I looked up the wave-length of Geneva and the intermediate transmitters. Michael set this wave-length on the apparatus and a needle on the dial began to move. If we were heading directly for Geneva the needle pointed to zero. Should we fly over the target the needle would travel once around the dial. It was as easy as pie. Unfortunately there are no trans-mitters in Central Africa, so that the instrument would be of no use there, but at the moment we were over Switzerland and had other worries.

Our aeroplane was a larger version of the Fieseler Stork of war years, but all metal and more modern. Normally it flew at about 140 m.p.h., but with full flaps you could slow it down to about 30—if you knew how. That is why we could land even in potato fields which could not be crossed by car. It had only one motor, but if it should fail we could put on full flaps and come down like a glider.

It was an incredibly safe 'plane—as we repeatedly told our wives. It also had very long legs, so that high grass and hummocks should not damage the propeller. We sat half-way below the high wings, entirely surrounded by Plexiglas. I sometimes felt that I was sitting in the air on a stool, for even the side windows reached far down, so that I could see a tiny village 3,000 feet below past my right knee.

Our machine was called D–ENTE. All German 'planes have the letter D, but the four letters after the hyphen were our own choice. Since we wanted an animal we plumped for ENTE (German for duck) and that remained her nickname.

The tail fin was painted, according to law, with the German colours: stripes of red, black and yellow. Apart from that the whole body was painted in black and white stripes, like a zebra. Perhaps it would not look so strange and mechanical to the animals in Serengeti who are used to zebras, but the real reason was to make the small machine easily recognisable from the air in case of accidents.

It was a little embarrassing to land this zebra-striped machine at the elegant international aerodrome of Geneva. Luckily we were not wearing tropical kit, or we really would have looked complete fools. Ten large air-liners stood on the runway and the waiting rooms were swarming with passengers. These big machines should have landed at Milan, but there was a large cold front over Italy with heavy storms in the Po valley, so the air-liners had been re-routed to Geneva.

In Nice the rain clouds were only 400 feet above sea level and visibility was less than a mile. Marseilles told us that we were not permitted to go anywhere near it, so we had to spend the rainy night at Geneva.

Two days later the grey clouds were still hanging on the slopes of the mountains, and only one valley to the south seemed reasonably clear. There was a hole in the clouds and we flew into it. The green trees on the slopes seemed uncomfortably close, and as we were afraid of sudden down currents we tried to climb a little, but were at once surrounded by milky clouds and had to fly blind. We immediately pushed the "duck" a little lower, until we found a clear path over the 3,000-foot mountains on the way to Lyons. Then we followed the Rhone for an hour and arrived in Marseilles in cool sunshine.

In the dim hotel room in Marseilles we covered the entire worn carpet with maps of Italy.   There was an enormous depression over Sicily, with consequent storms and cloud bursts.   We could not fly along the Italian coast because we would be constantly blocked by prohibited military zones.

So we got to know Marseilles, just before Christmas—without overcoats.   Across the road from the hotel there was a railway station which looked like a cathedral.   It was built eighty years ago.   Nowadays we build churches that look like railway stations.

The lines and flags on the weather chart in the control tower of the aerodrome refused to budge.   The black depression remained glued over Italy.   We were itching to get away from rain-washed Europe and finally decided to make a large detour via Spain and Gibraltar.

As we flew along the French coast we were tempted to try a short-cut across the Gulf of Lyons but the water looked so stark and cold that we edged the rudder to the right and hugged the coast line.

We had made the 600-mile trip from Marseilles to Cartagena in exactly four hours, aided by a tail wind and using up sixty gallons of petrol.   Hospitable Spaniards from the military aerodrome drove us into the town in a taxi with its gear box kept in place by wooden wedges.   We were driven, hooting loudly, through the narrow streets to the biggest hotel, where we had a princely meal: wine, three different courses, fresh crabs and coffee—all for five shillings.   Afterwards, for a further four shillings, we had lobsters, for at Christmas time there are no tourist prices in Spain.   Our bedside telephone only functioned if you kept the hook of the receiver lifted with your fingers, but it still managed to connect us with Frankfurt.   Our wives were surprised to learn that we were in Spain, in a comfortable hotel at the gates of a medieval castle. They were not to hear our voices again for a long time.

The Spanish airmen tempted us.   "Why go a long way round via Gibraltar?   Why not fly directly across the sea to Oran?"

"There is military law in Algeria.   Won't we need special permission to land in Oran?"

"Nonsense.   Many people fly there.   We'll simply announce you by radio."

Michael tightened his lips and wagged his head.   The cursed

depression over Italy had already cost us two days, and so we suc-
cumbed to temptation. I unpacked the reddish-yellow safety jackets, which we pulled over our heads and tied around our waists.
The English instructions seemed to be printed upside down but
were easily readable when you looked down at your belly. The
jackets contained a whistle, a battery which automatically lights
a bulb when in contact with sea-water, so that you are visible at
night, and a dye that colours the sea all around you. We also prepared our little self-inflating rubber dinghy. Michael wrapped
some bread, apples and biscuits, as well as a smoke cartridge and
shark repelling tablets (specially ordered from America) in a water-
tight packet.

We gained height above Cartagena by circling until we reached
10,000 feet. We did not want to go higher, for our progress in the
thin air would be too slow. Spain slowly became smaller and we
pointed the black and white striped nose of our "duck" dead
southward across the open sea.

The distance is less than 200 miles, or a good ninety minutes
of flying. It only seemed a stone's throw on the map, but we soon
lost sight of the coast and could see nothing but sea and sky. This
was not the blue, summery Mediterranean but grey water at 50 °F.
If you have to swim in it you become stiff and unconscious after
about two hours. At that time of the year there was not a ship to
be seen anywhere.

I had been listening to the motor, which seemed to be working
unsteadily. Involuntarily I glanced at Michael. I had come to depend on him to an ever-increasing extent during the last few years.
Now he was looking straight through the whirling blades of the
propeller at the blurred horizon. As yet there were no wrinkles
round his eyes, and a characteristic lock of hair fell over his forehead. There was another typical spike of hair standing up at the
back of his head. He had never been able to keep this tuft down,
even when he was a little boy taking Djingis, our pet wolf, for a
walk.

Suddenly the motor stuttered and stopped. My heart also
missed a beat. How could we got out of this metal "duck" if she
should hit the water?

Michael pressed the button of the booster pump and it sprang to life, forcibly feeding petrol into the engine. The motor had stopped for only five or six seconds—but they were very long seconds.

We dared not switch off the booster pump as long as we were over the ocean. Not a word was spoken until the needle of the radio compass responded to the signals from Oran. Then the North African coast line appeared and slowly, much too slowly, came closer.

Oran was surrounded by three dark, mountainous clouds, but where was the aerodrome? Our first guess turned out to be a barrack square. Another landing strip was lined with military aeroplanes.

We made two huge circles until we found the right place. I looked out for other aircraft while Michael listened to the control tower on his earphones. The controller in the tower is supposed to tell you the wind speed and direction, and also when to approach the landing strip. It is not always easy to understand a strange voice using the standard abbreviations, numerals and code words in English—according to international usage. Unfortunately this gentleman was speaking in French!

My forehead was clammy as we finally approached the right strip and started to come down. Suddenly an unexpected voice asked (in English this time): "How do you pronounce your name?"

If your name happens to be Grzimek you must get used to this question. In America and France I have often been told that no native could hope to pronounce it. I have reassured these people that the Germans were in the same boat—but in mid-air this question came as a surprise.

Oran has existed for 2,000 years. For 280 years it was a Spanish town, followed by forty years of Turkish rule, but since 1831 it has belonged to France. Our taxi driver was French, but had never been to France. Both his father and grandfather were born in North Africa.

"Oran is peaceful now," the driver told us, avoiding a heavily-laden donkey by a hair's breadth; "the rebellion is over."

The following morning the newspaper reported that the next taxi from the aerodrome had been ambushed and four people in it wounded. All the hotels were crowded with refugees and offi-

cers, so we were glad to accept a room in a third-class hotel, even
though the Moorish owner put us into an unheated chamber behind the kitchen.

The hotel porter was an artist at his job. While Michael was
talking to him his wide sleeves accidentally brushed one of our
travellers' cheques from the table. By the time Michael tried to
pick the cheque off the floor it was no-where to be seen, neatly
swept into one of the open drawers of the porter's desk — and con-
cealed by a book.

With its 200,000 inhabitants, large blocks of flats and modern
sky-scrapers, Oran appeared quite peaceful to us. The porter,
however, advised us not to eat in cafes which had windows facing
the streets. They were too frequently attacked by bombs. The
assassins themselves were usually killed before the Police arrived.
A really peaceful town.

We tried to push on to Algiers, but our "flying zebra" was beaten
back by the stormy rearguards of the deep depression. The wet
clouds dropped lower and lower, until we found ourselves in a
valley which was sealed by clouds at the top. We had only just
enough room to turn back.

A car can reverse when it drives into a blind alley, but to an
airman a cul-de-sac can mean death. Many have perished because
they could not climb the hillside in time, after the valley had
grown too narrow for manœuvring.

Next we tried low flying along the coast, but even here the
clouds were so low that they sometimes mingled with the foaming
sea.

After an hour and a half we grew discouraged and returned to
Oran. The officials — in a house surrounded by barbed wire —
shook their heads. "You should have stayed at least 1,000 feet
above the mountains. It's lucky you were not shot at, for only
three weeks ago they bagged an aeroplane."

Next morning we gave the dangerous mountains a wide berth.
When we had flown out to sea a little way we could observe some
of the damage the depression had left in its wake on its journey
eastward. Bridges swept away, swamped roads and floods. Not
a single large animal could be seen on the hills and mountains.
Long ago mariners used to be able to see antelopes and even lions

from the decks of their vessels. As recently as 1892 there were still lions on Mount Edough, close to the harbour of Bône. The black-maned Barbary lions were the handsomest of the African tribe and the last of these peaceful big cats did not become extinct in Morocco until 1922 — their descendants, however, still survive in many zoos.

We continued to meet some squalls. Michael wanted to fly uner them, while I preferred going around them. These desires were influenced by our positions in the "duck." The door above me leaked and could not be made watertight, because the speed of the 'plane forced the raindrops through the joints and sponge rubber. I therefore had to hold a rag above my head and wring it out from time to time. This made my arm ache and did not prevent some of the water from running down my neck. Michael's door was weatherproof.

We passed Algiers and beat along the coast as far as Tunis, then we turned south. At last we had escaped from the European cauldron of bad weather. As far as we were concerned the depression could wander along Italy and into the Balkans to rain on Marshal Tito. We were flying towards the sun with no rain clouds to stop us.

Once before we had had to wait in Tripoli in the middle of the night when landing there in a large air-liner. The corrugated hangar doors were still perforated with bullet marks from the African campaign. The paper money of the new Kingdom of Libya bears the head of the friendly old King, Idris-el-Sennussi, but we could not make out the value of the notes since they have arabic numerals. We, too, allegedly use "arabic" numerals, but there is a vast difference between ours and the real thing.

We wanted to make up for lost time. Our reliable old "duck" could cover long distances because it had a large extra tank in front of the two rear seats. With the aid of a little hand pump we could transfer the petrol from it to the proper tanks inside the wings. This would enable us to fly to Tobruk or even Alexandria without landing.

Progress through the air is rapid, but one tends to get stuck on aerodromes. Always the same old paper war. First find a tanker and refuel; then the customs, followed by a visit to the meteorologist to find out about winds and cloud cover, finally up the stairs to the control tower where one has to fill out and hand in a printed form before having it stamped.

I put the word Tobruk in the space left for "destination". The official told us that Tobruk was only a military aerodrome, so he crossed it out and wrote Benghazi instead.

Now it only remained to pay the airport fees and write out a cheque for the petrol. All this took at least two hours, even when Michael and I split the job between us. When we left at last, with a sigh of relief on being airborne once more, we discovered that we had forgotten to eat. I considered it my duty to look after Michael and offered him a cheese sandwich. He shook his head, not surprisingly, as it was quite stale, having accompanied us all the way from Marseilles.

Excitement always tightens his stomach, a trait he has inherited from his mother. This long trip had excited him, however calm he tried to appear. He did accept an apple and threw the core through the small sliding window. We saw it land on the road which Mussolini built along the coast. Behind the road there was desert and yet more desert — a vast kingdom of sand — Libya.

The road was completely empty except for an occasional military lorry every hundred miles or so. There were no villages, only a few Bedouin tents. At exactly fifteen-minute intervals we passed rest houses, all identical. Many years ago I saw photos of these elegant desert hotels in an illustrated weekly. Now they were occupied by Bedouins, with mountains of empty oil drums in the courtyards and goats living underneath the verandas.

The booster pump went on strike and we had to land in order to refill the main tanks from canisters. According to our map there was a landing strip at Marble Arch. This is not a settlement, nor related to its famous namesake in London, but merely a triumphal arch of white marble which Mussolini erected long ago. Close to the arch there is an airfield, probably built by Germans during the last war. We dropped down and crossed the asphalt runway at ten feet. The asphalt was cracked and large tufts of grass grew out of the fissures. All around there were ruined houses and mess-halls.

We landed on a piece of strip that was still reasonably smooth.

After we landed at Marble Arch, Bedouins with donkeys brought us petrol from an emergency store.

Some Bedouins who were watching grazing dromedaries close by produced two donkeys which accompanied us towards a tin hut. There, rather to our surprise—there was actually a store of petrol, contained in military canisters bearing the official marking "Filled May 1956". For eighteen months this aviation spirit had been stored beside the forgotten triumphal arch of the Duce. The donkeys carried the canisters to our waiting "duckling". The bill, with dozens of others from twelve different countries, reached us a year later in Frankfurt.

How long before sundown? One of the Arabs explained in sign language: "about two hours". When we were once again in the air, however, and consulted our books we found that the sun was due to set below the horizon long before that. We kept on flying, but the red ball sank with increasing speed towards the desert.

We could still see the sun, though it had set long ago for the Bedouins below, but twilight was falling when the radio compass made contact with Benghazi. They lit up the air-strip for us, two rows of pearls along the runway.

"Who is the captain?" asked the stern man in the control tower.

Then even more severely, "Where have you been?" The moustachioed Scot did not believe in our long stay at Marble Arch.

"If your flying speed is 140 miles an hour why did you give your flying time as seven hours in Tripoli? You only need four hours to reach Benghazi." They obviously thought that we deliberately gave the longer time in order to spy out the land.

We retired to the splended hotel in a depressed frame of mind until Michael saw the light. When the official in Tripoli crossed out Tobruk and substituted Benghazi he had not altered the flying time.

Above Cyrenaica Michael and I alternately took the controls and looked out for animals, but we only saw grazing camels. Apart from a few birds there was nothing else to be seen. The green colour of the country below us is a by-product of the last war. The seeds of a grass from the Australian semi-desert, an *Oinopodiacae*, was accidentally introduced in some horse fodder. While abandoned tanks rusted away, the desert around El Alamein started to grow green. Then the fertile carpet, up to six feet in height, spread to either side along the coast, as far as the Nile delta, and even began to move inland. The new green life adapted itself to the Mediterranean conditions and prospered, particularly among the deadly mines which Italian, British and German soldiers laid in a hundred-mile strip along the coast.

The mines are still waiting, and nobody dares to move among them, but the living grass has long since spread further than the zone of death. It is the only good thing left by the war. Below us there were endless trenches, burned out houses, strong points and a railway, 600 miles long, on which not a single train was running.

The asphalt road stopped at the Egyptian frontier, but instead there was a light turquoise sea with foamy breakers. There are very few moments in life when one is completely happy and without extraneous desires. This was one of them. We were alone between the glassy blue sky and the glassy blue sea, two men, one on the upward slope of life and one on the downward side, with but a single objective. The heavy veins of age were only just becoming visible on Michael's young man's hands as they lay on the controls. His hands would have to go on working, for mine were growing tired. There are few men who can leave their life's work in such good, capable, friendly hands.

Landing at Alexandria was easy because we had the whole airport to ourselves. Most of the big airlines flew around Egypt at that time and there were only a few Misrair machines standing about. When we braked to a halt we were met by nothing but five solemn dogs. It was just our luck to arrive on a Mohammedan holiday on which the restaurants and banks were closed. The customs officials, however, advanced us enough money for a taxi to the hotel.

Before this the officials had been very formal. They asked us about foreign exchange and I emptied my pockets of all their oddments of German, Swiss, French, Spanish, Algerian, Tunisian and Libyan money. Each pile was carefully counted and I was finally handed a long document, printed in Arabic, which I signed willynilly.

On opening the filter of our engine the capable Egyptian engineer found it full of small metallic grit. They had given us dirty petrol in Oran and the sand in it had corroded the piston of the hand pump, the metal pieces of which were luckily trapped in the filter. We bought funnels and chamois leather at once and always kept a watch when strangers filled the tanks of the "duck". After that the engine ran for 300 hours without coughing once.

The engineer apologised because he could not give us aviation spirit. Only the Egyptian air force was allowed to use the 80 octane fuel we needed. I ran up the steps to the commandant's office and showed him the official statement of his government that all kinds of petrol were freely obtainable on Egyptian aerodromes. The officer in charge personally telephoned Cairo and discovered that this only applied when paid for in dollars. As we did not possess American money we had to be content with ordinary motoring spirit—a most unpleasant experience.

On starting early next morning and flying up the Nile towards Luxor we discovered that Egypt resembles a moon-scape. Rocks and sand followed by more rocks and sand, as far as the eye can see. No tree, no leaf, no blade of grass. Narrowly embedded in this emptiness flows the Nile with its fertile banks, a thin strip of green running from North to South. Only a ribbon about two

This is how most of Egypt looks from the air—apart from the Nile it is a wilderness without trees or bushes.

miles wide on either side of the river is green. Behind that all signs of life stop abruptly and the desert starts without any transition.

We climbed to get a wider view and the endlessly stretching, stony desert gave an impression of breathtaking desolation. When we flew lower again the boatmen waved to us and their huge, brownish sails seemed to salute us, too.

The train journey from Cairo to Luxor takes twelve hours and the passenger must get the impression that he is crossing a green, fertile Eden. We did the trip in two hours and got to know Colonel Nasser's difficulties.

We arrived in Luxor and gladly accepted the customs officer's invitation to coffee. During the evening we took a trip to see the temple of Karnak; then we had a bath at the hotel and drank some wine with this friendly official, who was very lively and full of good stories.

Next morning, however, our friend was very worried. Our money was not correct. We had too many French francs and too few Libyan piastres. The document I had blindly signed in Alexandria was a few pennies out. Finally a solution to this dilemma was discovered and we were allowed to leave.

It was only a small incident, but it made us angry. Coming on top of the petrol affair it gave us a bad impression of the land of the Pharaohs. In order to get rid of our spleen we behaved like naughty schoolboys and flew some low, tight turns across the Nile to see the royal tombs at close quarters. This was against regulations and the radio from Luxor called us immediately and told us to climb to 2,000 feet at once. Well satisfied with our gesture, we obeyed and flew off.

We circled the high dam at Assuan and landed for a short time at Wadi Halfa, just inside the borders of the Sudan. Then we went on with our journey. Egypt lay beind us and we were on our way southward, leaving the meandering ribbon of the Nile to cross the Nubian desert. In this way we cut across the biggest loop of the Nile in three hours. Now we saw a real desert, like an illustration from a child's picture book—nothing but yellow sand, without even a stone to break the monotony.

We would never have dared to cross the desert if we had not been able to follow the railway, which Lord Kitchener built in order to fight the Mahdi. Every sixty miles we saw a station, like a toy house beside a model railway, one looking exactly like the next. When we met a train we flew low towards it and all the passengers waved from the windows. There is only one train a week, dragging itself across the sea of sand.

When we met the Nile again it was much narrower and the green banks had become threadbare. As a compensation, patches of desert began to show a faint green. We climbed higher to see the next loop of the Nile on the hazy horizon and to cut across it. Twenty minutes before sundown we landed at Khartoum.

Early the next morning Michael and I stood outside the great mosque in Omdurman in which the great Mohammed Ahmed el Mahdi lies buried. At night it is lit by garlands of coloured electric lights. Opposite the tomb the opponent of the Mahdi, General Gordon, rides on a bronze camel. When the Mahdi's mad dervishes captured Khartoum General Gordon's head was displayed on a spear. It was only in 1898, fourteen years later, that Lord Kitchener defeated the dervishes at Omdurman, a battle in which the young Winston Churchill participated. The gutted Khartoum

The single-track railway that cuts across the largest loop of the Nile gave us confidence to fly over the yellow sea of sand that is the Nubian Desert.

then re-blossomed as a modern city which is to-day shaded by 10,000 trees.

Gordon's statue has an adventurous history. At first it stood in London in St. Martin's Place. While on its way to Khartoum in 1902 it slipped and had to be raised from the bottom of the Thames. The same thing happened a few weeks later in the Nile. Even in the Sudan it once nearly sank into the ground. In Khartoum they tell a good story about the statue. An English official took his young son to see Gordon every Sunday after church, where they both stood for a few minutes in silence and meditated. When the boy grew old enough to be sent to school in England he wrote the following letter to his father: "London is very nice, but I miss my Sunday morning walks with daddy, and the visit to the statue. Please tell me the name of the man who rides Gordon."

I spent some time talking shop with my black colleague of the Khartoum Zoo, where many of the animals walk about on the lawns among the visitors.

In the meantime Michael was pottering about with our machine. When we proudly wanted to show the admiring Britons how slowly our "duck" could fly when throttled back, the temperature of the engine rose alarmingly, the needle nearly going off the dial. We were much concerned, especially when the engineers showed us the wrecks of three small aeroplanes, all powered by the same American Lycoming motor as ours. They had seized up. The cooling system could not cope with the oppressive heat in Khartoum. If Michael had not been alert our journey might have ended then and there. We at once telegraphed to Germany, for an extra cooling system which Michael could fit to the engine in East Africa, and decided never again to fly slowly in the searing heat. No, we are not allowed to endanger the task we have set ourselves.

Neither to-day, nor to-morrow, but in three or four generations' time when Bolshevism and Capitalism have long been forgotten and Eastern or Western blocs no longer matter, many people may be glad that during our era someone gave a thought to the wild animals in Africa. Who worries to-day about the struggles of the Guelphs and Ghibelines and the French Huguenots who were killed or exiled? In 1866 young Hanoverians were killed fighting against the King of Prussia, while four years later their younger brothers fought for the same ruler in his war against France. Most national and political ambitions for which men suffer and die are equally transient, but Nature is of abiding importance to us all. In a hundred years' time Kruschev and Eisenhower, political anxieties and hatreds will only have a printed existence in history books, but men will still consider it important that wildebeest should roam across the plains and leopards growl at night. It will matter all the more if human beings are increasingly condemned to live in soulless concrete cities.

We greeted the first free-living, wild giraffes we met by flying low over them. Perhaps they really took us for a flying zebra, for they did not flee, but merely stretched their long necks in amazement.

As we flew up the White Nile, the stream widened, grew even more complex with branches and showed succulent green carpets of floating vegetation. This is the home of the shoe-billed stork called *Abu-Markub* (father of the shoe) by the Arabs. Forty years ago the Swede Bengt Berg went up this river, in a steamer disguised with reeds as a floating island. He was the first to film this bird, but never found it nesting. No European has ever seen

To photograph a giraffe like this you have to fly very low.

a hatching shoe-bill. Five years ago we received a pair of these giant storks from Khartoum and they are still living in the Frankfurt Zoo.

We could see waterbucks on the banks and natives driving cattle with wide-swept U-shaped horns.

Finally we arrived at Juba, the capital of the equatorial and southernmost province of the new Republic of the Sudan. Two years before we wanted to drive here from the Belgian Congo in response to a kind invitation from the Arabian Government. Just at that time, however, the black troops mutinied and killed their Arab officers. They did not harm any Europeans, but we still thought it better to turn back. Tourists are not allowed in this province without special permission of the Central Government at Khartoum.

Juba is merely a large village. The radio operator in the control tower was an African, as at all Sudanese air-ports. He told us that leopards play on the modest landing strip during the early morning, because it is dry whereas the grass is still dewy. He has to approach his transmitter carefully because poisonous black mamba snakes like to lie on the warm tubes.

As we strolled through the village we were suddenly confronted by a proper concentration camp, surrounded by barbed wire and provided with high watch-towers carrying machine-guns. A European introduced himself. He had been there for two years and worked in Omdurman before that.

"The country is restive," he said. "The black tribes do not want to be ruled by Arabs who were once slave traders. The huge prison is therefore full of political prisoners. Now and then twenty or thirty of them are shot."

What would the world press have said if Great Britain had executed natives while they were in control here a few years ago?

The doctor was a German. Two days earlier his house-boys killed a poisonous snake in his house. A few days before that a leopard carried off his pet monkey from its perch in a tree. The monkey's belt was found torn into three pieces in the garden. Our hotel also lost two dogs to a leopard yesterday.

The hospital, staffed by eleven doctors during the British regime, now only had five. The natives seemed to be less impatient than Europeans. Some patients with strangulated hernias walked for eight days to reach the hospital, eating on the way. Despite this, half of them remained alive. A boy had been brought in not long before with a spear right through his abdomen. The iron tip had pierced the intestine in two places. His relatives had not pulled out the spear but tied it in position so that it could not move, and the boy remained alive.

The black tribes in the Southern Sudan would like self-government, within the framework of a Sudanese state, now that they are no longer ruled by Europeans, but some of them are still completely uncivilised and they have few educated leaders.

We had left early in the morning with nothing to eat but a buttered roll and it was late afternoon before we reached Juba. We were very hungry, and the Greek owner of our small hotel provided us with a welcome meal. At half-past seven the Governor of the equatorial province was giving a ceremonial dinner to celebrate Christmas, and we were cordially invited.

It was Christmas Eve, a fact which we had completely forgotten. The year before, Michael and I had also celebrated Christmas far away from home, in the Belgian Congo, but our wives were with us then.   Though both of us were bad dancers, we had to comply with Belgian custom and dance with them.

The black waiters were decorating the restaurant.   This was not expensive as they merely pulled palm branches from the trees and cut tropical flowers from the bushes.   The Christmas tree was a species of arbor vitae and had been brought by 'plane from the mountains of the Belgian Congo.   It was decorated with coloured lights, streamers and balloons according to English custom.

We sat near the festive table and waited.   Eight o'clock, half-past eight and the guests were still missing.   The air was moist and the thermometer read more than 105 °F.   The radio transmitted music from Omdurman, nasal songs, whining fiddles—very strange to our ears—played at a very fast tempo, hour after hour.

We supposed that the company were at a religious service, but when they finally arrived we discovered that they had all been to the cinema.   The Governor and his second-in-command were dark gentlemen, in their fifties, wearing smart white dinner jackets and displaying perfect manners.   Most of the guests were Greek merchants, many of them without ties and some in their shirt sleeves, but their wives were all in evening dress.   According to the menu there was soup *a la Nazareth* (strongly peppered), followed by a cocktail *a la Bethlehem* (containing a fruit like a cherry) and an incredibly tough turkey.   Rum burned with a blue flame all over the Christmas pudding which, as a surprise, was full of little Sudanese coins.

The Governor behaved like a perfect gentleman.   He was clearly conscious of his rank and listened with a smile to the artless prattle of the young lady on his right hand.   She appeared to be the village belle and complained that she would have preferred to spend Christmas at a grand hotel in Khartoum.

Next to me sat a man from Switzerland.   It had taken him six days' work in Khartoum to obtain permission to come to Juba. Now he had been there for eight days and could not leave because his money had not arrived.

The corners of the room appeared to be filled with large bunches of paper flowers, their colours clashing so horribly as to be painful. Michael discovered that in fact they were not made of paper at all, but were genuine African flowers—yet nature is said to be incapable of bad taste!

The British celebrate Christmas Eve as we do a carnival, and the Sudanese have taken over this custom. Each of us was given a paper hat, and had to put it on. The Governor declared that Michael looked very fetching in his. Then we were provided with crackers, piles of paper streamers and heaps of red, papier-mache snowballs. Some of the Greek merchants found it fun to dip these balls in wine before throwing them at each other. Unfortunately the dye in them was not fast and the snowy dinner jackets of the officials were badly stained. I had wrapped a tablecloth around my neck and could only marvel at the good-natured way in which the two Governors took having their clothes spoiled. But when some of the European guests started throwing bananas about, the fruit was politely removed.

We were both tired when we retired at midnight to a pavilion in the park. Above us two large propellers rotated on the ceiling. What a way to spend Christmas Eve! We needed a good night's rest for we were determined to finish our journey the next day, come hell or high water. We intended to fly to Entebbe on Lake Victoria, via Uganda. There we would take on fuel and fly across the wooded hills to Nairobi, the capital of Kenya in East Africa.

The elephants of Serengeti are found almost exclusively in the Ngorongoro crater and the highlands around it. This area was removed from the National Park in 1959 (see *After Some Years*, page 270).

CHAPTER 3

In the Ngorongoro Crater

---

*O Lord of love and kindness, who created the
beautiful earth and all the creatures walking
and flying in it, so that they may proclaim your
glory, I thank you to my dying day that you
have placed me amongst them.*

FRANCIS OF ASSISI

WE HAD arrived safely. There we were at our destination, in the
vicinity of Lake Victoria, 6,000 miles from home and about 250
miles south of the equator. We both felt a little apprehensive.
Would we be equal to the task we had set ourselves?

We were to explore the Serengeti National Park in Tanganyika,
an area of 4,500 square miles. This is not very much by African
standards, but it is nearly twice as large as Devonshire. The borders of this "Park" are not real, they are only lines on a map, but
they show it to be 120 miles long. The altitude of the region ranges
from 4,000 to 13,000 feet. There is only one road, which stops
half-way through the Park, and even that often cannot be traversed
by a jeep during three months of the year.

This wilderness is not thinly populated, for its inhabitants, according to books and brochures, are said to number more than a
million. These inhabitants are not men, however, but quadrupeds
varying in size from elephants to gazelles as big as a goat—not to
mention the smaller creatures. Serengeti is the last place in Africa
where there are still large herds of game roaming across the grassy

plains, as the bison once did in untold numbers across the American prairies. Its lions are the most numerous and the most handsome in Africa. We intended to make a census of this veritable ant heap, and to plot the movements of these huge armies.

Our first idea was simply to photograph the area in strips, piecing the photographs together like a map, and counting the animals. But on these photographs one would not be able to tell a wildebeest from a zebra, or a zebra from a gazelle. To differentiate between the animals we would have to fly below 3,000 feet and photograph much smaller areas. We calculated ruefully that it would take 50,000 photographs to cover the whole region from this height; translated into money, this would run to about £23,000, even if it was practicable. This was more than the total profits from our film, so we had to try and count the animals individually from the air.

To test the feasibility of this method and to discover its accuracy we tried it on a zoological garden from which the animals could not escape.

It is, in a manner of speaking, the largest zoo in the world, populated by over 9,000 large animals, and surrounded by walls 2,000 feet high. This zoo, which would accommodate a large part of Greater London, is nothing but a huge extinct volcano called Ngorongoro, the largest crater in the world. Where once the hot lava bubbled there is now a huge green meadow surrounded by enormous, steep walls.

First of all we wanted to see this marvel from ground level, for it is not easy to identify animals from above. We therefore drove our car from Arusha to the highlands of the giant craters. To get there on the road, which is even asphalted for half the way, we had to drive through the brush, round a range of mountains, down one side of a deep valley and then up the other. The trees became larger and denser the higher we climbed, until they formed a veritable forest. When the jungle cleared for a short stretch we looked to our right.

Michael stopped the car in amazement and we got out to have a better look. My son has the habit of throwing back his head a little and flaring his nostrils when he is moved. He was not the only one to be excited; I was equally gripped by the wonderful sight.

It is impossible to give a fair description of the size and beauty of the crater, for there is nothing with which one can compare it. It is one of the Wonders of the World.

We stayed the night with Gordon Harvey, one of the two game wardens of the National Park. His garden is overgrown with red, blue, and golden flowers, among which one can see glittering sun birds and brilliant green chameleons. The house itself stands in a clearing. There are damp patches on the walls of the living-room. With a few strokes of a brush Mrs. Harvey had transformed these into puffy-cheeked, trumpet-blowing cherubs, and zebras galloping across clouds.

After dinner we went outside and saw two male buffaloes chewing the cud and looking at us. Then to bed in a room with a wood fire in the grate. We were 9,000 feet above sea level, two-and-a-half times as high as Snowdon.

Next morning we drove our zebra-striped car along the edge of the crater on a track that is impassable to ordinary passenger cars. We had to drive around three-quarters of the circumference, which had a twelve mile diameter at the widest point and was ten miles across at the narrowest, before coming to a spot where the track winds down the steep sides. It took about two-and-a-half hours to arrive at a point 2,000 feet below the spot from which we had started.

Finally we reached the bottom. Large herds of wildebeest (gnus) unhurriedly gave way when our car was within forty or fifty yards of them. Zebras ran parallel to us at a full gallop and decided to cross our path at the last possible moment. It seemed as if they had sporting ambitions.

We sighted a rhino cow and calf in a little hollow and carefully drove to within forty yards of them. They stood quite unconcernedly and neither ran away nor attacked, for shooting has been prohibited in the crater for some decades.

I am quite used to dealing with rhinos, for we were the first in Europe to breed the "black" sharp-snouted African rhino in captivity. "Catherine the Great," our rhino cow in Frankfurt, allows

The wildebeest in the Ngorongoro crater took little notice of our car.

Galloping zebras; the animals in the rear are wildebeest.

herself to be milked, and we can even play with her child in her presence. She is about as tame as a domestic cow. The bull is a little more aggressive, but then one does not approach a solitary domestic bull in a meadow either.

Our tame Catherine nearly spitted me some time ago because I forgot an elementary principle known to every farmer and groom. I normally went between the wide bars of the cage to stroke her eyelids when she was dozing, for that was one of her favourite pastimes. One morning I did the same thing but forgot that I was wearing crepe-soled shoes. Standing quite close to Catherine I suddenly spoke to her. She started up at once, snorted and began to charge. When I called to her she recognised my voice and stopped a few inches from my body. She was friendly again and allowed me to pet her.

That taught me a lesson. Rhinos sleep soundly and do not like to be disturbed. The Masai boys have devised a game based on this sound slumber. They steal up to a sleeping rhino and place a stone on its back. The next boy has to remove it without rousing the rhino. Then it is put back again and so on until the animal finally wakes up. This game is not without danger, of course, but it is typical of the Masai.

I wanted to know how a free-living rhino cow reacts to an approaching man. I left the car, therefore, and got closer to the mother and child. Would she attack? Michael watched through our telephoto lens which we used instead of field-glasses. Four funnel-shaped ears turned towards me and the calf retreated behind its mother. Comparing it to our zoo-born rhinos I judged it to be about a year old.

I approached another yard, trying not to appear anxious, but my steps instinctively grew smaller. Suddenly the cow snorted and charged. One moment later Michael broke into loud laughter. The reason was that he only saw the angry mother on the ground-glass screen and at almost the same moment heard the door of the car slam behind me.

The cow stopped a few yards from the car, satisfied herself that I had disappeared and trotted back to her calf. If she really had attacked it would not have harmed our station wagon, which is big enough to hold ten people. Contrary to general belief, rhinos do

Rhinos are born without "horns." These develop much later.

not charge with the full weight of their one-and-a-half tons, but stop before they reach a car and prod at it with their "horn". Usually this only causes a dent in the coachwork. I have seen people who were killed by buffaloes, but during all our journeys I have never heard of anyone being murdered by a rhino, which of course does not mean that it has never happened.

Perhaps I could be considered biased in favour of the defence, and I would therefore like to call an expert witness, the German explorer Oscar Baumann. He was here seventy years before us, and in 1891 discovered the Manyara and Eyasi Lakes. He was also among the first Europeans to descend into our gigantic zoo.

In those days travelling in Africa was quite different. In Arusha Baumann asked a Masai the way and when the man said that he knew it, the explorer had him chained and guarded by armed askaris. This is what Baumann wrote about his experiences in the crater.

"We rested for a day at Ngorongoro and I took the chance to look at some Masai kraals. I was received in the friendliest fashion. In the meantime a crowd of tattered scarecrows, now typical of the

The "horn" of the rhinoceros is not dangerous to cars.

Masai country, gathered outside the thorn fence of our camp. There were women reduced to walking skeletons, out of whose sunken eyes looked the madness of hunger, children resembling deformed frogs rather than human beings, warriors who could hardly crawl on all fours, and moronic, emaciated greybeards. These people ate everything available; dead donkeys were a delicacy for them; but they also devoured the skins, bones, and even horns of cattle. I gave these unfortunate people as much food as I could, and the good-natured porters shared their rations with them, but their hunger was unappeasable and they came in ever greater numbers. They were refugees from Serengeti, where starvation had depopulated whole districts. They had fled to their countrymen, who had barely enough to eat themselves. Swarms of vultures followed them, waiting for victims. We were daily confronted by this misery and could do almost nothing to help. Parents offered us their babies in exchange for a piece of meat. When we refused to barter they artfully hid the children in our camp and escaped. Soon our caravan was swarming with Masai babies and it was touching to see how the porters cared for the

On the road from Nairobi to Mombasa a car traveling at nearly seventy miles an hour ran into a rhinoceros. Where nature and science collide, nature has to give way. The driver of the car was unhurt.

little ones. I employed some of the stronger men and women as cowherds and thus saved quite a number from death by starvation.

"On the 21st March we penetrated farther into the Ngorongoro crater. We halted in an acacia forest near the lake. The plain around us was populated by many rhinoceros, one of which I shot. Several others in my expedition have also shot these beasts, which is not nearly so difficult or dangerous as it is claimed to be by professional Nimrods. The rhinos are not shy, and if the wind is favourable one can easily approach to within thirty paces. To hit a rhino at thirty paces you do not have to be a spectacular shot, and if the bullet hits the chest or (with a smaller calibre gun) the head, the animal usually collapses without further ado. If wounded anywhere else it either runs away at such speed that there is little hope of catching it, or it attacks the hunter. This moment is usually the one described with vivid horror by the Nimrods. The companions flee and only the hunter bravely faces the charging colossus. This sounds terribly dangerous, but the 'charging colossus' is nearly blind and one step aside is sufficient to make it miss and charge past. When it stops and looks around for its enemy the hunter has plenty of time to kill it with another bullet at close range.

"I had hardly retired to my tent when I heard the crack of a rifle. Everyone ran to the fence and I lit a magnesium flare, specially bought for such a purpose. We captured two mother-naked Masai warriors who had tried to get into the cattle enclosure. We feared that we might be attacked, but there were no further incidents of this kind, except that our sentries once fired in the dark on some approaching figures. Next morning we were horrified to see two dead starvelings outside the fence. Beside them stood a thin old man with untidy white hair heaping furious curses on our heads. 'You wallow in milk and meat,' he cried, 'and shoot at us, who are dying of hunger. Curses on you!' I arranged for some meat to be given to the poor old man, which he swallowed raw, only to start cursing again. Even after the caravan had moved off, the cries of the pitiable fellow followed us for some distance."

Such starvation has since occurred only during wartime, when the Germans and later the British ruled Tanganyika. We found the crater unchanged by the passage of seventy years—the lovely acacia forest, elephants near the lake, rhinos, Masai kraals, girls hung with glass beads, and vultures.

Baumann needed twenty-three days to march through Serengeti to Lake Victoria. In all, he travelled 2,500 miles, and of the one hundred and ninety-five natives he took with him, forty died during the journey.

A zebra mare and her foal, with its childishly bulging forehead, were playing among green hills by the side of the crater, close to two ruined houses. This was the home of the German settler Adolf Siedentopf. His unmarried brother, Friedrich Wilhelm, built his house among the woods at the other side of the crater. Around 1908 they had about 1,200 head of cattle, bred ostriches and tried to tame zebras. I tried to discover their subsequent history but could find out very little. The German regional officer in Arusha, who is still alive, wrote to me that the two brothers and their friend Hartnung were the most awkward customers in German East Africa. Hartnung was fined two hundred rupees because he fired bullets at the feet of natives trying to escape. During the first World War he was assassinated by the Masai in the Ngorongoro crater, and "unfortunately nineteen Wambula workers shared his fate."

I received a letter from a former German official who took part in the hunts in the Ngorongoro crater which were organised by the brothers Siedentopf. This gentleman is over 70 years old and now lives in Munich. He recalls that parts of the crater were isolated by stretching ropes with coloured cloths attached, and posting strings of natives between the hills inside the crater and the north wall. Expert hunters counted about 24,000 head of zebras and wildebeest in the crater at that time. To-day the game amounts to barely 8,000 head, and this includes gazelles. Despite this there is talk of thinning out the herd in favour of the Masai cattle. In those days the lions inside the crater were still hunted and were much shyer than they are to-day, when one can approach them closely by car. Although one could hear them roar at night in times gone by, they were never visible in the daytime. The brothers Siedentopf tried to drive the wildebeests out of the crater by using long lines of natives as beaters. They wanted all the land for their domestic cows, but they did not manage to drive out a single wildebeest.

Our striped car wound its way back to the rim of the crater. We were trying to find a possible landing strip and when we drove our car down, light-coloured kongonis, a type of hartebeest, made room for us as we looked for a hundred-and-fifty-yard-long area free from hyena holes, rocks and hummocks. Finally we found one in a depression inside the three-mile-wide Malanja crater, a little above Ngorongoro. A few black hunters piled stones into heaps and whitewashed them for us.

Neither the two game wardens in the Park, nor their assistants, wanted to fly with us. They live eighty miles apart from each other, and even more from the Director of the National Park in Arusha. Every day at half-past six, half-past nine, and half-past one they contact each other via tiny wireless transmitters. They have their say, ending each announcement with the word "stop", and then press a button and listen to the others. The atmospherics are sometimes very bad, and occasionally they cannot understand each other at all. In that case they have to wait for the next "blow" a few hours later.

Kongonis, a species of hartebeest, have curiously curved horns.

When the men finish their official business the wives have a little talk. If you are surrounded by nothing but lions, storks and gazelles you eagerly snatch a chance to gossip a little. When these fond wives learned that we had only been flying for some months, they held a council of war and told the Director in Arusha that the "official wives' committee" would only permit the husbands to come with us in the striped 'plane if each of them was insured for £10,000. Since they insisted on this condition the director had to telegraph London and increase our passenger insurance. In the meantime Michael and I flew by ourselves.

We did not mind this in the least, since we could now cease being based on the commercial aerodrome in Arusha. We were flying across the wilderness and landing on our own little airfields. If you fill in a flight plan and do not arrive at the correct time at the stated destination they soon begin searching for you. Nobody was going to look for us now; we were all on our own.

The motor droned, the striped wings swept through the air and lifted us up. The wheels on their long legs still rotated after we left the ground, and then stopped. When I turned around I could see the clouds above the white glaciers of Kilimanjaro. In the whole of Tanganyika, the crater-pitted highland towards which we were flying is second only to this giant.

At some time or other, millions of years ago, the crust of the earth cracked in all directions. A large fissure, the "Great Rift Valley", runs north and south through the whole of Africa. This crack starts in the valley of the Jordan, water collected in part of the crack to form the Red Sea, then it runs across Abyssinia and far into East Africa. The dusky blue Lake Natron with its crust of red salt is bedded in it, and farther on in our kingdom, diagonally below us, the Manjara Lake, discovered by Baumann, is also in its domain.

Michael turned down the flaps because there were giant craters towering before us. Our "zebra" slowed down and climbed. We could not do this for long in the thin air at this altitude, for there was insufficient air to cool the engine.

Between Lake Natron and Lake Manjara the fissures must have been especially deep and the pressure from underneath particularly strong. The glowing lava welled groaningly upwards and bubbled viscously in the volcanic cracks. One fiery mountain stood beside the next. This gave rise to a fortress of blazing cauldrons sixty miles long and forty miles wide, giants towering 13,000 feet towards the sky; almost as high as the Jungfrau.

Tourists in Italy admire the world famous Phlegraic Fields near Naples, where one crater is next to the other, but these are only small hills 600 to 1,200 feet high with a crater diameter of a few hundred yards. Here the mountains are ten times higher and the diameters are measured in miles. The bases of the giants are quite bare, but the higher they rise the denser grow the forests on their sides. Their heads are hidden by clouds and surrounded by thunder and lightning. These volcanic mountains catch the east winds blowing from the Indian Ocean, milk them of rain and leave the land to the westward dry and bare.

The interiors of the craters are filled with forest-fringed lakes populated by pink flamingoes, as can be seen from the air.

The lava from the centre of the earth must have been quite liquid, for it quickly spread in all directions leaving the tops rounded and flat. When they cooled down the lava which was still liquid must have descended again so that the upper crust sank down in circular form. This, and not explosions, created the huge craters, which is proved by the fact that the slopes are of pure lava and not of ash and brimstone, as is the case with exploded volcanoes. There are still similar volcanoes in Hawaii in which the lava level is constantly rising and falling.

The 7,000-to-8,000-foot plateau created by the fusion of these volcanoes is not very old, geologically speaking, but it must have existed before the last Ice Age. At the equator this was a rainy era and the lake in Ngorongoro, which is now only up to five feet deep, once reached a depth of fifty to eighty feet and filled a third of the crater.

When flying horizontally across the jungle of the highlands beside the crater, we could see the tree-tops inter-twining to form a thick green fur. Suddenly the ground abruptly fell away for 2,000 feet and it was as if an abyss had opened before our feet. Luckily we were safely air-borne, so we only pressed the stick forward and glided into the crater. We stayed five hundred feet up inside this gigantic cooking-pot and flew backwards and forwards from one cliff side to another. In this way we divided the area into ribbons which we could later recognise.

The droning of our "duck" stampeded a herd of wildebeest. Michael yelled something, but I could not understand him.

Our aeroplane was not elegantly done up inside, like a car; it was completely bare so that the metal interior was clearly visible. Since the cabin was usually full of chests and boxes, any upholstery would soon have been in a sorry state. We hoped to remedy this when our "duck" was safely back in Europe and being used only for pleasure flights. The noise of the motor and propeller hit us with undiminished force so that we could not hear ourselves speak. The droning in our ears persisted late at night when we were in bed. If this was to go on for weeks and months we might have to get deaf-aids from Europe before we were finished. We put on our earphones and talked to each other with the aid of throat microphones.

"Dad, how many wildebeest do you think there are in the herd on our right?" asked Michael.

I looked down. Seen vertically from above the grey-black wildebeest resembled scurrying ants. It was impossible to count them.

Since the cabin was not upholstered we could only talk to each other via microphones and earphones.

I shrugged my shoulders, and Michael did the same. He also wrinkled his nose in disgust because we had imagined the job would be much easier.

Suddenly I had an idea and dug him in the ribs. "Fly over them once more." I had noticed a small splinter-group comprising ten animals. Farther away there was another group which appeared similar in size at first glance. I counted these, too—ten animals again. I trained myself to take in thirty animals at once and after that did not count them individually but in groups of a dozen to fifty head. At first we made mistakes of two to five either way, but slowly we became more expert.

We flew past the herd once more, each of us counting and estimating separately. Michael made the number 780 and I made it 820. After that we had to pull up the flaps and fly a little faster because the oil temperature had risen too high.

We took our time and each of us counted the same herds repeatedly. After putting down our figures we compared them. It was a disadvantage that there were only two of us, for we had to keep a sharp look out in order to avoid flying into the walls of

How many wildebeest are there in this picture? Nearly five hundred.

the crater, and so we could not wholly concentrate on our counting.
We also had to take care to fly at the correct level, as otherwise
we would stampede the herds into an uncountable chaos. On
top of all this we had to keep a watch on landmarks and fly in a
straight line to avoid counting the same animals twice over.

After dividing the eighty square miles of the crater into even
strips we counted only 5,360 wildebeest, not the 10,000 estimated
by the game wardens. We also saw 117 elands, 1,170 gazelles,
19 rhinos, 46 elephants, 24 hyenas (most of them had probably
hidden in their holes) and 60 baboons.

All this would have to be repeated once the game wardens were
insured, for with two people counting on each side the results
would be much more reliable.

Tired, half-deafened and a little dizzy from the constant turning, we rose above the walls of the giant pot and flew home. At
Malanja we found the white-marked landing field and settled down
into the green grass. The landing strip turned out to be too short,
for we had not reckoned on the rarefied air, but we managed to
get down safely.

When the machine had come to a halt Michael stopped the motor, and we got out and lay flat on our backs in the grass. We were completely exhausted. Inquisitive Masai with long spears surrounded us, jabbering away in excitement and spitting into the grass. Michael closed his eyes. Slowly the ground beneath us ceased to heave.

We were happy. There would still be difficulties and we would have to do better in future, but the method was feasible. The great census of the animal population could be done by these means.

We had not yet devised the square, barbed-wire fence which later we used to protect our "duck" from lions and to prevent hyenas from eating the rubber tyres. But we surrounded the wheels with piles of stones and securely tied down the wings and tail to prevent the aeroplane from being moved by a tropical storm.

As a further precaution Michael then climbed into the cabin and switched on the light. The book he chose to read was about the Mau-Mau atrocities in neighbouring Kenya. Not exactly a pleasant way to spend the night, alone in the Highlands of the Giant Craters. . . .

We had to build a barbed-wire fence around our "flying zebra" to prevent hyenas and lions from chewing on the rubber tyres.

Lions frequently rested in the shade of our aeroplane.

CHAPTER 4

The Serengeti Lions

Our Lord gave the greatest and loveliest gifts to the most common animals, but men do not seek them there.

MARTIN LUTHER

SERONERA SEEMED easy to recognise from the air—the almost dry river, the flat house surrounded by a few native huts, a hill sprinkled with trees and a landing strip. There was no smoke to be seen anywhere and no wind sock. Since we could not judge the direction of the wind, landing was difficult and a following wind could easily have pushed us into the sparse little trees. We cleared the tree tops at minimum height, pushed down all flaps and even then came to rest only a few yards from the trees at the end of the runway.

A Land-Rover at once arrived in a huge cloud of dust and Myles Turner, the game warden of Eastern Serengeti, stepped out of it. "A splendid landing," he said. "You are the first to come down here! The landing strip isn't finished yet and eventually it will be twice as long."

Michael and I looked at each other.

We had mixed up Seronera with Banagi, but at least we had come to the right spot. Myles Turner had built us a "tin hut" by screwing together a set of pre-fabricated aluminum sheets. It was a few miles away from his house, because, according to him, this was where you could sit right in among the lions.

Myles Turner loves lions and during the first night I realised that he had chosen the right place. I often lay awake at night, because in this part of Africa there are twelve hours of darkness, summer or winter. Once Michael's head touched the pillow he slept like a hibernating bear, but I could hear the lions roaring quite close to the hut. Funnily enough this made me feel quite at home since I live inside the Frankfurt Zoo. Here, however, the roaring seemed more resonant, for the walls were only thin metal sheets and the windows were wide open. My camp bed seemed to vibrate to the thunderous growling. Michael did not move, he slept soundly, lying on his stomach as he had done ever since he was a little boy.

I smiled inwardly, for only a few weeks ago I had received a rather incoherent telephone call from Abyssinia, asking what width of ditch was required to stop lions from jumping across it. Now I was lying in a flimsy hut with an unbolted door and the lions were only a few yards away.

I nudged Michael. At first he grumbled like a sleepy child, but on hearing the lions he at once became wide awake. He switched on the tape-recorder which stood, ready for use, between our beds. It seemed as if a lion was bellowing directly into the microphone placed twenty yards outside the hut.

Suddenly there was a bang, the recorder fell to the floor and disappeared towards the door which slammed shut. A lion was playing with the cable. The whole hut was in an uproar. We jumped out of bed and shone a powerful torch through a crack in the door. The lion outside was large but not yet fully adult since he had no mane, and he was very playful. He regarded us with interest, and in the background there were further pairs of gleaming eyes. We carefully closed the door and braced some chairs against it.

When the sun rose behind the Banagi hills we discovered that the photographic tripod which had held the microphone was bitten to pieces. The lion had played with it and pulled on the cable with such power that the door had been bent outwards. After detaching the door we jumped up and down on it until it was reasonably flat again.

A rubber water container with a tap at the bottom hung beside the door. We were proud of our "running water", specially as it as it became running "hot" water during the day-time. Now we found that one of the visitors had slashed it with powerful claws and we had to mend the rents with a bicycle puncture outfit.

Our colleague Richard, who was staying with us for a few weeks, had to visit the little outhouse about forty yards away from the hut. While he was unsuspectingly sitting there five lionesses unconcernedly strolled past, one behind the other, not more than four or five yards from him. Michael and I yelled as loud as we could: "Come out! Come out! Quick! Quick!" Richard appeared in all haste, imperfectly clothed, and we managed to photograph him while the last lioness was still visible behind him. The big cats were not at all upset by our yells and barely turned their heads.

During the next few weeks our Serengeti lions saw to it that there was always something exciting going on. One day we met a leopard who had just killed a Thomson's gazelle, usually nicknamed "tommies", and had anchored it firmly in the fork of a tree in typical leopard fashion. A little later a pride of ten lions arrived under the tree and appeared much interested in the victim. The leopard seemed to feel uncomfortable and soon climbed down the far side of the tree and made off. A big male lion climbed up thirty feet to the dead gazelle, but however hard he pulled and tugged he could not dislodge it. Finally the lion tore the gazelle into two pieces and descended with the hindquarters in his mouth.

One night a lioness caught one of the porcupines which nightly raided Myles Turner's garden, although there was nothing much to eat there. Vegetables and flowers cannot tolerate the horrible water of the Banagi river and there is not enough stored rain water to maintain them through the dry season. We could see signs of a fight and evidently the old porcupine had sold its life dearly.

Another pride of eleven lions killed an old giraffe bull so close to the motor track that we could watch them from the house in Banagi. It took them three days to finish this mountain of meat.

When Regowert, the black scout, camped out in the plains, two lionesses looked straight into his face through the mosquito net.

On another night an African cook who worked for Gordon Poolman, one of the game wardens, was preparing supper when he saw a hyena outside. When he opened the door to throw a stone at it, he looked straight into the eyes of a large lion which was lying in front of the door, barely ten feet away. The cook closed the door quickly, barred it by pushing a table across it, and climbed across the dividing wall from the kitchen to his bedroom. While this was going on there were yells, hisses and thumps outside. In the morning a dead hyena lay outside the door, but large tufts from the lion's mane showed that the *fisi* (the Swahili name for a hyena) had defended itself bravely. Richard stuck a tuft of lion's mane into his hatband instead of a feather.

If you had to be reincarnated as a lion, the best place for you to be born would be in Serengeti. There is plenty of game and large swarms of malarial mosquitoes and tsetse flies—as well as lack of water—make it uninhabitable by man. Even people who at home boast of their bravery as lion hunters admit that Serengeti is *the* place for lions.

When Tanganyika came under British control after the first World War, hunters from the older British colony of Kenya soon came into the Banagi region because Serengeti was so conveniently close. Nobody felt scruples about massacring the lions since they were simply regarded as dangerous pests. Some hunters returned from such safaris having killed one hundred lions on a single trip. Since they could not carry so many skins they merely hacked off the tails as trophies.

In 1929 ninety square miles of the open plains towards Lake Victoria were declared a protected area in which hunting was prohibited. In 1931 the small house in Banagi was built and occupied by the first game warden, Monty Moore. From that time to the present the lion's lot has steadily grown ever more pleasant.

Monty had many troubles. He soon found that it was not essential to photograph lions at a kill by flashlamps at night, as in the times of Schillings and Maxwell. It could be done just as easily in the daytime. In the thirties it became fashionable to shoot a zebra, tie it to the car by a long rope and drag it into the vicinity of some lions. The big cats soon appeared and tore the zebra to pieces while being photographed from the safety of the car.

Lions quickly grew accustomed to this new game and started to trot up from their shady resting place by the dry river bed as soon as they heard the engine of a car. Monty and his wife were most concerned because all their favourite lions, whom they had given nicknames, were fond of leaving the preserve and wandering into the surrounding country, where they could be shot at. They tried their best to entice their pets back to safety with juicy bait, but hunting parties frequently stopped outside their doors with skins of old friends and favourites such as "Simon" or "Greybeard". These animals had clearly been shot from the car, judging by the hunters' clear footwear, but Monty had to grind his teeth and listen in silence to the strenuous adventures which his unwelcome guests claimed to have experienced in order to kill these monsters. Nowadays the whole region is inside the National Park and from a lion's point of view the situation could hardly be better.

Dr. Gerhard Hass, one of my colleagues at the Frankfurt Zoo, took the time and trouble to spend days and nights in the lion house to find out how many hours our big cats slept. Even allowing for the fact that they are known to be lazy animals, the result was still surprising. According to age and sex our lions slept for ten to fifteen hours out of twenty-four. On top of this they dozed for an additional one to four hours and lay awake but unmoving for another one to five hours. They were thus active from one to seven hours per day at the most.

If you are acquainted with zoo lions you might assume that they are so indolent only because they have their food provided for them, but we noticed that the free-living Serengeti lions show a similar lack of activity. In the Zoo they spend twenty, or at the most sixty minutes actually eating, and this time is hardly increased when they are at liberty, for catching their prey is usually only a matter of minutes. Infectious diseases, such as those to which wildebeest and giraffes are susceptible, do not seem to occur among the big cats.

The life of a lion in the Serengeti would be undiluted joy if he did not have to grow old, but on reaching the age of fourteen or fifteen they become dodderers. We met such an old greybeard one day lying in the shade of a tree with no other life near him. His lips drooped to show his blunt yellow teeth, and each rib was visible through the skin. His lower eyelids sagged and his curved back and stiff legs showed that it hurt him to take even a few steps. Such lions are sooner or later killed and eaten by hyenas or wild dogs.

Myles Turner once saw a pack of wild dogs surrounding an old lion. They danced and leaped, like puppies at play, and made mock attacks. The old beast snarled and hit out at them till they withdrew.

I could not sleep at night thinking about the lonely old lion, and was deeply tempted to go out and shoot a gazelle for him. It is curious how often one wants to help one creature by hurting another. I have a suspicion that Myles Turner actually went to the free grounds outside the Park and shot some game for the old gentleman, for Myles' love of lions is unqualified. Many other people feel the same. The main principle of the game reserve, however, is that you should never interfere, but let Nature take her own course.

A few days earlier the other game warden, Gordon Poolman, who lives at Seronera, returned from several days' safari to the "corridor", our private name for the narrow part of the Park near Lake Victoria. Gordon told us that he had seen a lion lying on top of a freshly caught wildebeest. The game warden drove up in his car and chased the lion away. Then he got out and was just about to cut himself a nice steak from the hind-quarters of the wildebeest when his black companion shouted: "Turn round, Bwana! Turn round!"

The "dead" wildebeest had jumped up and nearly pierced him with its sharp horns. Gordon managed to grip the horns at the last moment and to get into the car before the animal freed itself, for no one can hold a struggling wildebeest by the horns single-handed for more than a few seconds.

Next day I met Gordon's wife Connie in their home at Seronera. I told her the story of the lion and the wildebeest, as if it had happened to *me*. "Only imagine, I came across a lion who had just killed a wildebeest and was lying on top of it . . ." etc., etc.

Connie's eyes grew rounder and rounder. She was speechless with amazement. Finally anger got the upper hand and she exploded: "But that happened to my husband!"

"That's true, Connie," I said, "but one should not tell such stories to men who write books about Africa. In print these things always happened to the author in person. Those who come from afar can get away with lots of things."

It is not too rare for an apparently dead animal to run away when the lion is driven off. This happened recently when four lionesses were forced to abandon a zebra foal, which ran screaming back to its mother. A few weeks before that, Myles Turner was an eyewitness at a similar event with a Thomson's gazelle. Just as a lion cub will remain completely motionless while the mother is carrying it about in her mouth, so there are many animals which instinctively stay quiet and do not struggle when gripped by a lion. If they struggled and tried to defend themselves, the lion would either kill them at once or paralyse them with a swipe of its paw, but by remaining still they have at least some very small chance of escape.

I even suspect that animals feel neither pain nor fear in the mouth of the lion. I could almost say I *know* it.

Most men have not been endangered by large predators for thousands of years, but stillness when captured is just as instinctive as the suckling of a baby or the narrowing of the eyes in bright sunlight. David Livingstone, the great African missionary and explorer, was once gripped and dragged by a lion. He reported later: "The lion growled dreadfully into my ear and shook me as a terrier shakes a rat. The shock caused a stupor similar to that of a mouse caught by a cat. It produced a sort of insensitivity during which I felt neither pain nor fear, although I was fully conscious. I was like a patient under slight narcosis who watches an operation on himself but does not feel the scalpel. This singular condition was not due to a mental process but to shock which wiped out all feelings of fear and pain—even when viewing the lion directly." Livingstone's companions drove the lion away in the next few moments.

During the first few decades the game wardens did not drive around by car but went on horseback, while their luggage went by ox-cart. They also took dogs along, and every evening the animals had to be placed behind a high thorn fence to protect them from lions.

To this day every game warden recalls what happened at that time to one of their number called Wolhuter in South Africa. He was overtaken by twilight while still six miles away from his camp. When he was crossing a dry river bed a lion leaped at his horse which jumped aside and threw its rider straight into the mouth of a second lion. This beast gripped Wolhuter by the right shoulder and dragged him away.

The game warden was completely paralysed at first and felt no pain. Then he considered that it was humiliating for an experienced hunter to die in this way. While his body was sweeping along under the belly of the lion his spurs kept on digging into the ground until they broke off. Wolhuter remembered his hunting knife, which usually dropped out of his belt even when he was getting off his horse, but when he felt for it with his left hand he was surprised to find that for once it was in its proper place. When the lion finally laid him down after dragging him for ninety yards (the distance was measured later) his right arm was powerless but he twice, left-handedly, stabbed it in the chest.

The lion retreated and snarled in his face. Wolhuter's dogs, who had followed him, barking like mad, set on the lion and drove it away. Despite his wounded arm the game warden climbed a tree and tied himself to a branch while the lion circled around the base of it. Soon after that his black companions arrived and finally put the lion to flight.

It was later found that Wolhuter had killed the lion, or rather lioness, which he had stabbed and that it was her companion, the one which attacked the horse, that had been circling round the tree. Propped up by his companions Wolhuter staggered back to the camp. He was carried by stretcher for two days before he reached the railway, and it took another day's journey before he saw a doctor. His arm remained permanently stiff, but he never blamed the lions.

The story of the game warden's adventures reached the ears of a reporter and was published, in tremendously exaggerated form, in all the newspapers. When one London daily stated that Wolhuter had strangled three lions single-handed, the game warden wrote to ask for a correction. He received the following reply. "We have investigated this matter. Our Johannesburg correspondent is extremely reliable and we see no cause to publish a correction." When Wolhuter was in London a few years later he went to the shop from which his hunting knife had come, to buy another and casually remarked to the assistant: "Your knives are very good, I stabbed a lion with one of them some time ago." If he expected astonishment or admiration, he was disappointed. The young man behind the counter replied in an offhand way: "I can well believe it, our knives are frequently used to kill sheep."

Myles Turner and his petite young wife live in an old clay hut at the foot of the Banagi Hills. Myles can be moody, specially on days when he has to suppress attacks of malaria by swallowing tablets, and feels like killing himself and all those around him. If his help is required, however, he will be there regardless of distance or time. Ever since his fifteenth birthday he has made notes every night of animal behaviour observed during the day. His evidence is therefore reliable.

Here are some extracts from Myles's diary:

"*9th October:* at four o'clock this afternoon I saw three half-grown lions, one of which carried something strange in its mouth. When it was dropped I saw that it was a tortoise. The three lions had chewed through the lower carapace and half eaten it.

15th March: I saw a large lion trying to kill a hyena. When it was dead the lion went off to stalk another, which barely got away.

21st March: A visitor claims that on the road from Olduvai Gorge to Seronera he saw seventy-five lions.

22nd June: Inside one hour a lioness stalked and killed four separate Tommies within sight of the house."

Many of the animal stories in this book were told to me by Myles. He was thirty-eight years old when I met him, and had been in Kenya since the age of three. His father had a cattle farm near Rumuruti, in the North. Little Myles got his first gun when he was nine and started to shoot zebras. At that time they were still as common in that region as they are in the Serengeti to-day, but not a single one now remains there. The farmers regarded the zebras as pests which stole their cattle fodder, so shot them in large numbers and the killer got a shilling bounty for every tail he delivered.

Myles went to school in Nairobi and then became a white hunter, accompanying tourists on hunting expeditions, until he grew tired of it.

Many game wardens started life as professional hunters, until they thought better of it and began to protect animals instead of shooting them. While working for the safari firm, Myles met his wife Kay who was there as a secretary. Since then they have lived with a little water and a lot of dust, surrounded by lions, mambas and zebras.

When Myles was thirty he went to Europe for the first time. What does a man from the bush feel like in a big city? Just as we were impressed by the lions close to our beds in the Serengeti, so Myles was struck by the crowds of people in the narrow streets, the tall houses, the large shop windows and the theatres. On his next leave, in three years' time, he has promised to visit Frankfurt.

I could only remain in Africa a few weeks at a time, for my primary job was, after all, the direction of the Frankfurt Zoo. Michael could remain much longer. It was good to know that during our absences the keen eyes of Myles, and of our other good friends in the Park, would keep a lookout for marked animals and other interesting events, and report to us by letter.

The large eland antelopes in the Serengeti would never let us approach closer than five or six hundred yards before running away. I only discovered much later that the reason for this was the Masai religion. Watching lions, on the other hand, is childishly easy, almost easy as in the zoo. One can approach to within a few yards or even feet as long as one stays inside the car. It was exciting and challenging.

One day we did not intend to go after lions. We drove out in our striped car intending to shoot Tommies—with narcotics. Suddenly we saw two large lions diagonally in front of us to one side, two lionesses on the other and a third lioness, which we had not noticed while driving, behind us. The third lioness rose slowly and stared unblinkingly into the grass by the dry river bed where a Tommy buck was grazing. The lioness crept towards him. If the buck raised his head the lioness froze, even the half-raised paw remained in mid-air. When the buck started to graze again she recommenced her stalking.

In the meantime the two lions approached the buck from the side. To do this they had to pass the car and one of them got so close that I could have leaned out and touched him. I went "pst", but the lion did not even turn his head away from the prey.

The unsuspecting Tommy was being stalked from three sides.

On the fourth side a half-grown male lion was also coming closer. The youngster, whose mane was beginning to sprout untidily, could not wait. Although the distance was much too great he charged and the buck naturally escaped.

If I had been one of the adult lions I would have cuffed the youngster's ears without pulling in my claws, but they did not seem to care. They just plumped down wherever they happened to be standing.

We followed one of the adults and drove to within eight yards, for it hurts one's pride when animals, even lions, regard one as so much thin air. When I opened the door and started to get out the lion rose, snarled, spat and came towards me. I naturally disappeared back inside the car again.

If one is attacked by a lion in the open it is best to stand quite still and look at him. He will usually lose courage, stop and finally go away. If one tries to escape he will attack at once and play cat and mouse. I have never had to put it to the test in Africa but drew on this experience the only time I experimented with training big cats in a menagerie.

It was always a joy to watch a pride of lions resting in the shade of a tree. To whom did the eight children belong? Three of them were nearly twice as large as the other five and must therefore have had different mothers. All the five adult lionesses, however, were equally friendly to all the cubs, and since they were lying down one could not see which of them was in milk. If one of the cubs passed an adult a rough tongue would carelessly lick its face or back. The cubs stalked the black tassel on the tail of one of the males in the best hunting style. When they "captured" and bit it with their sharp milk teeth they must have caused pain, but the lion merely snarled and did not punish his tormentors. When they passed the big male the cubs fondly rubbed their woolly heads against his chin, just like domestic cats rubbing against our legs. One of the males even condescended to play, toppling over one of the cubs and rolling it with his paw. The children seemed to be permitted to do as they liked, even to the extent of pulling at the meat in the mouth of the lord and master. Among lions such forbearance is almost incredible.

Lions belong to the cat family, but they are not like domestic cats. They cannot purr, and neither do they "wash" themselves as thoroughly. A lion will only wash his face after a meal as a rule, but merely around the mouth and hardly ever behind the ears. After that he will lick his chest and paws perhaps, but not his belly and flanks like domestic cats. Lions do not bury their dung and urine but merely scratch the ground with their hind paws a few times.

Lions certainly fight at mating time, leaving large tufts of yellow mane on the battlefield. Although they may scratch and wound each other I have never heard of one being killed during these battles. They kill zebras, wildebeest and other antelopes, but they do it quickly by breaking the neck or biting through it, so that the victim feels less terror than cattle when we put them to death in a slaughterhouse. It is almost unknown for a lion to kill one of his own breed, so that we humans, who murdered millions of our fellow men in Europe during the last war, could well learn decent behaviour from them.

On the 9th May, and on the 15th and 16th June as well, Myles observed a large male lion with a broken shoulder. It is probable that a buffalo or giraffe kicked him when defending itself. The lion could hardly move and had another full-grown male in constant attendance. Since the injured lion appeared well fed his companion must have hunted for him.

A few days later we saw a sick lioness not far from the abandoned gold mine of Kilimafea. She was with sixteen others and in this case they also seem to have provided for her.

On St. Nicholas day we saw a starved and weak old lion and three half-grown cubs near the track leading from Banagi to Seronera. When we passed the same spot two days later we saw the young ones in company with a healthy young male and a lioness. The sick old lion had apparently lost his family and died—but the children had found foster-parents.

Some visitors to the National Park picnicked beside their car in the open. Afterwards when they returned from the water hole, where they had washed their hands, they found a lion family among their hampers, Thermos flasks and crockery. The remnants of the meal had disappeared. The cubs had torn the luggage open and were playing with cameras and blankets. They were not easily distracted from these wonderful toys and the visitors had to watch the destruction of their property for two hours, before the lions got tired of the game and left.

I do not want to imply that lions are angels, and in any case I have only been writing about *our* lions in the Serengeti and the neighbourhood of Banagi. To chill your spine a little—as is only fair when talking about lions—I will conscientiously relate some of the tales about man-killers which have been part and parcel of the African record for generations.

In 1898 two man-killers held up the building of the Uganda railway for nine months, in the region which now belongs to the Tsavo National Park in Kenya. They devoured twenty-eight of the native workmen and finished up by eating the inspector himself. He had been sitting in a carriage armed with a gun in order to shoot them, but must have fallen asleep.

Even in 1955–6 lions are said to have killed forty-five people in the region of Ankole in Uganda. All the game on which they had lived had been poached by the natives. Several years ago a Mr. Bradshaw reported that he had seen a lioness regurgitate human flesh to feed her cubs. A visitor to this neighbourhood was also killed last year. He had just shot a lion and was about to be photographed with his foot on the body when the lion turned and clawed him before it died. The licence of the white hunter who accompanied the visitor was suspended for five years.

I am not writing about lions in general, however, but about those in the Serengeti. Here they have game in plenty and do not regard men as palatable. They are, after all, specially distinguished lions who have been born with silver spoons in their mouths.

This old castle near Ikoma, in northern Serengeti, was occupied by German troops around 1900.

CHAPTER 5

A European Castle in Africa

The missing links between apes and the human race are—men.

KONRAD LORENZ

I GRIPPED my son's knee and bellowed in his ear: "Michael, on the mountain on the right down below there's a castle!"

A real medieval castle in Central Africa? It must have been an illusion, especially since every other hill-top sported piles of broken rocks which looked like ruined churches or gigantic monuments. But this time we were not mistaken. We put the "flying zebra" into a right-handed turn and flew back to the hill with the castle ruins. It was really there and we could see the thick, crenellated walls and the massive watch tower. There were also crumbling houses and a large courtyard. All this ruined splendour among sparsely-wooded, desolate hills north of the Serengeti National Park, and far outside its borders. We flew lower and lower until the solid corner tower seemed to loom above us. It seemed inexplicable.

We were on our way to Masabi, a plain which lies in the narrow "corridor" of the Park, near Lake Victoria. We had intended to stay the night in one of the clay huts used by the native scouts and to watch animals at a nearby water hole in the early morning. Two scouts sat in the passenger seats behind us and another couple waited on the plain below. They stood close to a little copse, as arranged, so that we had to fly between them to reach the selected landing strip, an area which was free of stones and pot-holes. The excursion to the castle had taken so much time that we had to land directly into the setting sun. Since he was half-blinded Michael was afraid of hitting one of the men and, therefore, put on full flaps to touch down before reaching them.

There was a sudden, not too violent, jerk and the engine stopped. We found ourselves flat on the earth as if we had made a belly landing without an undercarriage—but our little 'plane did not have retractable wheels!

One of the wheels had run into a wart-hog hole and the supporting leg had broken off. This had caused the other leg to come away as well, which in turn forced the propeller against the ground. Apart from a slightly dented wing tip there was no damage to the 'plane itself. If you did not know that it normally stood on long stilt-like legs you might think that it was in its natural position.

The first thing we did was to spread out a long strip of orange-coloured cloth, and weight it down with bones and wildebeest skulls so that we could be seen from the air. Then a large area around the 'plane was cleared of dry grass to prevent it catching light in case of a bush fire. We could sleep inside the cabin.

Out pet bushbaby, which we had brought with us from Frankfurt to the land of its birth, refused to leave the cabin. As an arboreal animal it was afraid of the bare, open countryside. Our two passengers were quite unmoved. Evidently they thought this was the normal way of landing, for it had been their first flight.

The fatal wart-hog hole was half overgrown and not particularly deep. Two adult wart-hogs and four young ones stood about a hundred yards away with their tails vertically upwards, like flagpoles. As we looked at them fixedly they turned and ran off. We were going to have plenty of time to observe these animals.

Wart-hogs are charming creatures. If you see them in a zoo you might be repelled by the four to six inch long warts on the face of the boars and their razor-sharp, dangerously upward-curving tusks. Their faces are not pretty by human standards, but in the wild state they look like little rhinos or even antelopes. Unlike wild and domesticated European pigs they have no fatty layer under their skin, even when well nourished. They also start digging into the earth by folding their forelegs and "kneeling" on their wrists.

Since lions find wart-hogs delectable these pigs live in underground nests where they cannot be reached. Their favourite houses are tunnels dug by aardvarks in their search for termites.

The structure consists of a large chamber in which the parents and children sleep. Leading diagonally downward from it there is a tunnel to another chamber in which the charming piglets are born in September or October. These never number more than four and have a cosily warm nursery, the temperature of which remains according to the measurements of Professor Geigy of Basle at about 85° Fahrenheit. That is perhaps why so few wart-hogs have been reared in zoos.

Even after the young have grown up they prefer to stay with their parents, in fact they lead an exemplary family life. If two hogs belonging to the same family meet, the younger one approaches the elder, touches snouts, and gently pokes the old one's

This wart-hog insisted on crossing the road at the last possible moment, directly in front of our car.

This wart-hog boar was angry because we drove beside him. He almost attacked the car.

chin once or twice.   Another sign of affection is to nibble gently at the head or mane of a companion.

If a mother with a young family is chased, the young ones sometimes fall down and play dead. If you pick one up, however, it will squeal as if you were murdering it. This usually brings the mother back on the scene. If you then release the piglet it rushes back to its mother and the whole family makes off again.

A game warden once saw a wart-hog mother being chased by a leopard. The sow suddenly turned and attacked the leopard—putting it to flight. On another occasion an elephant was irritated for some reason or other by a wart-hog. He trumpeted and attacked. This proved too much for the wart-hog, which turned and rushed at the elephant who retreated in surprise. Nor were the wart-hogs on the lawn of a game warden's house intimidated by his big dog; they chased him off the premises.

We had wrapped ourselves in our blankets and were just about to go to sleep when two lights appeared in the far distance. This turned out to be Myles in his car. He had brought *everything* with him, hot coffee in Thermos flasks, brandy, bandages, food, a collapsible stretcher, splints and blankets, and not to mention his wife and young baby in a carry-cot. Since we had not returned by sundown he had at once set out to look for us. This is typical of Myles, who can always be depended upon to turn up when he is needed. Since he did not want to leave his wife alone all night he had brought her with him, which meant the baby had to come, too.

Next day we sent telegrams, via the Nairobi radio connection, to Germany, and airmailed photographs of the aeroplane, taken from all angles, to Munich so that the factory could decide what replacements and spare parts were needed.

Then we made camp and waited for two engineers from Nairobi to arrive. They took three days to reach us. One of them had injured his spine in a flying accident five years ago. He had been almost paralysed for nearly a year and had sworn that he would never fly again. He was quite sprightly now. The two of them, a Londoner and a Scot, worked like Trojans, but we had to keep them supplied with large quantities of beer. They were very eager

Our "flying zebra" lay with broken legs for several weeks.

to learn German swear words, and we taught them some magnificently resounding ones.

It would be at least three weeks before our striped zebra could take the air again. In the meantime we had to crawl along the ground feeling slow and clumsy. It did give us time, however, to take another look at the incredible castle we had seen from the air. It lay in the territory of the Ikoma tribe, of which Mgabo, our driver, was a member. His father had been a foreman in a mine during the German rule, and as a child Mgabo had often played in the ruins of the German fort, which was then still occupied by German troops. There was a bitter fight between German and British troops, he told us: "Look over there. On that hillside there was a pile of bodies."

As we drove across the old, weed-infested road between the trees a small herd of topi antelopes made way for us. Then we saw a gap in the thick high walls. Although only made of stone blocks and clay most of the walls had survived for fifty years, since there is no frost and little rain in this region.

As we went through the gap into the large courtyard three startled zebras galloped through the entrance gate. The walls of the houses were still standing, except where they had been split by the trees which were growing up all over the site.

Mgabo took us on a guided tour of the fort. The Lieutenant lived in the large house with the free-standing staircase. The kitchen was nearby and the sergeant's little house opposite. The deep cistern still showed the water-level marks and two red flowers were growing at the edge of it.

A crumbling trench ran all round the old fort. Michael dug in the N.C.O.'s living quarters and unearthed a few coins. After cleaning them we could see the inscription: "D.O.A. 1916. Fünf Heller." This was the colonial money of the former German East Africa, and it had been minted during the war (D.O.A. = Deutsch Ost-Afrika, German East Africa). Our bank in Frankfurt when we returned home offered us nearly £ 1 each for these low denomination coins. A few weeks later Mgabo's uncle brought us a fifty-rupee note bearing the portrait of Kaiser Wilhelm with his up-twirled moustache.

According to Mgabo the Germans buried their guns and ammunition in a deep shaft before leaving. The weapons were then covered with a layer of cement and the shaft was filled in. There they lay for forty years, until the British dug them up again, perhaps in case ammunition fell into the hands of the Mau-Mau in nearby Kenya.

As Michael and I leaned on the breastwork and looked across the green-blue hills we thought how lonely the German troops must have felt so far from home, especially as the endless distances had to be covered on foot. There were no cars, no radio and no proper tinned food. Since the German Colonial administration had insufficient money for a telegraph system, isolated posts used to communicate with each other by heliograph. When our film *Serengeti Shall Not Die* was shown in Germany, a retired General, P. Diesener, wrote to tell me that he was in command of the Ikoma fort from 1900 until 1913 as a young lieutenant. He had to defend the natives against the war-like Masai, to look after the prospectors, and to hold court over the Africans. This fort was only ten days' walk from Uwanza. The old General never imagined that he would see his old fort again in full colour on the screen.

But the history of Tanganyika began long before the Kaiser signed the protective agreement in 1885. The first to discover it were probably not Europeans at all but the Chinese. It took us thousands of years before our little ships could round the Cape, but the Asians had a very much easier task. Every year the monsoon blew them towards Africa from November to February and it blew them back towards Asia just as reliably from April to September. The Arabs and Indians reached the shores of Tanganyika in this manner many centuries B.C. Chinese coins minted twelve centuries ago, and even older Chinese pottery can be found in Tanganyika. A Chinese writer left a description of the country and the people in about A.D. 1000, and four hundred years later a Chinese expedition took a giraffe back to China as a present for the Emperor. Arabs from Shiraz in Persia founded towns in the islands off the coast, and in Kilwa there is an Arab chronicle dating from A.D. 1060 up to the arrival of the Portuguese five hundred years later.

Vasco da Gama, the first man to round the Cape, landed at Kilwa, in Tanganyika, on his third journey to India in 1502. He promised Emir Muhammad Kiwabi safe conduct, but broke his word and kept him captive until the Emir had acknowledged Portuguese suzerainty and paid 5,000 crusados (about £ 2,000) ransom. From this money Vasco da Gama ordered a gold monstrance to be made to the greater Glory of God, which can be seen in the church of Our Lady of Belém in Lisbon to this day.

In 1593 the Portuguese built the proud Fort Jesus in Mombasa. There were wars, rebellions and butcheries of the cannibals from the interior until 1696, when the Arabs came from Oman in the Persian Gulf and captured the fort after a siege lasting thirty-three months.

The new Sultans of Zanzibar loved their second kingdom on the shores of Tanganyika, but they constantly had to return to the Persian Gulf to protect their thrones from usurping relatives.

The Arab Sultans never really ruled anything but the coast of Tanganyika, but they sent slave and ivory hunters into the interior.

These finally reached Lake Tanganyika in 1860. Their caravan route passed Tabora, and along this road the Germans later built a railway. Although the red Arab flag flew above the trading posts on the trade routes, the two or three Arab traders who sold their goods at fantastic prices really depended on the goodwill of the local chieftains.

The Arab slave hunts in East Africa never reached the frightful proportions of the similar trade in human beings carried out by Europeans and Americans on the West Coast, and the lot of the slaves in Arabia and in India was not so harsh as that of those in the plantations of North and Central America. The Arab slave trade was, however, still extensive enough to completely disrupt tribal traditions and depopulate whole areas, such as the region near Lake Tanganyika. If you travel by railroad from Dar-es-Salaam to Lake Victoria, via Tabora and Mwanza, you cannot tell that the land all around has been fertilised by the blood, flesh and bones of slaves who collapsed by the road, under Arab whips, during their endless marches, and that the soil had been wetted by the tears of mothers separated from their husbands and children.

Before the Suez Canal was built European ships bound for East Africa were rounding the Cape in increasing numbers. Said ben Sultan, one of the Arab rulers in Zanzibar, therefore signed treaties with many nations. First with the United States in 1833, followed by Great Britain, France and finally in 1859 with the German Hanseatic League. Each promised not to buy ivory and gum arabic on the Tanganyika coast, but to respect the monopoly of the Sultan. This was the only thing that mattered to him, he did not care about the ruling of the country. Meanwhile the cruel ivory and slave trade was taking the Arabs farther and farther into the interior. In 1850 a certain Said bin Habib bin Salim Safifi left Zanzibar and did not return for sixteen years. During that time he had visited Loanda, on the African West Coast, three times, and was therefore the first man to cross the whole continent, long before Stanley did so.

Reports of such exploits stimulated the curiosity of Europeans. Two things particularly drew Europeans at first to Central Africa during the nineteenth century: the wish to convert the poor ignorant heathens to Christianity, and the desire to explore unknown territory. Trade and greed did not come till later.

The first explorer, a French naval officer called Maizan, started in the rainy season—of all times. He carried such splendid provision boxes that he was murdered before he had covered fifty miles. In 1848 two German missionaries, Johann Rebmann and Ludwig Krapf, were the first Europeans to set eyes on the icy cap of Kilimanjaro. An Englishman later wrote: "These two missionaries lacked nearly all the physical attributes required for expeditions, and had no scientific knowledge. Krapf carried a gun which caused constant accidents and his mounts usually bolted under him. The most remarkable part of his equipment seems to have been an umbrella under which he and his companions slept during rainy weather. He scared away a lion by suddenly opening it, and on another occasion did the same to a band of robbers. But whatever their shortcomings, these were more than compensated for by their knowledge of languages, their sympathetic understanding of the natives and above all by their rugged determination and bravery."

Missionaries' tales about large lakes in the interior stimulated protests (but also the curiosity) of professional geographers. In 1857 the two Englishmen Richard Burton and John Speke discovered Lake Tanganyika. While Burton lay sick in Tabora, Speke went on and in August 1858 saw the largest lake in Africa, a sheet of water larger than the whole of Ireland, and named it Lake Victoria. The bay at which the Serengeti touches the lake is called Speke Gulf in honour of the explorer. When Burton heard Speke's story he doubted whether Lake Victoria really gave birth to the Nile, and therefore set out again in 1860, accompanied by James Augustus Grant, who gave his name to a beautiful gazelle. In July 1862 these two stood, deeply moved, and saw the waterfalls in which the Nile flows from Lake Victoria.

Before starting from the coast the two explorers had met a citizen of Hamburg called Albrecht Roscher. The deposed King Ludwig I of Bavaria had supplied Roscher with funds "To look for the innermost African lakes." The amount of money cannot have been great, for Roscher was only accompanied by two servants and two porters. Nevertheless he was murdered for his miserable possessions. The power of the Sultan was still extensive enough to have the murderers caught and brought to the coast for trial.

The great missionary and explorer Livingstone had travelled up the Zambezi and discovered Lake Nyasa a few weeks before Roscher (believing himself to be the first) reached it. From 1866 to 1869 Livingstone pushed farther into the interior. When he returned to Ujiji, by the shores of Lake Tanganyika, after an absence of three years, looking like "a ruckle of bones" he was deeply disappointed to discover that the provisions he had ordered had either been stolen or were still two hundred and fifty miles away in Tabora. No letters from Europe had reached him.

Since nothing had been heard of him in Europe for five years the *New York Herald* sent their correspondent Henry Morton Stanley to look for him in 1870. Stanley succeeded but could only move the seriously ailing missionary as far as Tabora. Livingstone refused to return to the coast and to Europe but set out once more to explore the east side of Lake Tanganyika. One morning his two black servants found him dead, kneeling beside his bed. These faithful souls, James Chulla and Abdulla Susi, took the emaciated corpse and all his notes and instruments to the coast. Livingstone now lies in Westminster Abbey, among the greatest men of the land. His two servants later guided expeditions into Central Africa.

In the 'eighties A. G. Fischer, a German doctor, travelled into the region round Lake Victoria. On the depopulated eastern shore, where the Serengeti is situated, he could raise so little food that he died of the effects of his journey soon after his return. Another careful observer was Joseph Thomson, the Englishman after whom the handsome yellow, white and black striped gazelles are named. Fischer and Thomson were the last truly scientific explorers for a long time. The men who followed them usually had secret, secondary motives.

Although German merchants had been in Zanzibar since 1840, and German explorers such as Roscher and von der Decken had been the first in Tanganyika, the German government remained quite uninterested in that country. In 1870 the German Consul in Zanzibar wrote to inform the Foreign Office in Berlin that the

Sultan was quite prepared to accept German protection.   He never received a reply.

In England things were not very different.   In 1884 the geographer Henry Hamilton Johnston, who had travelled on the slopes of Kilimanjaro, bought some land in Moshi and wrote telling the British Foreign Office that the local tribes would favour British protection.   The British Government sent enquiries to the Consul in Zanzibar who had never heard of the matter and advised against it.   When Johnston returned to England he had no notion of the events which had occurred in his absence.

The German Colonial Company advocated the acquisition of German Colonies despite the opposition of Bismarck.   In 1884 they sent Dr. Carl Peters, Count Otto Pfeil and others to Zanzibar. They travelled third class from Trieste disguised as mechanics and with false papers.   Although a telegram from Bismarck awaited them in Zanzibar, warning them that they could in no circumstances depend on the protection of the German Government, they went inland, established contact with the local chieftains, and persuaded them to sign undertakings that they were not subjects of the Sultan.   It became a race between them and General Lloyd Mathews, whom the Sultan had sent to the same region with one hundred and eighty soldiers.   The chiefs alternately declared for Peters and the Germans, and for Mathews and the Sultan.   One of them even stated that he was in favour of whichever gave him the prettiest flag to hoist on his flagstaff.   Sometimes these "chiefs" were only village elders or unimportant relatives of the real rulers. When Peters returned to Berlin with his "documents" Bismarck had to bow to public opinion and change his attitude completely. He gave the German Colonial Company an Imperial letter of safe conduct for the newly acquired territories.   Although the Sultan of Zanzibar maintained garrisons in some of these areas, his protests were vain, a German squadron forced him to recognise German protection.

Carl Peters made another secret journey to Uganda and collected more signatures.   When he returned to the coast he found he had been wasting his time.   Bismarck and the British Government had agreed on German and British spheres of influence in East Africa; Uganda had gone to the British.   A commission consisting of an

Englishman, a German and a Frenchman, and on which the Sultan had no representative, decided the future of the Sultan's Kingdom. The British ordered the Sultan to cede the Kilimanjaro region to the Germans. In return for Heligoland, Germany agreed in 1890 that Zanzibar should come under British protection. On 1st January 1891, the German Government took over the control of the new protected area of Tanganyika, which was given the name German East Africa.

The densely populated cemetery of the Benedictine monks in Dar-es-Salaam bears evidence of the many deaths among the Germans who flocked to the new colony.

The first rebellion broke out as early as 1888, while the Germans were nominally only in charge of the customs and excise on the coast by arrangement with the Sultan. The rebel leader, Bushiri, behaved in a chivalrous manner at first. He protected a Bishop from the raging mob and sent him and five European women to the coast. Later the struggle grew more bitter. The German Imperial Commissioner, von Wissmann, had to intervene with troops from Egypt and Zulus from Portuguese East Africa. Bushiri's stronghold was forced, the rebels were routed, and finally Bushiri himself was captured, half-naked, hiding in a hut. He was bound and taken to Banagi where he was hanged on 15th December 1889.

The rising led by Mkwawa, chieftain of the Hehe people, consisting of twenty-nine tribes which his father had unified, proved more serious. Mkwawa's demands for tribute from all caravans crossing the territory soon brought him into conflict with the new German administration.

Finally a force of 400 askaris was sent out to subdue the powerful black ruler. Mkwawa was conciliatory at first, and sent messengers with gifts. But his emissaries were fired on, perhaps due to a misunderstanding, and only one of them returned to Mkwawa. As a result the king laid an ambush in a thickly wooded valley and killed two hundred and fifty black and ten white soldiers, as well as capturing three hundred guns, three field guns and a lot of ammunition.

Mkwawa maintained himself until 1898, when the new German Governor put a price of 5,000 rupees on his head. This too had no effect. But a lad who had been captured by the Germans disclosed that he was Mkwawa's servant and that the king was seriously ill and hiding in the bush quite close by.   Two bodies were observed at the indicated spot by a Sergeant-Major Merkl who at once shot one of them through the head.   It was Mkwawa, but he had been stiff and cold for hours.   He had shot himself in the head after first killing his old servant.

The head of the great king was cut off and sent to a museum in Germany.   His tribe ceremoniously buried the body, but the Hehe did not cease to sing laments on the anniversary of Mkwawa's death.   When the territory came under British rule the Hehe's first plea was that the head of their chief should be returned to them.   The German Government replied that it could not be found.

After the second World War the new Governor of Tanganyika took the matter up personally and wrote to the Director of the Overseas Museum in Bremen.   This was my friend, Dr. Helmuth O. Wagner, who at once agreed to send back the bullet-shattered skull.   In 1953, after more than half a century, the head of the chief was returned to his people.   As a reward for his being so understanding, Dr. Wagner received a whole collection of valuable ethnological objects from Adam Sapi, Mkwawa's grandson.

Another great fighter for liberty was a Chief named Siki, who, when he was defeated, took his family into a powder magazine and blew himself, and them, to pieces.

When Carl Peters became Imperial High Commissioner for the Kilimanjaro region, ugly rumours of intimidation, robbery and beatings soon reached the Central Government at Dar-es-Salaam. The worst story was that a young African had been hanged, allegedly for stealing cigarettes, but actually because of his friendship with one of Peters' concubines.*

Peters was recalled in 1893, and after investigation lasting three years, was relieved of his post because of "abuse of his official position".   Later public opinion swung in his favour; in 1914 the

---

*In order not to libel a dead man I would also like to give the other side of the picture.   According to his detractors the English Mission in Moshi had written to the Central Government in Dar-es-Salaam about the alleged execution of the concubine and her lover in 1882.   It is said that an official investigation found no grounds for such accusations and stated this in writing.   It was only when Peters tried to enter the Reichstag and made speeches attacking the Social Democrat Party in 1895 that Bebel attacked him in the Reichstag using as evidence a letter from Peters to the

Kaiser gave him a pension as a civil servant, and Hitler, describing him as a "strict but exemplary government official", went so far in 1934 as to put his portrait on a postage stamp.

In an English book on Tanganyika it is stated that it would be a mistake to regard him as typical of the German colonist.   The book further states that it was unfortunate for his country and the good name of his people that he should have had the opportunity to undo in a few months all the good work done by von Wissmann and Lieutenant Ehlers with endless patience and good faith, after the German flag had been raised in 1890.

One of the greatest German colonists was Emin Pasha.   Born Eduard Schnitzler, at Oppeln in 1840, he studied medicine and while working in Albania became a Mahommedan.   He entered Egyptian service in 1876, soon became an Effendi, rose to a Bey and was finally made a Pasha.   He gave up medicine and was appointed Governor of the Southern Sudan.

When the Mahdi's reign of terror began, Emin Pasha escaped to Central Africa and nothing was heard of him for many years. Finally Stanley discovered him there.   Von Wissmann, who was Governor of German East Africa at the time, had sent him into the region of Lake Victoria in 1890 to prevent the British from gaining too much influence.   He took with him Dr. Franz Stuhlmann, who like Emin was deeply interested in ethnology, zoology, botany and astronomy.   They were accompanied by Captain Wilhelm Langheld and a German lance-corporal named Kuhne.

Emin Pasha's journey was not only extremely valuable scientifically but also resulted in the capture of Arab slave caravans, the freeing of slaves and the virtual abolition of the slave traders near Lake Victoria.   It was Arab slave traders who, two years later, while he was travelling in the Belgian Congo, cut Emin's throat. They resented the fact that, as a Muslim, he had worked for Christians.

English Bishop of Uganda, Dr. Tucker.   In this letter Peters openly declared his guilt.   Later Dr. Tucker, it is said, denied under oath that he ever knew Peters or received a letter from him.   Bebel is also said to have stated in the Reichstag that he was the victim of a forgery.   In any case the journey which Dr. Peters took to relieve Emin Pasha of his post resembled, according to his own description, a military campaign rather than an expedition.

Emin brought much greater areas under German influence by peaceful means than Peters ever did, and British authorities on East and Central Africa are the first to agree that Emin and his colleagues were by no means exceptional examples of good German colonial administration.

An official handbook issued a few months ago by the British Government of Tanganyika lists the numerous rebellions during the first period of German administration. It comments that the Germans were the last European power which tried to gain colonial possessions. Everything had therefore to be done in a hurry, and most of the first colonial officials were military officers who had only seen European service. The native soldiers were not East African but Zulus, Sudanese and Swahilis from the coast. They marched through the interior as "masters" and antagonised the native tribes. It is only fair to add, states the handbook, that many German officials were interested in the people they governed; they were sympathetic towards them and took a conciliatory attitude.

Certainly numerous rebellions gave the Colonial administration a lot of trouble between 1905 and 1907. These risings caused particular concern in Germany as the government had only just managed to suppress the rebellion of the Hereros in South-West Africa. When the Benedictine Bishop, Cassion Spiess, was assassinated together with two monks and two nuns, the German government sent out two light cruisers, a company of marines and native troops from the Pacific Islands. Nearly 100,000 people are said to have perished as a result of this war which ruined the harvest and drove the cattle away.

To restore order, Germany created an Imperial Colonial Office. The first Minister was Dr. Bernhard Dernburg, a Darmstadt banker. After touring the protectorates he reported to the Minister of Finance in the Reichstag that "the planters are at war with everybody; with myself, the government, the local officials and the natives. It makes a very bad impression to see so many white people running around carrying whips of hippo hide."

He replaced the military administration with a civilian one, but this was only to survive another seven years.

The British handbook closes the report on the German administration with the Shakespearian quotation: "The evil that men do lives after them, the good is oft interred with their bones," and it particularly praises the German school administration which was far ahead of all neighbouring colonies.

General von Lettow-Vorbeck arrived in Tanganyika six months before the outbreak of the first World War. He had seen service in the Boxer rising and in the Herero rebellion in South-West Africa, during which he had been wounded. He had also commanded colonial troops in the Cameroons.

This experienced veteran had two hundred and fifty German officers and 2,500 native troops under his command. The cruiser *Konigsberg* was opposed by three British ones. Despite this the German cruiser twice slipped out into the open sea to coal, and sank one of the British cruisers before escaping up the Rufiji river. The British cruisers could not follow because of their greater draught. They had to send for howitzers from England in order to destroy the *Konigsberg*. The crew of the cruiser escaped, taking their heavy guns with them, and carried on the war under von Lettow-Vorbeck. Twice German supply ships broke through the coastal blockade and brought guns and ammunition.

Tanganyika was under German rule for four decades. A Masai woman brought us this old banknote.

Small bodies of men under his command destroyed railway tracks in Kenya and Uganda, and others stirred up unrest in Rhodesia and the Belgian Congo. He defeated troops imported from India, drove them back to their ships and remained undisturbed until 1916.

In the meantime German South-West Africa had surrendered. This released General Smuts and his troops, but so many of them caught malaria, that few of them ever went into action against the Germans. In 1917 von Lettow-Vorbeck crossed into Portuguese territory with his small army. There he carried on a guerrilla war for ten months, suddenly reappeared in the German colony in September 1918, once more attacked Rhodesia and did not surrender until the 25th November 1918, a few days after the German Empire had given up the fight.

Despite his small army and lack of supplies he undoubtedly tied down a large part of the allied forces in East Africa and kept them from being moved to other theatres of war. The natives of Tanganyika, whom the Germans and British had vied to "protect", got only blood and misery from a European war which was no concern of theirs. This was not the last of their tribulations.

The 1917–18 influenza pandemic killed 80,000 natives when it reached Tanganyika; and when the rains failed in 1924, the railway tracks were lined by the skulls of people who tried to reach the train before dying of thirst.

The British received Tanganyika in trust from the League of Nations, excepting the overcrowded Watusi kingdoms of Ruanda and Urundi, which were incorporated into the Belgian Congo. During the German regime the population of Tanganyika was estimated as three million. Since Michael and I intended to count hundreds of thousands of wild animals, we were professionally interested in how such an estimate was reached in a wild country where there was no register of births and deaths, and no national census. The count of 1931 was carried out as follows: each chieftain had to deliver four types of seed corn. Thick black seeds represented men, brown seeds with two hairs stood for women, small round seeds meant girls and elongated grass seeds represented boys. One seed went into the pot for each subject of the local chief. This type of "census" was much more accurate than all previous estimates and revealed a population of five million black people, an increase of two per cent per year.

The extradited and dispossessed German settlers of 1914 were allowed to return to Tanganyika in 1925. Hitler encouraged emigration to Africa by loans and advances, and by 1939, just before the outbreak of World War II, there were 3,205 German settlers owning 558 farms, as opposed to 4,054 British settlers owning 499 farms. The next most numerous group of Europeans were the Greeks, of whom there were 893 settlers owning 260 farms.

The last census in 1957 showed a population of 8.6 million black people—their number had trebled in the last fifty years. There were also 72,000 Indians, 20,000 Europeans and 19,000 Arabs. The Indians were primarily introduced as coolies and cheap labour for railway construction. Since they are modest and industrious they opened shops in the remotest areas, where no European could make a living, and soon became quite affluent. Nowadays they control a large proportion of the country's trade.

One of the most courteous of the Indians was the British customs official in Arusha, who always inspected our goods and instruments on arrival. He was as meticulous as any Prussian official, entirely incorruptible and invariably friendly and helpful. An admirable representative of his people, in fact.

The herds of Thomson's gazelles seemed innumerable.

CHAPTER 6

Counting the Animals

*The fate of animals is of greater importance to
me than the fear of appearing ridiculous; it is
indissolubly connected with the fate of men.*

EMILE ZOLA

EVERY MORNING we had a race with three thousand yellow, black
and white Thomson's gazelles.

A spare tyre was placed on the flat bonnet of the car. I sat inside it on a cushion and braced my legs against the two water-cans
which were strapped to the front of the car beside the headlights.
Wedged in this way, I could not be thrown off easily, even if the car
made a tight curve or bucked on the uneven ground. Our black
chauffeur, Mgabo, drove fast and boldly, but he never went into a
pot-hole or let thorny branches whip against my face.

I only wore bathing trunks, since I had long lost my fear of the
equatorial sun and gave up wearing a hat many years ago. I felt
waves of warm air sweeping past my body.

Some of the grazing gazelles ran beside us. This infected the
others. Hundreds, sometimes thousands, wanted to emulate the
original runners, and all of them seemed to enjoy the race. Their
maximum speed seemed to be 35 miles an hour. If we did not step
too hard on the accelerator they insisted on crossing our path close
to the bonnet of the car, at full speed. The tall and slender impala,
with their wide-sweeping cork-screw horns, did this on principle,
leaping off the ground with all four legs at once.

Each morning we drove for two-and-a-half hours from our tin
hut to the lame "duck", which was being fitted with new legs by the

Two full-grown impala bucks.

two mechanics. In the African plain this was an exhausting business. There was no electric current and each of the several hundred screw holes had not only to be drilled through the steel by hand, but had to be accurate to within a fraction of an inch. Although both the engineers had been in Africa for many years they had lived in Nairobi all the time and were thrilled by zebras coming close to the 'plane during the day, and hyenas howling near their hut at night. Their greatest wish was to see a lion at close quarters. This could be arranged quite easily, as we had only to drive them little more than a mile from the 'plane by car.

They slept in a clay hut with a conical straw roof, which the black scouts used as a shelter on their travels through the park. Three months ago two of these brave men had found a trail of blood leading from the closed door of the hut. They followed the trail until they found half the skull and jawbone of a woman. She must have been wounded or seriously ill, and hoping to find protection inside the hut. Instead she was killed at the very door, and her identity was never discovered.

One day, while we were driving across the country near Ikoma, outside the boundaries of the Park, a little boy stopped us and

Our camp in the Masabi plain.

asked for help. We took him into the car and he showed us the way. Inside a large hut we found a seriously wounded old man groaning on the floor. His relatives had placed him on some cattle hides and he was breathing stertorously. Although his wounds had been bandaged the pool of blood under his body grew larger. Outside the hut the black medical orderly who ran a small "hospital" in Ikoma was vainly trying to start the small van which he used as an ambulance. We jacked it up and Mgabo spent two hours helping to repair it. The villagers assisted cheerfully, chatting and laughing, while inside the hut the old man panted for his life. When the van was finally mended the old man obstinately refused to leave his hut. "Please let me die here, among my wives," he said, and a few hours later, still on his bed of skins, he did so.

The villagers told us that he had been attacked by a buffalo while working in the fields, and that the animal had gored his stomach. Probably he had been poaching and shot the beast with a poisoned arrow, for buffaloes do not as a rule attack without reason. We ourselves have always found buffaloes to be harmless, and I have photographs showing us in the centre of buffalo herds. I consider them about as dangerous as domestic cattle, not forgetting that tame bulls, and even cows, have been known to attack people, sometimes with fatal results.

I asked Myles Turner about the viciousness of buffaloes. He did some mental arithmetic and said: "Well, I must have shot eight to nine hundred buffaloes in my time and was only once in danger. That was when the buffalo was wounded. He fled into the bush two or three times, but we always followed and drove him out again. Finally he grew tired of that and went for us."

You can never tell what is going on in the mind of an old buffalo. One day we flew across Myles' house to land in a field nearby. The noisy aerial monster roused a buffalo to such fury that he jumped round and ferociously attacked a bush.

Four old buffalo bulls regularly went through the gap between the warden's house and our hut every day. One of them seemed to be nearly blind, for he followed every movement of his companions and kept his head close to the flank of one of them. Another nearly blind old bull blocked the road from Banagi to Ikoma two months ago. Nearly every day he stood under a tree about fifty yards from the track, greatly alarming any cyclists who came along.

The black students at the Kampala Engineering College do field work in the Queen Elizabeth Park in Uganda for three months of

In Uganda and the National Parks of the Belgian Congo buffaloes are as tame as cattle and Michael could approach them in order to make films. Their shyness in Serengeti is connected with the habits of the Masai.

the year, usually connected with road building. One of them was cycling home on a Friday night, with a friend on his luggage carrier. On the way they roused an old buffalo who got angry and attacked. The cyclist turned round and pedalled away with all his force, but the buffalo caught up and was just about to use his horns. In fear and desperation the passenger pushed his hat over the animal's eyes. This shocked and frightened the buffalo so much that it jumped aside and ran away.

When *rinderpest* sweeps across the land sick buffaloes sometimes become vicious. They can attack without reason and have been known to butt cars. They never lack courage at any time. One bull has been seen counterattacking a lion, goring it through the belly and leaving it to be eaten by crocodiles.

On another occasion a small herd of buffaloes drove off three lions who had just hunted and killed two wildebeest. The lions were kept from their dinner for a whole hour, during which time vultures had eaten most of it. Buffaloes and elephants have one habit in common, they sometimes refuse to abandon comrades that have been shot. Buffaloes prod the fallen animal with their snouts in an effort to rouse it to its feet.

Unlike rhinos, hippos and giraffes, which are easily killed,

Hippos and buffaloes are not afraid of each other. Despite this the mother keeps her baby on the side away from the buffalo.

buffaloes are tough customers. Unless they have been hit squarely they can run for long distances. Frequently they will hide in the shrubs and then suddenly attack their pursuers. This may be what makes some people call them "treacherous" and "vicious".

For a long time our "winged zebra" hung on a tackle suspended from a large tripod, but it finally had legs of its own again. We invited the two mechanics to share the first test-flight, since as they had fixed the legs they should be the best judges of the machine's airworthiness. They declined with thanks. When I went to the machine I noticed that Michael had not put the second pilot's seat in position.

When I asked him if he proposed to fly alone, he replied: "Should anything happen, one of us must stay alive, otherwise all our work will have been in vain." He had the impudence to add: "You know perfectly well that the pilot always has the last word about whether to carry passengers or not."

This was too much. I lost my temper, as fathers so often do when they are being bossed about by their sons. But there were people looking on, and I did not want to make a scene. Instead, when Michael bent down to pick up some water canisters I took aim and slapped his khaki-clad bottom with all my might. This inelegant way of unexpectedly smacking each other at unsuitable moments has long been a family habit, and one of which both our wives have vainly tried to break us. Strangers did not realise that Michael and I understood each other particularly well at these moments. And in this case the buffoonery as usual broke the spell. The second seat was screwed into position without more ado and we rolled across the grass to find a level piece of land. Down went the throttle and a peacefully droning motor took us into the air.

Everything went well. Things *always* go well when you are prepared for trouble, the real disasters hit you out of a blue sky.

Yesterday morning, at half-past seven, we contacted Colonel Molloy in Arusha on the field radio, asking him to send out a small commercial aeroplane to take our two mechanics back to Nairobi.

These radio conversations were not easy. Our people in Frankfurt wondered why we always telegraphed to them in English. Have you ever tried sending a message, letter by letter, on a squeaking, hissing, raucous radio when the receiver at the other end does not know the language you are spelling out?   Once the Director in person tried to get an endless telegram of over a hundred words to us.   The letter by letter transmission took two hours, and after the sun had fallen we were still trying to make sense of the verbal hotch-potch.

The reply said that we were to supply a room for a lady.   Apparently the pilot was bringing his wife or girl friend.   We were annoyed, for, after all, it was we who were paying for the charter flight, and we required all the seats.   Our anger was unjustified, however.   When the small Cessna landed the pilot proved to be alone—but a woman.

We celebrated our return into the air.   That night we prepared a punch bowl outside our hut.   Michael knelt down, and Gordon "dubbed" him across the shoulders with the broad side of a Masai sword, giving him a smack that could be heard for yards.   Then Michael was presented with a small, striped and winged horse. Mrs. Harvey had cut out and painted this tin Pegasus, and with it went the following testimonial:

THE SERENGETI WINGS
presented to
MICHAEL GRZIMEK

by the officers of Eastern and Western Serengeti and their wives, in appreciation of his low flying and high-flying spirits; for scaring the life out of man and beast; for his ever readiness to fly anyone anywhere any time; for smiling at our madness; for never complaining and above all for his untiring service for the cause of our wild life.

The punch bowl was strong and had diverse effects.   Hermann Gimbel released a thunder-flash on the tin roof and the noise nearly threw us on the floor.   Michael was draped with ribbons and with the yellow nylon cloth which we normally used for marking zebras. As the Poolmans and the two mechanics started to leave, a bowl of water which Hermann had placed on top of the jeep just in front of the opening in the roof, slowly slopped over and drenched them. They were feeling so merry by then that at first they really believed it was raining.

Later Connie Poolman told me: "It was a wonderful party, just like Christmas."

It was nice having a house right in the plains. On our occasional returns to Europe, we used to bemoan the dull, wintry weather and having to see so many people; we found ourselves longing for the wide, soft, undulating countryside of the Serengeti and our second home, the grey tin hut among the lions and zebras. It was so small that you could barely see it from the air. To find it you had to fly along the Seronera river until you came to Banagi hill and then search for it among the sparse trees.

Our hut had no floor. The metal plates were simply screwed together and erected on the ground. You never had to sweep up, for the soil was a fine, reddish dust. It was best not to look at your feet before retiring to bed, for water was very short. It was also inadvisable to scratch your head if you wanted to avoid black finger nails. Michael and I often asked ourselves what our wives, Eri and Hilde, would say if they could see our domestic arrangements.

It was cool at night, but by noon it became unbearably hot. Luckily we were out almost all day. Even the boys in the small, open, corrugated-iron shed a few yards away sizzled in the heat. Inside we had piled empty boxes against the walls so that the open sides faced into the room. These were used as shelves and contained bags of soup powder, tins of vegetables and meat, piles of fresh pineapples which were still ripening, cabbages, apples and oranges, each article in a different box. Since we had our own aeroplane we could fetch fresh supplies from Nairobi or Arusha every few days. Other shelves of boxes contained books, cameras and cine-cameras, typewriters, ropes and tools, in short it looked like a typical Indian *duka* or village shop in Africa.

Besides this we had an extremely modern refrigerator which ran on paraffin, since no electricity was available. We even had ice-cream, but we had to explain the directions on all the tins to Desusa, our capable black cook, who could not read English.

Desusa was an attractive man, intelligent and industrious. He never walked from the hut to his kitchen, but always trotted. When asked about this constant haste he replied: "*Bwana makuba* eats dark bread so as not to get fat. I don't want to get fat either, so I trot." *Bwana makuba* is Swahili for "great master" and meant me. Michael and our occasional assistants were addressed by their Christian names.

Pictures of our tin hut. It grew unbearably hot during the day, but at that time we were always away from home.

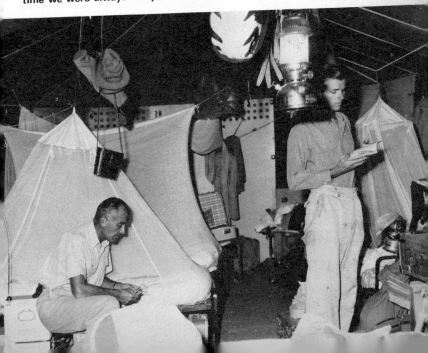

Our refrigerator had to be de-frosted when it no longer worked efficiently. This was done by turning it upside down and leaving it for a day—a domestic hint which I proudly offer to the housewives of Europe and America!

Once even this drastic measure did not help. The paraffin lamps also failed to function properly and their sharp, yellow light grew progressively dimmer. These lamps were expensive, but good illumination was essential during the long African evenings.

Michael took the lamps to pieces and fitted new incandescent mantles. He filled the little pans with methylated spirits for preheating. He followed all the instructions and still they failed to burn. We finally discovered the cause of the trouble. The new assistant in the Indian grocery had sold us insect repellent instead of paraffin. We were lucky that the stuff burned at all, and had good reason to be glad that he had not given us petrol by mistake, since all the canisters looked alike.

Our bushbaby could jump about everywhere in giant leaps, including the tin roof where things we wanted kept out of the way were suspended on hooks. When we were at table it jumped from one head to the other, reached for its own portion of food from our plates and ate it while sitting on our shoulders. At night

The bushbaby hopped across the grass like a miniature kangaroo.

It had to investigate every bottle.

it had to return to its cage, otherwise it clambered all over our mosquito nets. It was not easy to recapture it. The favourite haunt was the box where we kept our drugs and clinical thermometers. When you tried to catch it there it bit your fingers. I had to wait till the little fellow was feeling playful, then he would attack my hand, stand on his hind legs, open his arms, swear at me and fight my fingers. On such occasions I could put him into his cage and he would be quite happy about it.

One night the bushbaby hopped through the open door. It had not the slightest intention of running away, but anything, from snakes upwards, might attack it outside. We could hear our pet scrambling along the tin walls. It was clearly trying to get in, but the windows were screened. We took out our big torches and tried to recapture it. The little fellow decided to play tag, climbed up a tree and sat there fifteen feet above the roof of the hut. We could see it quite clearly in the beam of our torches, for at that time of year there was not a single leaf on the tree. We called it and carefully tossed stones at it, but our little truant took no notice. Finally Michael climbed on to my shoulders and from there to the roof. I handed him a long stick which he beat against the branch on which the bushbaby was sitting. Suddenly there was a plop, and our pet had landed on the roof. To an excellent jumper such as a bushbaby, a leap like that presents no difficulty.

It was not easy to feed our bushbaby correctly after bringing it with us for six thousand miles. Since we could not buy mealy worms we had to provide a diet of grasshoppers. This was harder than it sounds. For one thing grasshoppers look exactly like blades of dry grass. You only notice their presence when you are walking through grass if they leap to avoid you. If you try to catch one in a hat or with your hand it always escapes at the last moment.

We slowly discovered two basic methods of catching grass-hoppers. One is to spot the exact position to which the grasshopper has jumped. Then you approach very slowly, inch by inch and millimetre by millimetre, until your hand is just above it. Grass-hoppers do not seem to detect such slow movements. The other way is to tire the leaping insect. You follow it until it has made forty, fifty or even sixty leaps and feels worn out.

Our boys had to catch these *dudus* for us every day. They were kept in an empty marmalade jar, so that we could check whether the boys had really been doing their job. Our bushbaby was also fond of dry cheese biscuits and liked poking its head inside the marmalade pot.

Lest too many people write and ask me to supply them with bushbabies, I had better mention that they have one very distinct drawback—the inelegant habit of urinating on their hands and feet, rubbing them together and then jumping directly at your face with wet palms. All the walls and the furniture which they touch become "perfumed" and, unless a window is kept permanently open, the stench is considerable.

The Seronera is only a "river" during the rainy season, when sometimes you have to wait for days before you can cross the raging torrent by car. In the dry season, from June to October, the river bed is empty, leaving only occasional pools to provide drinking water for all the animals. The families of the scouts near Turner's house did their laundry in these water holes as well as washing themselves from head to foot every day. You can imagine the colour and smell of the stagnant water.

We obtained the precious fluid in large iron drums which were brought by car. Our boys washed our clothes in these drums and that was the reason why all our laundry slowly turned to a yellow-ish khaki. When we take our freshly-laundered underpants home to Frankfurt, our wives fastidiously pick them up with their finger-tips and drop them into the dirty linen basket.

You could only get your laundry white if you used rainwater, and that was very scarce. During the wet season the rain from the roof is led through pipes into concrete, subterranean cisterns. In Banagi and Seronera these are also fed by concrete channels from the great rocks in the surrounding country. The cisterns were under lock and key, and we collected one ton of water a week for cooking and tooth-brushing. As a precaution we percolated the water through a bacterial filter before use. One day Jambuna, the cook's assistant, forgot to fill the reservoir above the filter. I scolded him, but a little later I caught him as he short-circuited unfiltered water into the sterile container below "to make it go faster".

Jambuna either made you laugh or cry. Sometimes he stood beside some boiling eggs studiously looking at the mechanical egg-timer in his hand, although he had neglected to wind it up. Then he used the egg water for making tea, which turned it a curious blue-green. Every night we had to drive him by car to the huts where the other boys slept, because he was afraid of lions. If we did not see to his taking his medicine regularly he constantly came down with attacks of malaria. We ought to have sacked him long before, but never had the heart to do so.

All the boys were very fond of sugar, and our supply of matches also decreased at an astonishing rate. Desusa, the cook, told me with a grin how one housewife taught him not to scrounge sweet things when he was a young man learning his job. Although she never caught him in the act she once deducted the price of a pound of sugar from his monthly wage. He had not noticed that she had put a live fly into the sugar box every day. The next time she opened the lid later she could always tell whether Desusa had been at the sugar again.

One evening as we sat outside our door by lamplight we suddenly heard galloping hooves. We had barely got up when a full-grown wildebeest raced into our camp and stopped within six feet of our table. When we yelled at the animal it stared at us before turning tail and running away. We had hardly sat down again when we heard the hoof beats once more. This time the wildebeest stopped

There were no proper maps of Serengeti, and we had difficulty in dividing the area into smaller regions for purposes of an animal census.

barely two feet away. We threw our jackets at its head and it disappeared into the darkness. This was enough for us, we collected the signalling pistol from the hut and waited. The next approach of the ghostly wildebeest was more impressive; the thundering hooves grew louder and came closer as the animal appeared once more. This time it rushed past us, knocking over the chair and missing the table by inches, and jumped into the waterhole in the river bed with a tremendous splash. We *never* discovered what had got into that wildebeest.

Michael and I were busy every day with the great census of the quadrupeds. Since they had by now been insured at Lloyd's, the game wardens often flew with us. We had divided the huge territory into thirty-two districts, which we tackled one by one. This was not easy, for there was no proper map, only a sketchy one which did not show many of the rivers and hills. Some of the distances were also incorrect. We therefore looked for recognisable rocks and river beds to use as boundaries or we took bearings from volcanoes on the horizon. When neither of these methods was feasible we dropped a paper bag of lime and used the white circle as a marker.

Michael was the pilot. He had to take devilish good care to stay in the same district and fly across it in equidistant strips. We always flew directly due west or east, for then the constant wind from dead eastward could not cause any lateral deviation. We usually flew at 150 to 300 feet, for at that height you could comfortably survey a 500-yard strip, differentiate between the various types of animal and distinguish the young ones from the adults. Besides the pilot there were usually two passengers in the 'plane, doing the counting, and I was invariably one of them. Michael and I always watched from the same side so that we could compare afterwards what we had seen. This was a good insurance against inaccurate numbers. Each of the observers had a list with twenty columns in his lap, one for each of the most important animals.

If there was little to be seen but an occasional hyena or a group of ostriches we flew at 130 m.p.h. If the plains were thickly populated, however, Michael put on full flaps and our speed decreased to thirty miles an hour. We could not fly for very long at this low speed because, as I have said, the motor got overheated in the rarefied air. Each observer had to be able to calculate the exact width of a 500-yard strip. We had marked this distance with white stones in Banagi and had flown our helpers across them dozens of times, until they could judge it correctly. At the end of each strip we would bank and turn, which tends to upset the stomachs of people who are not used to flying. Michael had nothing but glass in front of the pilot's seat and could slow down at once when animals appeared in front of us. We flew across the whole of Serengeti, including the highlands of volcanic craters, in flights spaced exactly one thousand yards apart. If you add to that the flights to and from our base you can calculate the seemingly endless distances we covered, and the gallons of wickedly expensive petrol we used. Aviation spirit has to be imported from overseas. Then it goes by train on the Tanganyika railway to Lake Victoria, across the lake by boat and finally, if the roads are dry and passable, it is carried inland by lorry. It gets more expensive with every mile and at the end of the journey most of the canisters and drums are half empty. Our hard earned money disappeared in noise and fumes.

How did the animals react to our droning "flying zebra"? Single

kongonis, wildebeest, topis and zebras took remarkably little notice. We even had to fly over our landing strip once because a
Thomson's gazelle buck did not deign to get up at our approach.

Small groups of five to fifteen wildebeest or zebras galloped
parallel to us, but rarely for more than a hundred yards. They
often tried to cross our path at the last moment, just as they did
with our car. Large herds of over fifty head fled much farther,
quite often for several hundred yards, before stopping and looking
up at us. From the air we could see quite clearly that single, over-
anxious animals started the stampede, which then quickly spread
to the others. The more animals there were in a herd the greater
the chance that it would contain one of these hyper-sensitive
creatures. Large herds therefore took to their heels more often
than small groups or single beasts.

The yellow gazelles usually remained quite calm. They only
fled if we went very low, down to fifty or thirty feet, behaving
quite differently from the large wildebeest and zebras. When the
little fellows did run they fled in all directions, in zig-zag runs,
rather like startled hares. This is probably meant to confuse striking eagles.

Zebras noticed us 150 feet away, even if we cut the motor and
glided past them. Giraffes near trees ignored the 'plane when it
was silent; even when we were using the engine they ran no more
than fifty yards at most. It was the same with ostriches. They
usually started to dance with raised tail and beating wings, trying
to create an impression and threaten us. Baboons made a bee-
line for the nearest trees.

It was difficult to count a herd of wildebeest amounting to perhaps 5,000 head. If we flew too low they would scatter and then
they resembled a hurrying ant-hill. As soon as we saw such a herd
we climbed steeply, our good old "duck" moving upwards almost
like a lift. We could then circle high above the herd and take a
leisurely count. We also took a note of the direction in which they
were heading, in order not to re-count them the next day.

We frequently flew for three hours on end. This took a great
deal of energy and concentration, for we had to look at the ground
for every second of that time. We also had to perform feats of
rapid mental arithmetic and to remember the numbers until there

We grew apprehensive when faced with task of counting this scurrying
ant-heap.

A wildebeest at full speed. Taken through an aperture in the bottom of the aeroplane during a low flight.

was a spare moment to jot them down. We dared not take a rest, for landing and re-starting the 'plane on strange territory is not to be recommended, especially when carrying three or four passengers.

We began to mumble numbers in our sleep. One evening I feared that my ears had become affected, for there was a constant humming, whining and singing. I later found a tiny radio set under my pillow, where Michael had surreptitiously placed it. A manufacturer had given us the set to try out in Africa. Although it received all the European stations clearly at home, in the Serengeti it produced nothing but interference, howls and weird noises.

That same night I dreamt that Michael and I were flying across Brussels, a town we had often visited before going to the Belgian Congo. We landed very skilfully in a narrow street, but our wings were caught on two wires. One wing broke, and our passenger, whom I did not know, climbed out and said: "I'll never fly in that thing again." As we unloaded our luggage a poisonous gaboon viper climbed out of the crate and bit me. Michael ran to the nearest pharmacy, but the owner said: "We haven't got anti-snake-bite serum, but I will order it from Paris at once . . ."

Vultures and other birds of prey sitting on carrion usually remained on the ground when we flew over them, but we kept a sharp look out for birds in the air. Storks and birds of prey always took evasive action at the last possible moment, for they probably underestimated the speed of our metallic bird.

While the observers looked downwards and counted, Michael looked for flying vultures. He always gave them a wide berth, for collision with even a small bird could mean certain death. Herr Repple, our flight instructor at home, nearly crashed during the last war because a flying wild duck tore a large hole in the metal wing of his large Junkers machine. He later found the duck still inside the hole. Birds of prey avoided us by flying downwards. They turned on their sides until their fully-spread wings were in a line vertical to the ground.

Buzzards and vultures gliding beside us showed no fear, they merely watched us with interest. They probably have no enemies in the air. Since we overtook them so quickly I always had the impression that they were flying backwards, with their tails in front.

The large bustards on the ground ducked when we shot towards them and stretched their necks forward horizontally, turning their heads at the same time so that one eye was directed upwards and could keep us in sight. They kept this curious position while they ran to one side and rarely took to the air. The European storks, which spend the winter here, and the beautiful crowned cranes also made only short flights of about twenty yards to one side, even when we were a bare hundred and fifty feet up.

The bustard always turned her back on us so that she could run away or take to the air if necessary.

We were glad that the census of the animals showed numbers which agreed quite well. Although I nearly always counted from the left and the other observers alternated on the right, it turned out that the left-hand observer counted nearly as many animals as the right-hand one (48.7 per cent to 51.3 per cent). It had always been assumed that the Serengeti contained about a million large animals. After flying for many weeks we found the following numbers:

Thomson's Gazelle	Gazella thomsonii thomsonii. Gunther 1884	
Grant's Gazelle	Gazella granti robertsi. Thomas 1903	194,654
Wildebeest (Gnu)	Connochaetus taurinus albojubatus. Thomas 1892	99,481
Zebra	Equus burchellii Boehmi. Matschie 1892	57,199
Topi	Damaliscus korigum eurus. Blaine 1914	5,172
Eland	Taurotragus oryx pattersonianus. Lydekker 1906	2,452
Impala	Aepyceros melampus melampus. Blyth 1866	1,717
Black Buffalo	Syncerus caffer aequinoctialis. Blyth 1866	1,813
Kongoni (Coke's Hartebeest)	Alcelaphus buselaphus cokii. Gunther 1884	1,285
Giraffe	Giraffa camelopardalis tippelskirchii. Matschie 1898	837
Waterbuck	Kobus defassa raineyi. Heller 1913	284
Stork	Ciconia ciconia ciconia. Linné	178
Oryx antelope	Oryx beisa callotis. Thomas 1892	115
Elephant	Loxodonta africana africana Blumenbach 1797	60
Roan antelope	Hippotragus equinus langheldii. Matschie 1898	57
Rhinoceros	Diceros bicornis bicornis. Linné	55
Ostrich	Struthio camelus massaicus	1,621

The grand total of large animals living in Serengeti was therefore 366,980. Perhaps there were up to 10,000 more which we had overlooked, but in any case there were only about one-third as many as had been expected. Even 366,000 is an almost inconceivable number. Would the animals be able to go on living here? Were there enough plains, mountains, river valleys and bush areas to maintain the last giant herds still in existence? We had already noticed that large herds of wildebeest roamed outside the present boundaries of the Park, and it was intended to change the borders and lessen its area. Nobody can follow these huge regiments of wildebeest and enormous armies of gazelles, and no one knows where the hundreds of thousands of hooves will march. We were filled with fear and foreboding.

Together with the wildebeest, Thomson's gazelles and zebras form the greater part of the Serengeti population.

Catching zebras from the roof of the car with a noose attached to a bamboo pole.

CHAPTER 7

Zebras Dyed Yellow

If you nurse a sick dog back to health, he won't bite you later. This is the chief difference between men and animals.

MARK TWAIN

WE HAD big plans for the day.

At breakfast I remembered that it was tablet day. As we arrived in Africa on a Thursday, we had to swallow two tablets of *Resochin* every time Thursday came round. Hermann relied on his travelling calendar and maintained that it was only Wednesday. He bet me a bottle of gin (of all things) and lost, since he had forgotten that I wear a Swiss calendar wrist-watch. This shows the date, the phase of the moon and the day of the week, all of which are more important on an expedition than knowing whether it is nine o'clock or merely half-past eight.

Resochin tastes like gall, but down it had to go. One of the two mechanics who recently repaired our 'plane collapsed a year ago and had to stay in hospital for five weeks with a severe attack of malaria. As he lived in Nairobi, which is healthy and free from fever, he had not bothered to take any tablets when he flew to Lake Victoria to exchange a propeller.

"*Jambo, bwana.*" A fourteen-year-old boy stood in the doorway and wanted to sell us four hen's eggs. We gratefully declined, since we preferred to collect fresh eggs from Nairobi by 'plane. The young man generously declared that he would *give* us the eggs. We naturally did not wish to appear mean and made him a present of money worth more than the goods. Later it was found that all four eggs were so rotten that they contaminated our cooking pot.

We were going on a serious zebra hunt. We had known for a few weeks that there were 57,000 "tiger horses" among our 367,000 wards, and Michael and I wanted to study the habits of our striped little horses.

We would never be able to do this from the air. Our notes of 25th January last year, for example, say: "herds of gnus behave most peculiarly. When they come to a small dried-up rivulet—only about two feet wide and eight inches deep—they run along the bank for quite a while before crossing it in Indian file. Why don't they simply cross it on a wide front? Even when chased by a low-flying aeroplane they spread out on either side of the bank and finally turn right about."

Four weeks later Michael wrote "Nonsense!" in the margin, and with good reason. For in the meantime we had visited one of these "rivulets" on foot. It proved to be more than six feet deep and six yards across. The grass, which from the air had appeared to be two to four inches long, was two or three feet high.

Zebra presented another problem. How could we know whether the herd which we saw at Lemuta hill to-day was the same one we observed 25 miles away yesterday? Were the herds which graze in the National Park in July and in December the same ones? We wanted to find ways to recognise individual zebras and whole herds. That was not so easy!

Good advice was plentiful: "Construct game pits, or put narcotics in the drinking water." I am a veterinarian and know only too well how long a horse will suffer thirst before it drinks such stuff, and also how carefully the quantities have to be measured. If an animal drinks too much it will die, and the amount required for a zebra will kill smaller animals using the same water hole. In the rainy season, from July to December, there is abundant water everywhere, but even in the dry season one would have to cart narcotics about by the hundredweight.

There were some good animal catchers in neighbouring Kenya. The most experienced of them was Carr Hartley, whom I had known for a long time. He had not caught many animals lately, because most zoos now breed the more usual grazing animals of his region such as zebras, wildebeest and the commoner antelopes themselves, or only pay low prices. He always keeps a few half-tame lions, leopards, hyenas, buffalo and giraffes on his farm however, so that American and German companies can film their adventure stories without too much effort or loss of time.

Gordon Poolman, our Serengeti game ranger, is Carr Hartley's half-brother. He worked with Carr for many years, and as a result one of his fingers is stiff to this day. One Sunday an American arrived and insisted on filming a fight between an African and a leopard. In reality this was only a tame, immature leopard playing with his keeper, a teenage boy, photographed in such a way as to look very dangerous. Carr Hartley does not work on Sundays, but the American kept offering so much money that Carr finally capitulated. Since the leopard boy was at church, a substitute had to be found. This boy did not really trust the leopard, got frightened during the play, and started to run away. The animal at once gripped his neck, started to bite in earnest and clawed the boy's chest. Gordon put his hands in the leopard's mouth, pressing the lips over the teeth. The farther the animal's mouth was forced open, the harder it lacerated the black skin with its claws. The film people did not dare to intervene. Finally Carr Hartley had to shoot the tame leopard and the black boy had to be stitched up in hospital.

What adventures we had with Gordon Poolman at the steering wheel of our zebra-striped car, going cross-country at thirty or forty miles an hour! Gordon either had a sixth sense, or a special guardian angel, for he never drove into holes made by honey-badgers, nor ran into termite hills.

Once we were driving beside a large cock ostrich. The bird was nearly eight feet high and took eleven-feet strides with ease. Gordon adjusted the accelerator so that, despite the high speed, I could comfortably take photographs at 1/1000th second exposure with an ordinary lens. Michael had taken out the side door and lay on his stomach, tied down with rope. He was taking slow-motion films, so that we could later study the movement and musculature

Ostriches are the most indefatigable runners of all the animals of the plains.

of the bird in detail.   The speedometer registered thirty miles an hour.   The cock ostrich did not seem to mind the race.   When we stopped after twenty-two minutes he carried on running for another mile or more, showing that he was by no means exhausted.   Ostriches must have extraordinarily efficient hearts.

They also have *brave* hearts, when called upon.   Not long ago we met a cock, a hen and eight chicks.   A hyena tried to grab one of the youngsters.   There was a great to-do, the cock looked after the children while the hen attacked the hyena, routed it and chased it for nearly a mile.   A few days later we met the same family, but there were only six chicks left.

On another occasion two ostriches stood on the completely bare plain with their wings spread, providing shade for their children.

Sometimes an ostrich can suddenly disappear while running away, without going anywhere near the horizon.   On following, one can see him sitting on the ground with his long neck stretched flat in front of him.   This may be the origin of the fable that ostriches hide their heads in the sand and believe themselves unobserved.   The old Arabs recorded it and since then, throughout the centuries, Roman and other authors have copied it from each other.   Half-grown ostriches are especially fond of this trick.   If they are approached when in this position they start up and streak away.

Ostrich cocks can roar and growl like lions.   To do this they blow air from their trachea into their mouths, keeping their beaks tightly closed.   The air is then forced down their necks back into the esophagus.   The opening into the stomach is tightly closed to prevent the air from entering.   The red, completely naked neck expands like a balloon and a low, far-carrying roar is heard.   They probably want to tell other cocks, or even hens: "This is my territory!"

An ostrich cock in love behaves just as oddly as a man in the same predicament.   The ostrich sits on his long legs and rhythmically beats his wings alternately on either side.   He puts his head back and rubs the nape of his neck along his back.   His neck and legs are a shining red colour at this time.   To us this may seem a strange way for the largest living bird to behave but the hens know its meaning.   They run away playfully, and he chases after them with giant strides.

The old Egyptians regarded the ostrich as a symbol of justice, for they noticed that its feathers are the only ones having vanes of exactly equal width on either side of the shaft. The feather of any other bird has a wide and a narrow vane, and is thus "unjustly" divided. The old Egyptians also discovered that ostrich feathers make attractive ornaments for humans. As long as their plumes were only needed to decorate the helmets of medieval knights, wild birds were reasonably safe, but when the feathers became fashionable for ladies during the last century, things began to look black for the ostrich. In Arabia and Persia they had been exterminated long ago, and in Africa, north of the Sahara, one can only find remains of ancient eggshells.

The fact that only *cocks* were hunted did not improve matters, but only made them worse. The cock not only fertilises the eggs but acts as nursemaid as well. He scratches a depression into the soil and sits on top of it. The hen lays her eggs in front of his chest, and he places them under his body with his neck and beak. The husband broods from late afternoon to morning, far longer than his wife. Even now we do not know whether wild ostriches are monogamous or whether they have several wives. When too many cocks have been killed, however, the hens nearly come to blows over the remaining ones. In any case the brooding cock is then inundated with so many eggs that he cannot cover the whole pile. As a result none of the eggs hatch out.

Ostriches were saved from extermination when people learned to breed them in captivity. Many other animals whose fur became fashionable had a similar fate, such as the chinchilla, coypu, silver fox and mink. All our limited knowledge of the breeding habits of ostriches comes from zoological gardens and ostrich farms. The first farm was started in South Africa in 1838. When the price of feathers rose this was soon followed by others in Algeria, Sicily, Florida and even at Nice in Southern France.

I hope the 1,606 ostriches in Serengeti will not share the fate of their fellows in South-West Africa. Before the first World War the birds were strictly preserved because their feathers were so valuable. During the war nobody had enough time to shoot them, and afterwards the feathers became unfashionable and cheap. It was decided that protection could be removed because there were too many ostriches. Business-minded people at once pursued them in motor cars and shot them. They often returned from these trips with four to five hundred skins, which were then turned into grained wallets and handbags. Nobody wanted the two or three hundred pounds of meat on each bird, especially as some of them were up to thirty years old. The carcasses stank out the neighbourhood, because even the vultures and hyenas could not cope with such an unexpected windfall.

The love and favour of men is not to be relied on. When the purse or fashion takes a hand they are easily reversed. That is why we wish this wilderness, in which men cannot make a living anyway, to remain a sanctuary where a few hundred thousand wild animals can live in complete independence. Our grandchildren, as well as those of the Africans, should see what Africa was like before we Europeans brought Christianity and slavery, human rights and machine-guns, medicine and motor-cars.

We decided that the solution of our problem was to catch zebras and paint them. Fifty or sixty were grazing in the wide, tree-fringed plain of the Grumeti river, and took little notice of our striped car. Michael steered the car towards six zebras grazing a little apart from the herd. They started, raised their heads, pointed their ears towards us and then turned about and galloped away. It was not hard to catch up with them.

Gordon Poolman crouched on the roof of the car with a long stick of bamboo in his hand. The upper end of it was notched, and the notch held a rope noose. The noose was tied with a thin thread so that it remained open, but when the noose was tightened the thread broke.

Michael navigated so that the zebra galloped close beside the bonnet. The rope had to be passed over the nose, under the chin, and finally around the neck of the zebra. We were travelling at a fair speed and the car jumped and danced over the grass, so that we frequently bumped our heads. The slipstream blew the noose backwards, and the zebra constantly veered to the right. We were going so fast that we could only turn in a gentle arc while trying to keep close to the animal. If we braked too violently, Gordon would be catapulted over the bonnet. Sharp turns would fling him off sideways, and he did not want to be tied on, as that might have been even more dangerous.

Finally the noose was over the zebra's head, Michael braked very gently to prevent the noose from slipping off. Gordon jumped down, all of us followed, clutching the rope and letting ourselves be dragged slowly and protestingly forward by the stallion until he stood still. Then he was held and painted.

We did not think it would be difficult to paint a zebra green or red for, after all, the art of dyeing feminine hair is highly developed. But there was a surprise in store for us. Steam and heat are required to dye a woman's hair permanently. Mere washing, painting, or powdering is not enough. We consulted the greatest experts in the dye industry, but they could not give us any advice on how to give a zebra a cold hair-tinting. Horse hair is very short and there was no question of steaming a zebra, even had we possessed a model hairdressing salon. We therefore had to fall back on the old stand-by, picric acid, which stains the hair and hide a bright quince yellow.

The most permanent of all stains were those on our hands and trousers; the zebras could have the satisfaction of knowing that they were not the only ones to turn yellow. Unfortunately the bright colour later turns a dirty brown, and when the short hairs fall out they are replaced by white ones. Painting is not the real solution. We already had the remedy, but it was still in transit. To-day, we wanted to see how the other zebras treated their yellow colleague. Would they regard him as an outcast, avoid him, or even bite him? If that were the case there would be no point in marking.

We released the stallion and followed at a distance, observing through field-glasses how the herd reacted when he rejoined it. Would they ostracise him or bite him? Nothing of the kind happened. They behaved as if he had always been yellow. So far so good; at least we had made some slight advance.

It takes three or four minutes for a zebra to run out of breath and slow down. Despite this the second chase never really got going. The zebra repeatedly escaped into groups of trees, and although the trunks were widely spaced, there was always one that got in

At first we dyed zebras yellow so as to recognise them from the air.

the way of the car. Michael could not get close enough to our quarry.

Gordon and Michael exchanged places. I did not want my son to play cowboy on the roof of a dangerously swaying car. Mgabo volunteered for the job and Gordon Harvey also wanted to have a go. Michael, however, insisted. "You must realise, Dad, that one can't always leave the slightly dangerous jobs to other people."

All right, I gave in. We hunted a mare. Whenever the noose came close to her eyes she lowered her head until it nearly touched the ground or got between her forelegs.

Michael knocked. We stopped. The noose had become twisted and had to be retied. We were quickly back in the car and close to the mare again.

There was a sudden jerk. Gordon braked violently.

Michael had been thrown from the car. The next moment I was beside him. "Misha!" I saw a hole in his neck. Blood. Michael seemed stunned. The two wardens lifted him and seated him against a wheel. I investigated the wound. It seemed deep but did not bleed strongly. I was afraid the wind-pipe had been damaged, an artery torn, or that there was internal bleeding.

Michael was growing visibly paler and weaker. I lifted his eyelids to see if the lining membranes were still pink, which would be a good sign. They were greyish-white.

Michael lost consciousness. I quickly put him flat on his back, but he had to be moved under the car because that was the only shady place. It was noon and the sun was directly overhead. The first-aid kit, which was normally kept in the 'plane, was luckily in the car for once.

In the prone position Michael soon came to. His first words were: "Did you make a note of everything and photograph it?"

"Don't talk, Michael, you mustn't talk."

Only later did I realise what had happened. The zebra lowered its head. Michael lowered the bamboo stick with the noose, until the swaying truck forced the stick against the ground. The other end struck Michael, and as we were travelling fast it pierced his neck. Fortunately the impact threw him over the back of the car. If he had been tied down he would have been spitted. But the wound? I anxiously considered what might be inside it. There were dirt and splinters at least, and perhaps some muscles had been torn.

We put Michael into the car and drove towards the aeroplane. This took twenty minutes. Diagonally opposite us two lions were standing under the canopy of a tree. At any other time we would have stopped to photograph them.

At last we reached the 'plane. I supported my son and pushed him into the second pilot's seat. Then down with the hood. Ignition started. Booster pump tested. Impatiently I waited for the oil temperature to get high enough. Finally we were off.

We flew cross-country towards Lake Victoria. There was a small hospital in Musoma, and the Indian surgeon in charge had an excellent reputation.

Michael had to sit up perforce, and started to feel worse. I grasped the joy-stick, looked at the compass and peered forward to catch a glimpse of the gleaming surface of the lake. I also watched Michael. His head sank forward again and again, though in between he straightened up for a few minutes. His hands were covered with sweat.

I had never been to Musoma, and had to take care not to lose my way among the many hills and native settlements. Michael sensed my anxiety and knew that I was afraid, afraid for him. He grinned at me and moved his hand—"Don't worry, Dad."

I counted the minutes and waited for Musoma to come into sight.

The landing place of the little town appeared enormous and very modern from the air, but that was an illusion for it was anything but level when we touched down. As soon as we bumpily rolled to a stop a native appeared with a book into which I was supposed to make entries. I left him standing and rushed away looking for a car. There was none to be seen anywhere; everything was empty, deserted and flat. No car, no European, nothing.

A house at last. I knocked. A young lady opened the door and I called to her that I had to have a car at once, to take a wounded man to the hospital. She understood. Two minutes later I sat in a Volkswagen without a windscreen.

Now the hospital. The Indian doctor made a good impression. He looked at the wound, shook his head and said that he would have to anaesthetise Michael at once to see what had happened inside the neck. His African assistants tied white masks over their faces.

The operating theatre was just like the rest of the small hospital: modest, no tiled walls, but spotlessly clean.

I had to wait outside.

It took time and still more time. After two hours they finally carried Michael, still fast asleep, to his little room. The friendly black nurse had already made the bed. The doctor had taken a long wooden splinter from Michael's neck, cleaned the wound and sewn it up. He would have to stay at the hospital for at least three days.

I sat beside his bed and looked at him. I could not read. I realised how easily this could have turned into tragedy. I pondered: *"Is it really worthwhile to endanger your life for zebras and lions? Will the Government reduce the size of the park, despite all our efforts, and re-draw the boundaries so that the wild herds cannot be maintained? Will a later, independent government of natives destroy everything with one stroke of the pen?"* Question upon question, and no answer.

Michael awoke and insisted that I go to the hotel; visitors were not allowed after ten o'clock.

It was dark. There were no street lamps and on top of that we had a new moon, a fact indicated by my wrist watch and confirmed by the sky. In this, as in every African town, the houses were far apart. It was planned for cars and not for pedestrians.

The only small hotel was said to be by the shores of the lake. I wandered all over the place before I found it. Here, at Lake Victoria, it was hot even at night, and I had been spoiled by the high plateau of the Serengeti. Everyone at the bar naturally knew what had happened but I was too tired to explain it all over again. I quickly took a hot bath and went to bed, but I could not sleep.

Next morning the owner of the hotel drove me to the shopping centre of the town. An Indian tailor measured me for a pair of shorts and I bought needles and thread, as well as buttons of all sizes. At last we would be able to button up our shirts again.

I intended to go to the hospital at about eleven to take Michael some fresh South African apples, but found him already sitting at the hotel, angry at having to wait for two hours. Since he could

The Ngorongoro crater is a huge zoological garden containing a great many wildebeest and zebras.

Topis (a type of hartebeest) have blue-black thighs and yellow stockings.

Crowned cranes resemble walking flowers.

The tall, slender impala has wide-sweeping corkscrew horns.

We counted 57,199 zebras in the plains of Serengeti.

Grant's gazelle is the larger of the two common gazelles found in Serengeti. It is named after the British explorer James Augustus Grant, who searched for the sources of the Nile from 1860 to 1864.

Lions are always kind to their cubs. Even old males are considerate to the children.

not bear to be in hospital I was to give him injections for the next three days and take the stitches out after a week.

Twenty minutes later we were on our way back to Banagi. At first we followed the shores of the lake until we reached Speke Gulf, where the Serengeti Park touches the lake. Then we flew east over the "corridor" where the rivers flow towards the lake. The banks of the rivers were marked by narrow strips of forest and between them spread the grey-green grasslands. It is in these tsetse-infested lowlands that the animals have the greatest chance of finding water and forage during the dry season. Next came the hills which were not on any map as yet, and many of which had not even been named. Their rounded tops were strewn with trees, and here and there a rock cliff was visible. We knew every one of these 1,000 to 1,200 footers, for we had flown up, down and across them many times during the last few weeks. The mountains ended and the treeless plains began. We throttled back the motor. On the far side of the grassland was the highland, the giant crater Ngorongoro. We glided across the shoulder of Banagi hill and touched down.

A week later we were catching zebras in the Ngorongoro crater. We wanted to know whether the herds climbed out of it and grazed in the broad plains during the wet months. This is the story told by hunters down the ages, and it is also the theory of Professor Pearsall of London, who two years ago wrote a report on Serengeti for the Tanganyika Government. During the rainy season these herds are said to wander to the middle of the great plain. The herds from the "corridor" are also reported to travel into the plain until they almost meet those from Ngorongoro.

If the National Park is truncated, and a line is drawn down the centre of the free grassland, the great herds from the "corridor" could, in theory, still wander freely inside the new boundaries. It is said that they only use the western half of the grassland during the rainy months. The animals grazing on the eastern half are supposed to come from Ngorongoro.

Up till now nobody has really observed or proved this. In the rainy season you cannot drive around the prairie. According to the able geologist, Professor Fritz Jaeger (who is still alive in Zurich), the Siedentopfs repeatedly tried to drive the wildebeest out of the crater with the help of Masai hunters as far back as 1906. The settlers wanted the crater for the sole use of their cattle. They never succeeded. The herds evaded them and remained inside Ngorongoro. During our many flights we never saw a single herd migrating across the rim of the crater. When we observed six to seven thousand wildebeest grazing in the eastern Serengeti during our animal count, we flew at once to Ngorongoro and had another count there. According to the old theory these herds had come from the crater, but the number inside had not diminished. This alarmed us, for the plans for a smaller park are based on these old theories.

We wanted, therefore, to mark wildebeest and zebras in the crater, to see whether they would be found later on the grasslands outside. We flew into the giant crater and landed on a strip of grass, at the corners of which Gordon Harvey had already placed his boys. He himself had travelled down by car for two-and-a-half hours from his house at the edge of the extinct volcano. Mrs. Harvey accompanied him, and had brought a large hamper of food. Both of them live up in the clouds as if in a paradise. They not only grow flowers but strawberries, lettuce, cress, leeks, tomatoes and many other kinds of vegetables. The Harveys are charming, hospitable people. Their grown-up sons are scattered in British colonies all over the world.

Our zebra hunt in the crater was a failure. It was cooler up here and the animals had more stamina and did not tire so quickly. They quickly learned that it was best to escape the car, not by galloping forward, but by running sideways in increasingly tight circles. On the slippery grass and at high speed we could not make such sharp arcs and our victims slowed down to a canter and finally to a walk. Some even stood still and watched our maneuvres with interest.

Then it started to rain, and on top of it all our truck turned over. My camera and I fell face downwards into the mud, but luckily no one was thrown under the car. When we tried to right the vehicle it slid away on the slippery surface. We had first to dig pits under the wheels and then lift it from the side. Success. When it stood on four wheels again we discovered that all the oil had run out. Without oil Gordon Harvey could not make the two-and-a-half hours' drive back home.

Michael had a brilliant idea. He ran for half an hour to our zebra 'plane, which had been filled up only two days ago. There were still two gallons of oil in it. Since we only needed about one and a half gallons we could safely spare three pints.

Unfortunately the correct spanner had been "organised" some time ago in the Nairobi workshop, but one of the car spanners fitted. Michael undid the nut and the boiling-hot oil poured over his fingers. Despite this he forced himself to screw it up again quickly before it had all escaped, otherwise we would have been held captive in the crater for another day. We transferred the black gooey substance.

In the meantime a thunderstorm was raging in the eastern part of the crater, and it started to rain where we were. Before the blanket of cloud closed completely we managed to start the 'plane and slip out through the last hole. We could not fly inside clouds, because of the danger of crashing into one of the volcanoes.

The sky above the plains was clear. We roared towards Banagi hill which appeared far away on the horizon. Our plans had miscarried, but we were already busily making new ones.

The Masai call this volcano *Oldonio L'Engai*, the mountain of God. It is still occasionally active.

CHAPTER 8

We Discover Poachers

*There is only one untruthful creature on earth,
and that is man. All the others are honest and
upright in that they openly declare their nature and do not simulate emotions they do not
feel.*

ARTHUR SCHOPENHAUER

MANY PEOPLE nowadays sleep while flying high above the ocean,
or eat duck and green peas miles above the marvels and mysteries
of the jungle. Such heedless users of aerial omnibuses should
really *fly* sometimes, as Michael and I did.

It was the morning of a bright new day. We did not want to
count animals, we did not have to fetch supplies from Nairobi, we
simply wanted to take to the air. We circled upwards until the
Banagi and Seronera hills grew smaller and smaller. The pointer
of the altimeter slowly crept round the dial because our 250 horse-
power engine had to lift nearly two-and-a-half tons' dead weight.
As Banagi lies 5,200 feet above sea level, which is higher than
Ben Nevis, the air is rarefied and we took four minutes to climb
the first 3,000 feet. The second 3,000 took six minutes, and after
that the climb grew consistently slower.

We could see increasingly larger portions of the Serengeti.
L'Engai, the "mountain of God," came into view, from the sharply
conical top of which smoke issues in some years, and on our other
side we saw the twinkling, silver strip of Lake Victoria.

We set our flaps for maximum lift and adjusted the pitch of the
propeller to 3,000 revolutions per minute as our trusty "zebra"
climbed slowly into the sky.

When we reached a white cumulus cloud we flew straight into it. We were surrounded by a glaringly white mist, but we knew that the rising air was constantly lifting us higher. In the meantime a needle on a small gauge was steadily drifting towards the yellow "danger" line. This meant that the engine was overheating because we were flying too slowly in the thin air. There was not sufficient forward speed to cool the laboriously working motor.

We pulled in the flaps and set the pitch of the propeller for horizontal flight. The altimeter needle came to rest and after ten minutes the engine temperature fell to normal. Then the struggle for height started once more and we climbed foot by foot and yard by yard.

Michael finally said: "We can't get any higher, the air is too thin." We were 18,800 feet above sea level and 13,600 feet above our tin hut in the plains. This, however, was invisible for we flew about the white clouds in a world of unreality. We stopped the motor and switched off the ignition.

The silence was uncanny. The propeller slowed down and stopped until it looked like a thin plank with yellow tips. The landing flaps were set at forty-five degrees, the angle of maximum lift. Now our "duck" was a glider and we had the feeling of sailing through the sky on silent wings like soaring eagles. The air rushed past our thirty-nine foot wing span. The altimeter showed that we were dropping at a rate of between ten and thirteen feet a second. When we fell into the lower and denser atmosphere this rate would be even slower. I calculated that we could glide for fifteen minutes before reaching the Serengeti again.

The glaciers of Kilimanjaro towered above the white cloudscape. Even when truncated by a layer of water vapour the mountain still looked regal. In this silent world we could talk without the use of microphones. We looked down on the soft valleys and rounded hills of the clouds below us. It seemed an other-worldly realm, shaped by a Deity to compensate for the harsh reality below it. We longed to land our 'plane on the soft white cloudscape, to stretch out on it and to listen to the whispering voice of the Spirit. We closed our eyes, the only two men in this higher, second world . . .

Slam! I suddenly felt a stinging pain in my left thigh. Five fingers appeared in red outline on my skin, but Michael's blue-grey eyes were looking straight ahead. He could barely conceal his triumphant grin. This was another instance of our old game, to catch each other unaware at a specially emotional moment. Michael had succeeded and we were one all, as in a football match.

We shivered a little in our shirt-sleeves, missing the warmth of the motor, but it was good to know that by pressing a button we could make the engine come to life again.

Six months before, a pilot had flown a little Cessna machine across the mountain craters and salt lakes. He climbed above the clouds to cross the peaks in safety, but he probably did not find a hole in the sheet of cloud through which he could see the earth. It is very dangerous to descend blindly through clouds. You never know how close they are to the ground, or whether they even reach right down and touch it as mist or fog. Nor can you tell whether mountains protrude into them. The radio in Nairobi heard the pilot say that he had only enough petrol for another five minutes' flying and that he did not know where he was. That was the last that was heard of him. Nobody knows whether his aeroplane dived into the caustic water of one of the salt lakes or lies shattered in one of the mountain ravines.

We glided into a black-lined crevice inside the cloud bank and sank down, as if in a lift, near the flank of the huge white monster. Then we suddenly saw the plains below us again, stippled by sunlight and shade.

Michael nudged me. "Dad, can you see what's going on straight underneath?"

A curious thread stretched across the grassland between two tree-fringed river beds. The men running beside it did not notice our silent approach. They were erecting a fence made of thorny branches right across the plain. Every twenty or thirty yards they left a gap through which the roaming wildebeest, antelopes and zebras could pass.

We knew that these gaps were filled with wire snares. Here the animals would slowly strangle themselves, or be eaten alive by hyenas and jackals. Hundreds of vultures were waiting in the trees by the rivers.

"Game poachers!" exclaimed Michael furiously.

Poachers shooting at wildebeest with poisoned arrows.   Taken with a 1,000-millimetre (39-inch) lens from a long distance.

We kept the motor off and came closer and lower. Five of the men below were dismembering a zebra. They put the red hunks of meat across a pole, which was carried by two of them to a shelter among the trees.

"I'd like to have a machine-gun which fired through the propeller," said Michael.

I pressed the red starter-button and after stuttering once or twice the engine came to life again. We roared across the ground at twelve to fifteen feet. The poachers were not prepared for a sudden interruption out of the blue sky. We pulled back the stick to clear the tree tops at the edge of the plain, banked, and flew back again. A few of them were running for shelter among the trees, but at our approach they threw themselves flat on their faces.

A few moments later some of them rose to their knees and shot at us with their bows and arrows. This was ridiculous, as their arrows would hit the empty air far behind us.

Our fighting spirit was roused. Should we land and capture some of these wild-life murderers? We decided against this as

Diving "attack" on poachers.

we could not tell where there were warthog holes which might damage the 'plane. Also we were unarmed, and the poachers were sure to have poisoned arrows. Besides that we were not policemen and had no powers of arrest, and we did not want to get on the wrong side of the authorities.

We did own a signalling pistol, however, for cases of emergency. It was not a deadly weapon, but it might give these robbers a real fright. I undid my safety-belt and reached backwards for some ammunition. Michael took one of the red cardboard cylinders, pressed it into the brass tube at the bottom of the cabin and screwed it down. Then we flew over them once more.

Ready, steady, go! Michael pressed the trigger. The result was startling, not for the men below, but for us. Before we knew what had happened a sudden gust of wind rushed past our faces. The air whistled through a hole the size of a dinner-plate in the curved Plexiglas windscreen. Instead of startling the poachers the shot had gone upwards, between our heads, for the catch in the fire-work pistol had been faulty. What if the cartridge had hit one of us instead of the windscreen? We shuddered.

To save our pride we swooped on the robber band once more, before climbing to five hundred feet and heading for home.

The game poachers had hit us after all! After we had rolled our machine into its protective corral of thorn twigs we discovered an arrow in the wing. The tip was bent, so that it was hard to remove. Michael climbed on my shoulders and carefully pulled it out with pliers.

"Take care," I told him, "the tip is probably poisoned."

If you cut your finger with one of these arrows you are lost, as there is no known antidote for the poisons with which they have been treated.

Arrow poison is obtained from a tree (*Apocanthera frisiorum*) which looks quite harmless, rather like a withered Italian olive tree. It has little berries which redden when they are ripe, and from which quite a pleasant jam can be prepared. Not all the trees of this genus are poisonous, and it is difficult to identify the few that are. The natives probably trace the lethal ones by the dead insects and rodents lying near the trunk. The poison is prepared by cutting branches and roots into small pieces and boiling them into a thick stew. This is carried on until the messy mixture reaches the consistency of thick treacle. The final product is poured into boxes, wrapped in leaves and sold to poachers. A small piece of it, just sufficient for one arrow, costs a shilling.

You do not have to be a good marksman if you own poisoned arrows. You only have to wound an animal or a man in the leg, and your victim is doomed. This method is slightly more dangerous than shooting a lion with a modern rifle, but it still makes you the lord of life and death on the plains. The meat from animals killed with poisoned arrows is quite palatable, provided you cut away the meat near the wound.

Really sharp business men who are out for a quick penny dilute the poison with black soil, or any other doughy substance which resembles it. I was told that it is easy to spot the genuine article. You make a small cut in your calf, let the blood trickle down and touch the blood farthest away from the cut with the poison. If the poison is real thin blisters appear at once and run up the streak of blood. The material must then be wiped off before

The poisoned arrow in the wing had to be removed very carefully.

reaching the open wound. I tried this method, but obtained no blisters.

Gordon Poolman had just returned from a trip to the "corridor". He was the only one amongst us who always carried a pistol in his belt. He, too, had had an adventure the previous day. He found an old man, quite alone, in the country near the Duma river. Filled with suspicion and compassion at the same time he had invited him into the car. Why was he all by himself in this desolate country? The feeble old man said that he had had a young companion, but that the lad had been bitten by a snake in the river bed and had died within ten minutes. The old man had placed him underneath an overhanging rock and covered him with branches.

Gordon drove to the forest-covered river bank of the Duma, close to the spot where the accident was said to have occurred. The old man shivered and did not dare to alight, he merely described the exact position of the corpse. Gordon found only a few bones—and many hyena tracks.

We glued and screwed a plate over the hole in the windscreen. Then, at two o'clock, we dictated a telegram to Munich—via Arusha—on the radio. It was not so easy to express all this in English, for we did not know the right word for "windscreen".

We were the proud owners of a whole library of technical books, lexicons, dictionaries and maps. Since air freight between Africa and Europe is so expensive, we had long ago decided to keep a duplicate set in Serengeti. The same applied to our shirts, linen, suits and shoes, specially as we could not wear khaki in Europe. We were therefore running what amounted to a second household in the Serengeti, for one of us or one of our English colleagues was nearly always there. It also meant that we had the drawbacks of two domestic staffs, white in Europe and black in Africa.

I constantly run across Germans and Englishmen who declare they can no longer bear to look at black faces. Their spoons disappear, their crockery is smashed, and anything that is not locked away is stolen. The boys maintain that they have malaria or must visit their sick parents. Given leave for two days, they do not reappear for a week; they are presented with clothes and shoes but are ungrateful and insolent. They thieve like magpies and do not even know how to clean boots unless you show them how.

I have found that the people who complain the most vociferously are generally those who have never had servants of their own in Europe. They imagine that all white servants are polite, industrious and honest, and they refuse to believe that they would have exactly the same trouble in England or Germany. Their words have a familiar ring. I can remember them from my childhood, forty years ago, when I spent my holidays with relations on the large estates of eastern Germany. Every day I had to listen to the same complaints which are made about coloured Africans now—only at that time they were made about white farm labourers.

I am not a politician but a biologist and can only speak as such when discussing the black and white question.

It is conceivable that negroes are more easy going and less intelligent than Europeans or Asiatics, just as their hair is shorter and their beards grow differently, but up to the present time there is no scientific evidence whatever to support this view. What we have found is that all peoples and "races" have about the same proportion of criminals and murderers, of brilliant men and idiots.

Not long ago an African-born European told me how impressed he was when he saw Italian cathedrals for the first time when he was fifty years old. "Only compare them with the miserable huts of our African natives."

This is no evidence that natives will never be able to build such edifices. I replied that the Egyptians of the era of the great pyramids would have had the same opinion of their Western contemporaries, in their rough skin clothes and crude wooden huts, as we have of the Africans to-day.

Frederick the Great of Prussia could not write in German without making elementary mistakes. He always used French and all his experts and architects came from France. The Frenchmen of that time—and perhaps those of the present also—therefore considered themselves cleverer and more talented than the Germans. German books once stated that the Germans were superior to the Poles and Russians because German artists had created masterpieces in Cracow, Moscow and Kiev in past centuries. Hitler's *Mein Kampf* even states that Russians are so racially inferior that they would never be able to build a car that worked. Who can foretell what the black races will be capable of in a hundred years' time, even though they may be running around naked to-day?

Hitler's *Mein Kampf* stated that it was "against Nature" for black and white people to intermarry. According to him it was like crossing horses and donkeys to produce sterile mules. This, of course, is nothing but ignorant nonsense. The hybrid between a horse and an ass would be akin to that between a man and a chimpanzee. There is only one human race and Mongolians, Caucasians and Negroes are merely different types within it. If they intermarry they do not produce hybrids but intermediary forms. If it should happen to a large extent we would create new peoples. All our present peoples and nations were produced by the intermingling of older ones. In South America, at the present time, you are getting an intermediate sort of man who happily combines the sunny temperament and resistance to tropical disease of the Negro with the adventurous spirit of the European. From a scientific point of view there is no possible "cross-breed" which combines only the *bad* characteristics of both parents. The children of Amerindians and Europeans or of negroes and whites are only "inferior" if they are condemned to grow up among beggars and criminals.

On the average, Europeans have a slightly heavier brain (1,360 grams) than Negroes (1,315 grams)—which fact seems to please most Europeans. Unfortunately for them the Europeans are outdone by the Chinese (1,430 grams). This has nothing at all to do with intelligence which is determined by the number of brain cells. This number is the same in all three cases, namely about fifteen thousand million. The individual cells of the negro are only a little smaller than those of the European, while those of the Chinese are larger.

If you trace your family back for two or three generations you usually find that your grandparents or great-grandparents looked for their husbands and wives in the nearest village or local market town. The whole group of relations lived in the same district. Nowadays we have relations in the north and south and quite often in America or Australia. Decade by decade people move farther and marry at greater distances from their places of origin. This addition of fresh blood is probably the reason for the greater size and earlier maturity of present-day children. Statistics show that the average height of military recruits has steadily increased during the last century. Medieval armour in the museums would fit very few men to-day. Animal breeders know that the children of a cross between two pure, and therefore inbred, type of poultry are larger and healthier than their parents; they show "hybrid vigour". The interbreeding of human types should have the same result. The future of whole continents depends on the friendly inter-mingling of different nationals, giving rise to ever-increasing talent and genius. It is to be hoped that the Africans and Indo-nesians will not follow the European examples of nationalistic pride and racial hatred.

A coloured man is the equal of a white one and has equal rights as long as his inferiority has not been proved. This proof cannot be achieved (as is constantly tried) by comparing an illiterate African village boy with a European visitor. If we compare a black bank clerk with a Bavarian peasant or even an African Uni-versity professor with a British docker or a Russian serf of two hundred years ago, matters appear in a different light. This makes it insupportable for an Indian minister to be refused hotel accom-modation while an uneducated, unshaven European farmer is gladly given a room. For me a Negro is an equal and a brother.

This is the reason why I am not sure whether the over-hasty conversion of coloured colonies into independent democratic States is good for the inhabitants. This may be the fashion to-day, and an easy road for colonial administrators, who may thus rid themselves of many annoyances, expenses and difficulties. They would have the world press solidly behind them, but in fact they would be shirking their responsibility towards the governed peoples, however hard those peoples' own educated political lead-ers may agitate.

Europeans have abruptly pulled these people out of a well-adjusted primitive existence and in some cases have abolished the slavery, tribal wars, pestilences and starvation which beset them. One cannot, however, suddenly grant independent, demo-cratic self-government to a people who are 98 per cent illiterate. They could very easily be at the mercy of a corrupt clique of chief-tains, merchants and opportunists, who would exploit them. Democracy had a slow growth in Europe and took hundreds, even thousands of years to come to full flower. It had all kinds of transitional forms, from elected rulers to the Prussian three-class voting system. A colonial nation must be at least half literate before it can govern itself in a modern way. It must possess tens of thousands of doctors, lawyers, technicians, teachers, nurses, road engineers, railway men and radio experts. I know that many Africans and Europeans disagree with this because they could make more money during the corrupt regime of the initial maladministration.

Things are not improved by quickly founding a few universities which have more professors than pupils. What the coloured countries need are teachers and tens of thousands of elementary schools. After ten years these should be followed by thousands of secondary schools, and they in turn by high schools and universities. Should those who love and honour the coloured people like brothers lay down their appointed task in anger only because they are urged by the native politicians and their own countrymen at home? The right to vote and a voice in the affairs of the nation should not depend on the colour of the skin, but on literacy and learning. Under these conditions the law would be the same for black and white, and the African would take part in the government as soon or as late as he was capable of doing so.

Many Europeans in Africa misanthropically state that everything is useless because the Africans will take power in a few years and throw them out. I regard this attitude as irresponsible and undemocratic. If the British left Tanganyika to-day, without leaving any European help and influence, that country could lose one of its greatest assets, a possession which is envied by all other lands and to which multitudes of people in coming decades will make a pilgrimage: the gigantic horde of animals in Serengeti. Such a well-educated and clever man as Dr. Julius Nyerere, the leader of the Tanganyika African National Union, certainly may realise its value for his country, but will new and uncivilised nations follow moderate politicians? To-day most Africans regard wild animals merely as so much meat, hides and grazing land. *We Europeans must teach our black brothers to value their own possessions, not because we are older or cleverer, but because we do not want them to repeat our mistakes and our sins.*

I had finished this chapter when I received a visit from a young African medical student in Europe, who intended to go into politics later on. I asked him to read the last section.

"Although everything you have written is correct," he said, "there still remains a big BUT. If our countries remain colonial possessions we will not have the schools you mention in fifty or even three hundred years. Only look at India. That was a colony for three hundred years. What happens to our countries is *our* concern—even if we ruin them. We'll manage all right, because we *want* to manage, but first of all we must be free!"

During my life I have had a lot of contact with simple black villagers, because it was part of my job. For that reason I always forget the big political questions and think primarily of their concerns. They want to have enough to eat all the year round and see their children growing and learning instead of dying. Most of them do not even know the name of their capital, or who is ruling there.

It is well known that wise men cannot pass on their wisdom to their grandchildren; each one must learn by his own mistakes and stupidities. This probably applies to nations as well. The young nations of Africa will have to find their own William Tell and Frederick the Great, Napoleon or Stalin, their own heroes; they will have to make their own wars and bury their own dead.

CHAPTER 9

Concerning Poisonous Snakes

No animal is cruel for the sake of cruelty, only man. This makes his character devilish, which is much worse than mere beastliness.

ARTHUR SCHOPENHAUER

ONE DAY in October Michael was sitting under a leafless tree in front of the tin hut reading a book. After an hour he was startled by the approach of Tambura, our black house boy, along the path leading to the hut. The young man shouted, gesticulated and looked around for a stick. This led Michael to examine the leaning tree-trunk, on which he discovered a black mamba leisurely creeping downwards, about three feet from where his shoulder had been. The snake was twelve feet long.

While the reptile was gliding across the bare space in front of the hut and towards some bushes, Michael tried to deflect it with a bamboo pole. The snake protruded its tongue, raised its head about two feet from the ground but refused to be diverted. Michael did not dare to grasp it by the tail, and so it disappeared into the thorny undergrowth. We were not pleased about the presence of our poisonous neighbor, for the black mamba is notorious and deadly. Our main concern was for our bushbaby, so we burned down the shrubbery. The snake, which had probably gone to earth, did not reappear. We had to leave it where it was, willy-nilly, but we gradually forgot all about it, since we never saw it again during the following weeks.

This was the sum total of our personal contacts with the feared mamba, in Africa at least, for there are plenty of poisonous snakes in the reptile house of our Frankfurt Zoo. Although mambas are by no means rare in Africa, I have never seen one out of captivity. This does not mean that no mamba has ever seen *me*.

I can tell you the most hair-raising stories about these snakes, which I have heard from others or have read in books. These reptiles seem to have most efficient press agents.

For instance: A bridal pair were on a honeymoon ride in Africa. They saw a black mamba in the grass which raised itself higher than the horses' heads. They immediately turned around, spurred on their steeds and galloped away—the mamba overtook them all the same and bit the bride, the bridegroom and both horses. All four died.

Or: A farmer met a mamba and shattered its head with a volley from his shotgun. Thinking to frighten his young wife he took the dead, but still wriggling, reptile and placed it on the floor of their bedroom. After two hours the merry company downstairs noticed that the young wife had not returned from tending her children. The horrified spouse found her dead on the floor, next to a second mamba, still very much alive. He killed the second snake, too. "I should have known that the mate of the dead mamba would come to avenge his wife," he cried.

Further: A government official drove through the brush in his car, saw a mamba on the track and tried to run over it. The snake rose, pursued the car, jumped into it through the side window and killed two of the occupants.

I would only like to add that snakes do not have "husbands" or "wives" and only meet briefly during their mating. If you see two of them they are just as likely to be two males or two females as a pair of opposite sexes. If one snake finds another one dead it does not know who killed it and in any case does not thirst for revenge.

Poisonous snakes do not hunt men. As they cannot take bites out of their victim and have to swallow their prey whole, a man is much too large for them. The comparatively enormous human being remains alive much longer than the usual small fry which form the snake's main food, and therefore constitutes a danger once he has been bitten. That is why most poisonous snakes avoid us and creep away into bushes, holes or rock crevices if given a

chance to do so. Even when they approach us they are not necessarily agressive. Sometimes we are between them and their hole,
and they may slide between our legs, or over our shoulders into a
tree to seek shelter, without biting us.

I have spent hundreds of nights in Africa, many of them in native
huts, tents or even out in the open. I must confess that I have never
woken up, bathed in sweat because a coiled-up cobra lay on my
chest searching my face with its tongue. Nor have I ever found a
puff-adder in my boots when I tried to put them on. I must admit,
however, that I never wear boots in Africa, as I prefer gym shoes or
sandals. This does not mean that such things *cannot* happen.

This spring one of our native workers was in bed with a severe
attack of malaria. He felt a movement underneath him and on
groping for the place was bitten in the arm by a mamba. Our
friend Myles Turner at once brought his "snake kit," a cleverly
constructed metal box sold by the Fitz-Simons Snake Pack in Dur-
ban. (We also had such a box handy in the car and aeroplane.)
Myles made some deep cuts in the arm, parallel to the muscles so
as not to damage tendons and blood vessels, rubbed potassium per-
manganate into the wound and injected anti-snakebite serum.
Finally the man was taken to hospital in Ikoma.

It was two months before the patient returned. The tissue-
destroying snake venom had caused a large portion of the muscle
to degenerate, so that the man could push a little stick into his arm,
the end of which then protruded again about eight inches farther
down.

Kay Turner, Myles's young wife, disliked the fact that a large
mamba crept around on the thin ceiling of their bedroom every
night. It was hunting for bats and small rodents. Kay finally became so annoyed that Myles and his black assistant took off half the
roof and crept into the space with a cocked shotgun. They found
two complete skins, including corneas, which the reptile had shed,
as well as the remains of many victims. Myles did not capture the
snake, however, which still crept about on top of the ceiling. In
the meantime Kay had got used to it.

I do not mean to convey that snakebites may not be lethal. The
Spaniard, Louis de Lassaletta, was a good friend of mine. He
caught two young gorillas now in the Frankfurt Zoo, and also the

huge frogs from the Cameroons.   Last January he was bitten in the neck by a poisonous snake which he was transferring into a cage. He died within five minutes.   But most people in Africa neither catch poisonous reptiles nor put them into cages with their bare hands.

Another acquaintance of mine was nearly killed twice.   He is Marlin Perkins, the Director of one of the two big zoos in Chicago. When he was still the reptile curator in the St. Louis Zoo he was bitten by an African gaboon viper.   These reptiles can hiss so loudly that it sounds like air escaping from a punctured tyre.   Luckily the bite was in a favourable position, the index finger, and only *one* of the two poison fangs had gone home.   The puncture mark was at once cut and sucked.   The director then telephoned New York for advice.   Since no specific serum for the gaboon viper existed at that time, Perkins was injected with rattlesnake, cobra and fer-de-lance serum in succession.   Despite all this the patient became unconscious, and the pulse rate fell to fifty.   The strongly dilated pupils no longer reacted to light and the urine was tinged with blood.   When death seemed imminent a blood transfusion was given.   This helped and after three weeks Perkins was allowed to leave the hospital.   In 1951 he was again bitten, this time by a South American snake during a television programme, and several blood transfusions were needed.

Ordinary people, who do not appear on such television programmes, get bitten when they step on snakes in long grass or in bushes, or when they disturb a branch on which the snake is lying. Accidents are even more frequent when people try to kill or catch snakes, and force the reptiles to defend themselves.   Unless the snake bites unexpectedly the best method is to run away.

We constantly overestimate the speed of small creatures, and no snake can move as fast as a man.   James Oliver, the curator of reptiles in the New York Zoo, has written a whole book on facts and superstitions about snakes, and I have taken many of my details from that book.   He once timed a black mamba, allegedly the fastest of these snakes, with a stop-watch, and found that it moved for forty-seven yards at a speed of circa seven miles an hour.   Men as well as horses can manage eighteen to nineteen miles an hour for short distances.   There is not much sense in running away from

elephants, lions, gorillas, rhinos or hippos; in fact it can be dangerous, for it might incite the animals to attack, but it is easy enough
to get away from poisonous snakes.

Snakes can bite in any position, even under water, and it is said
that a severed head can still make deadly bites; on the other hand
they do not strike like "lightning." The striking speed of a rattlesnake was timed and found to be eight-and-a-half feet per second.
A cobra is six times as slow. A second is a long time—an untrained
man can move his fist at twenty feet a second, more than twice as
fast as a rattlesnake. A trout swims at seven-and-a-half feet a
second, a bee flies at nine, and a dragon-fly at nearly twenty-five
feet a second. A golf player can reach forty-three feet a second.
Skilled "snake-charmers" can easily pat a cobra on the head whilst
it is striking. Most snakes can only strike about a third of their
own length. African snakes which spit or squirt their venom can
hit your eyes at six feet with great accuracy and get uncomfortably
close at ten feet. This is excruciatingly painful and causes severe
inflammation. You cannot see for two or three weeks and cases of
complete blindness have been reported.

"Snake-charmers" who display their cobras at the roadside and
play to them on their flutes utilise this slowness. If you know
them you can avoid their deadly bites, and cobras usually strike
with closed mouths—during the daytime anyway. The fakirs
look for animals which do not crawl away but tend to remain upright. The "charmer" moves his flute and head from side to side
to keep the snake irritated and erect. Snakes cannot hear the tune
of the flute since they have no earholes and cannot perceive sound
waves. When a cobra had its mouth tied and its eyes covered it
still got into a striking position when people approached although
it remained completely indifferent to a tin can which was beaten
with a stick quite close to its head. Snakes depend on smell and
vibrations transmitted through the ground. These facts have not
displaced the fallacy that snakes can be "charmed" by music.

Most "snake-charmers" are eventually killed by their charges,
despite their skill. It is the old story of familiarity breeding con-
tempt. Exactly the same thing can happen to curators in zoos. I
kept some common European adders in my house more than
twenty years ago. The deadliness of these snakes is usually exag-

gerated, except in rare cases they can only kill small babies or old and weak people. At that time I was completely unfamiliar with poisonous reptiles and picked the snakes up close behind the head, with my bare hands. Then I read somewhere that they could push their lower jaw aside and still strike the fingers with the fangs in their upper jaw. I put on gloves the next day and the first snake I picked up demonstrated that it could bite my finger despite my grip in its neck.

Most people over-estimate the danger of being struck by snakes in the tropics, but they under-estimate the horror such a bite can involve. The small victims of the snake die with amazing rapidity and probably feel little pain, but a man is twelve to a hundred times as big as the usual prey. The agony can go on for minutes, hours, or even days. Not all the different venoms have been investigated in detail, but we know that some act on the nervous system, others attack the tissues and the blood vessels. There are also all kinds of intermediate types.

Nerve poisons lead to cramps and paralysis, especially of the respiratory centres and sometimes the heart will go on beating for a little while after the breathing has stopped. Other constituents of the venom cause the veins and arteries to "leak". The blood enters the tissues, limbs become red or black and swell enormously, the victim coughs and vomits, and blood enters the urine and stool. The eyes become bloodshot and blood can even flow into the abdomen.

Other parts of the venom decompose the tissues—they are intended to prepare the victim for digestion, as the snake cannot chew its prey but eats it whole. It took four days for a snake to digest a rat it had bitten, but a freshly-killed, unbitten rat lasted for thirteen days. Even if the victim is saved by serum the consequences can still be serious. Whole limbs may wither or become gangrenous; long-lasting infections can ensue and lead to deafness, blindness, or partial paralysis.

The Kioka of Tanganyika are experts at handling poisonous snakes. Some years ago a young American, who was collecting snakes for museums back home, made friends with Kalola, the chieftain of the tribe, and his nephew Njoka. One day the American was horrified when a black mamba bit Njoka in the leg, and he remained unperturbed, maintaining that he was immune.   He was, however, so touched by the concern of the American that he promised to initiate him into the rites of the tribe.

The American took part in many magic ceremonies during which incisions were made all over his body.   These were then rubbed with a powder called *lukago*, consisting of all manner of weird ingredients, including dried and ground snakes' heads and tails. Finally he had to catch a mamba with his bare hands and permit himself to be bitten.

The young man was sure that he had made a great discovery, which he wanted to pass on for the benefit of mankind.   It was fortunate that he took some of the snakes to the headquarters of the expedition.   An expert herpetologist examined them and found that their fangs had been removed.   He had been bitten by a harmless snake.

It must not be assumed that all African "snake-charmers" use harmless reptiles.   Sometimes travellers touch these snakes protected by such beliefs and the "charmer" halfheartedly protests only just enough to save himself in case of accidents.   A real disaster would be a good advertisement for him.

One such "snake-charmer" offered magic potions against snakebite in the streets.   He had a cobra and two gaboon vipers with him to make matters more interesting.   After "charming" the cobra he gave it to a spectator to hold.   The snake bit the spectator in the cheek and within one hour the man was dead.   An investigation showed that all three snakes still had their fangs and full poison glands.   The vendor was sent to jail for three years for manslaughter by negligence.

Taking it all round, snakes in Africa are just like elephants and lions: you never see them unless you go out of your way to look for them.

During the dry season hundreds of thousands of animals are obliged to use the few remaining water holes in the "corridor," the low-lying district of Serengeti near Lake Victoria. Death may be lurking near the water.

CHAPTER 10

Miracle Guns

Whole aeons of love are required to compensate the animals for the services they have rendered us.

CHRISTIAN MORGENSTERN

EVERY DAY our most pressing problem was becoming increasingly clear—I remember how, morning after morning, while shaving with our battery-driven electric razors, Michael and I used to discuss it: "How are we to keep track of the moving herds?"

We now knew that all the 367,000 large quadrupeds in the Serengeti National Park roam about restlessly and cross the intended new eastern frontier of the Park during the rainy season. This process may take weeks or even months so that the herds, which are the prime reason for the existence of the Park, may live outside it for a large part of each year. During the wet season the smaller groups coalesce into huge herds and drift through the open grassland. It is easy enough to follow them by 'plane, but one cannot keep track of individual groups.

During the dry months things are quite different. The large herds break up again into groups of 100 or 150 beasts. Many of these live in the low-lying "corridor", while others can be seen far to the north, outside the borders of the Park. Are they all a part of the great army which wandered across the grasslands during the rains? We were consistently plagued by the same idea: "Let's paint them, so that we can follow them." We toyed with the idea of driving them between funnel-shaped fences, at the end of which there would be a pool of dye through which they would have to swim. We realised that this would unfortunately be impossible, since the animals' coats would have to be de-greased first. Besides that our 99,481 wildebeest were black, and you cannot dye black hair. They would have to be painted, and probably with oil paint at that.

Michael ground out the butt of his cigarette in the loose soil of the floor. A sandy floor is very practical in a male household, it obviates sweeping. Odds and ends are merely pushed into it and scratched over loosely.

Michael said, "Incidentally, do you remember trying to drive wildebeest and zebras between two cars? As soon as they realise that they are being driven in a definite direction, they veer round and escape."

Ear-tags were too small for our purpose. Even reasonably large and coloured ones would not distinguish one zebra among thousands. Electrical devices which send out signals were also impracticable, for the battery would only last a few weeks, so we finally decided on collars. The leather ones we tried at first were useless. They suffered from sun and rain. The paint scraped off and the collars were soon indistinguishable.

The material of our choice was a synthetic plastic, the kind you see on gaily-coloured, striped deck-chairs and garden seats. It is light, durable, and persistently loud in colour. We measured the zebras and wildebeest in the zoo at home and made them collars of four or five thicknesses of cloth. They do not worry the animals, are not easily lost, have no tendency to catch on anything and can be quickly recognised from the air. There is only one drawback: First catch your wildebeest!

This is no easy matter, for the animal must not only be caught but caught quickly, otherwise the herd wanders too far away for the captive to rejoin it. Once the animal is collared, in both senses, it is easily recognised. A zebra provided with a red collar and an earmark bearing the number 21 on the 4th May was seen by a game warden on the 12th November. It was spotted in a herd, seventy miles farther eastward, outside the borders of the park. On the 31st October it was back at almost the identical spot where it was first caught. We picked it out very easily, although it was inside a herd, and we were more than 1,500 feet up.

During the previous two years the technical press had been

praising a new "miracle" gun. It was said to be just as efficient as sprinkling salt on the tails of evasive birds. A white hunter in Africa offered to sell me one for $600. He maintained that I could use if to stupefy any gorilla, elephant or lion for a few minutes, long enough to get the animal into a cage before it regained consciousness.

We bought such a gun, of course, but we obtained it direct from the American manufacturer at a quarter of the price quoted by the gentleman. This weapon looks like an ordinary hunting gun, but instead of gunpowder it is charged with carbon dioxide from two small steel cylinders. When the trigger is pressed a puff of the gas is released at several atmospheres' pressure. This ejects the "bullet" for twenty to thirty yards.

The "bullet" is a steel hypodermic, a hollow needle that penetrates the skin of the animal. The shock of firing mixes a tablet of carbide with water in the rear of the missile, and the gas evolved from this mixture pushes forward the plunger of the hypodermic needle, forcing the narcotic charge under the skin.

A very clever invention, but apparently it had only been tried on captive animals. Our zebras did not let us come close enough

The "miracle gun" was difficult to load.

to use it, and generally galloped off when we were still a couple of hundred yards away. The hypodermic bullets were also extremely sensitive to shock. They could not be transported when fully loaded with carbide, water and the narcotic, but had to be freshly prepared before each shot. We felt like chemists in a dispensary, and wild animals are not inclined to wait about while one gets the bullets ready. On top of all this the flight of the bullets varied between twenty and thirty-five yards, and worst of all, they usually missed their mark.

One day we finally managed to plant a missile squarely into the rounded hindquarters of a zebra stallion. Michael and I waited for ages, but nothing happened. We had to pursue the animal by car and pull out the needle by hand at a full gallop. It had failed to detonate! If we had not recovered the missile we would never have understood this failure, and assuming that it contained insufficient narcotic might well have doubled the quantity of the next shot, thus probably killing the "patient".

After a prolonged trial we decided that the gun was too dangerous, and we took it home with us to Frankfurt.

Michael pondered, made sketches and then disappeared into the workshop of an instrument maker for two weeks. On his return he hung five thicknesses of wet woollen blanket over our clothes line and shot at them. He bought whole quarters of beef from the butcher, hung them up in our garden, and used them for target practice.

Now we really did possess an American miracle gun, but reconstructed by Michael. It was connected by a small tube to a large cylinder of compressed air at two hundred atmospheres' pressure. The bullet carried for more than forty yards and had a much more accurate trajectory than the earlier model.

We also changed the injection mechanism of the syringe. Previously the carbide and water had been mixed as the missle left the gun, and the narcotic therefore began to ooze out of the needle before it hit the animal. Now the plunger was activated by the impact of the missile on the hide, so that all the drug entered the muscles of the victim and none was spilled in flight. The bullets could also withstand the shocks and vibrations of a vehicle, so that there was nothing to prevent our preparing ten or fifteen of them at home in advance and taking them along with us in the car.

Mgabo, our native driver, was much interested in our preparations. He was most concerned that everything should be in perfect order. Besides acting as a chauffeur, he also knew all our belongings, our tripods, cameras, trunks and chests and never forgot a single item of equipment. When Hermann joined us for a few weeks Mgabo was deeply impressed by the fact that Hermann's *Leica* was much smaller than my *Praktisix*. *"Hermani camera kidorko,"* he constantly exclaimed mock-seriously in Swahili, extending the first O in sympathy. "Hermann's camera is sooooo small."

The next question was what drug to put in the bullets.

The obvious answer seemed to be one of the narcotics used for human operations, but the matter was not quite as simple as that. When operating on human beings, doctors carefully select a vein into which they inject the drug directly. There could be no question of our doing this, so we had therefore to choose a medicament which is effective when injected directly into muscular tissue. This necessitated using twice as much drug as an intra-venous injection, but at the same time the drug had to be more dilute to avoid intense local irritation. All this implied a large volume, whereas the capacity of our bullet was limited to five cubic centimetres. The anaesthetics used for human operations cannot be concentrated to such an extent. Despite expert advice from pharmaceutical manufacturers we could not find a drug sufficiently soluble in water, of which five cubic centimetres would send a horse to sleep.

On top of all these difficulties was the fact that the drug must act quickly, within a few minutes at most, otherwise the beast might panic and escape us by crashing through shrubs and rivers. Also its action must be very short-lived and it must leave no side effects, so that the animal can catch up with the herd before it moves too far away. If a zebra remained dazed it might be attacked and killed by predators who are always on the lookout for weak animals.

When Colonel Peter Molloy asked us the year before to solve the riddles of the Serengeti, we certainly never suspected that we would have to become expert pharmacists.

There are very few substances which act quickly enough, and one of the few is *curare*, the notorious South American arrow poison. Since it not only paralyses the muscles of the limbs but very easily also those of the diaphragm, with consequent danger of asphyxiation, we did not even attempt to try it on our animals.

A drug which knocks out men does not necessarily act on dogs. Ether sends cats to sleep, but it only excites cows. A horse weighing ten times more than a man will need much more than ten times the amount of the same drug to anaesthetise it. Since a horse's brain is simpler and therefore not so susceptible to poisons as a human being's, a vet would have to inject one hundred times the human dose to achieve the same effect.

Michael and I were tense with excitement as we approached a herd of wildebeest. We did not drive straight at them but pretended to go past, at the same time getting as close to them as possible. Mgabo slowly stopped the car. At the exact moment that he finally cut the ignition Michael fired the gun. Within a fraction of a second all the wildebeest raised their heads and galloped away, stopping again very soon.

Before coming to Africa we had tested our drug* on goats. They tolerated up to 4.5 milligram per kilogram body weight without any ill effects, but for safety's sake we only gave the big, well-fed black antelopes one-third of this dosage. (The ration of milligram per kilogram is one in a million and is usually abbreviated mg/kg.)

The wildebeest had been hit in the right upper thigh. The wound did not bleed. I started my stop-watch and waited, full of expectation. . . . The animal did not seem at all concerned and even started to graze again.

After five-and-a-half minutes it gave a small shiver, began to act strangely and then, after a further ninety seconds, collapsed. When Michael approached, the bull tried to rise and attack on wobbly legs. As its horns were as sharp as daggers we threw two ropes over its head and pulled it to the ground.

The bearded fellow had an aluminium clip placed in his ear carrying the number 25, and was entered as such in our books. The clip carried the message: "Ten shillings' reward. National Parks, Arusha."

* Nicotine salicylate.

A chameleon found in Gordon Harvey's garden.

Our bushbaby accompanied us on our 6,000-mile journey.

The markings and colour of giraffes vary considerably even within the same herd. Working on single skins in museums led Europeans to believe at one time that there were several sub-species.

We counted 1,606 ostriches in Serengeti.

Buffaloes are not nearly as ferocious as most books on Africa make out.

African fish eagles on a candelabra euphorbia.

During an intermediate landing in northern Serengeti the whole village turned out to admire the aeroplane.

As it was doubtful whether lions and hyenas would leave the marker in decipherable condition, we also strapped a bright green collar on the wildebeest. After making sure that the collar was not too tight we packed away our hypodermics, spare collars, ear clips and the rest of our paraphernalia and drove our zebra car to a point fifty yards away from the sleeping wildebeest bull. There we waited for it to rise and rejoin the herd.

We were still waiting after eight hours. We had tried during that time to raise the bull to his feet but he remained unsteady and sat down again. He was still bemused although he no longer lay on his side but was resting on all fours with his head off the ground. It had grown dark during our vigil.

We dared not leave the bull by himself as he would at once be attacked by hyenas, in fact these *fisis* were already waiting in a large circle. As soon as we switched off the headlamps they boldly advanced. The wildebeest seemed to be recovering slowly. At eleven p.m. Michael advanced to check the pulse rate and temperature, but the bull jumped up and attacked. He collapsed again, however, after running ten yards.

The waiting continued. At one-thirty A.M. we roused the wildebeest again. He began to wander in a large circle and took no notice of the car. He also ignored our pocket torches. If we stood in his way the wildebeest walked straight at us and made no attempt to step aside. He was completely insensitive to sounds, although he walked quite normally and without staggering.

We extinguished our torches and retired to the car, as we did not want to excite the animal unduly.

After five minutes a hyena jumped at our "patient" and hung on to his tail. The wildebeest neither defended himself nor tried to escape, he simply kept on walking in a straight line. Our torches soon frightened away the *fisi*.

After a further thirty minutes of aimless circling the bull lay down again. There was nothing for it but to keep on watching over his slumbers.

Finally, at half-past six, a full hour before dawn, the bull rose. He walked sedately and deliberately in a straight line for over two miles. We followed. By now the animal had begun to take notice of us and speeded up when we got too close. As the sun rose the old fellow joined a large herd of wildebeest. Apparently it was the same herd, and the other animals took no notice of the bright green collar.

Although wildebeest look so vital and tough they do not tolerate as much of our drug as domestic goats. Since we did not desire an all-night vigil with every animal we "shot", we reduced the dosage. After many days of shooting, catching, marking and waiting, we discovered that the correct amount for a wildebeest is 1 mg/kg. This was just sufficient for us to catch and mark the animal, which then recovered before hyenas had a chance to attack it.

If we gave a similar amount to the jolly little Thomson's gazelles they simply took no notice of it. By gradually increasing the quantity, shot by shot, we discovered the correct amount. This turned out to be 5 mg/kg. About seven minutes after the bullet had gone home the buck began to shiver and arch its neck backwards, until the slanting horns were almost parallel to the ground. After a further minute the animal collapsed. We marked it quickly and two or three minutes later it rose to its feet again with the whole matter forgotten. A buck must be caught just at the moment while it is lying down. If it is running away at thirty miles per hour the drug does not seem to take effect.

We could now catch wildebeest and "tommies" with the aid of the miracle gun, but had no luck with zebras. They did not permit us to get close enough. We dearly wanted to put gay collars round the necks of a few dozen striped little horses, for they are the second most prevalent nomads of the Serengeti plains. We had long ago realised that you could not simply go out into the bush and capture any animal you wanted with the aid of narcotic bullets. It took days and weeks before the correct dosage of drug for each type of animal was worked out, quite apart from the difficulty of getting close enough to shoot.

Once we had to take two of the little bucks home with us for the night, because they had been given too much narcotic. When we reached the tin hut our bushbaby was terrified of these huge and dangerous monsters.

On another occasion, when on our way home, we unwittingly flushed two cheetah cubs. Suddenly the furious mother rose from

When Michael slowly and carefully approached the Thomson's gazelle buck while it was still stupefied, he could stroke it.

the grass fifty yards away and rushed at the car, running beside it for a while at over thirty miles an hour. As cheetahs usually avoid men, I had not thought it possible for mother love to generate such courage.

Two giraffe cows watched us inquisitively from their stately height of fifteen feet. Four calves of equal age also stared at us from the lower, but still respectable, level of six feet. There were no other giraffes to be seen anywhere. Do giraffes have twins, or do they form nurseries where they look after each other's children? In Africa there are still unsolved questions regarding wild animals wherever one looks.

We stopped to watch thirty or forty baboons frolicking among the higher trees along the dry river bed of the Grumeti. The clumsy, lean baboon children were playing tag, catching each others' tails and climbing up bushes, only to pull each other down again. A half-grown bushbuck wanted to join in the game, but the little baboons were only interested in themselves. The small buck invitingly lowered his head, until a baboon grabbed the back of his neck. The bushbuck was evidently delighted and at once started prancing comically about.

One game warden saw baby baboons jumping on the backs of young impala, and the antelopes did not seem to mind the game at all.

We saw a zebra stallion nipping a mare on her forelegs. She ran away for a few paces, but since he was persistent she knelt down with her legs hidden under her body. He then put his neck across hers and pressed downwards. It became a trial of strength. When he stopped for a moment she put his head under her neck in turn; she succeeded in pushing him over, so that he lay flat on his side. He slithered away and jumped up. The playful mare plucked at his mane and knelt before him, inviting him to another bout of "wrestling". When he accepted the invitation and approached she started up, pretending to flee and lashing out with her hind legs. She was evidently in love, for her ears were laid back and her mouth was open to its fullest extent. Among horses and donkeys this is a sure sign that they have lost their hearts.

We do not as yet know a great deal about zebras. A short while ago the biologist Heinz Giebel trained a zebra to recognise twenty

Zebras used this rock for scratching their hides. One is giving a friendly nibble to the mane of its companion.

Zebras do not neigh like horses; their calls sound more like the barking of dogs.

different patterns—beams, crosses, circles, triangles, etc.—and only to look for food when the right pattern was shown. The animal still remembered which was the right one after nearly a year—a remarkable feat of memory.

I always used to worry in case the zebras in our zoo grew too fat, but the wild ones in the Serengeti are even more corpulent. Their hindquarters are so well padded that one longs to slap their sleek rumps.

In many parts of Africa, including Serengeti, it is impossible to keep European horses because of the *nagana* pest *(tryponosomiasis)*. Before the advent of cars many people therefore tried to harness zebras or break them to the saddle. German troops in Africa tried this experiment before the first World War, so did the Siedentopf brothers, since they had so many zebras almost on their doorstep in the Ngorongoro crater. The zebras became quite tame and pulled at the traces with all their might, but they did not have the stamina of horses. After looking up the old reports I was not surprised at this, for they were not given the strengthening foods supplied to horses, but had to make do with the thin grass of the plains.

Perhaps collars and markers might help us to find out how old a zebra grows in the Serengeti. In zoos they reach a ripe old age. A quagga lived in the Amsterdam Zoo from 1867 until 1883, and during the last of these years it was the only living quagga left on earth. All the other hundreds of thousands had been killed by white settlers who used the hides to make sacks for their grain. A Chapman's zebra in the Dublin Zoo even lived to be forty-six years old.

Mgabo left the track and drove cross-country towards some wild dogs squatting in the shade of an umbrella acacia. These dogs have irregular black, white and yellow markings, but all of them have white-tipped tails. They surveyed the scene in a bored way. We had no fear that they would run away, since they are not afraid of cars, or even of men. When I got out of the car most of them rose to their feet, but remained in the shade of the tree.

The large-eared wild dogs are curious, eerie creatures. If they decide to attack an eland, waterbuck or wildebeest, the animal is doomed. One morning, when Michael and I were living in the Masabi plain beside our crippled aeroplane, we saw seven of these

Zebras frightened by our "flying zebra."

animals attack a female Thomson's gazelle. Two of the dogs separated it from the herd and drove it aside, without any particular haste. The gazelle jumped in the air with all four legs but grew tired in a few minutes. The leading dog increased the tempo and the others approached from the other side. Before we had realised what had happened the gazelle was seized and torn to pieces.

Not long ago Myles witnessed a similar chase and observed that afterwards four of the dogs ran to some holes in the ground and whimpered. Four youngsters appeared from the holes, whereupon the adults regurgitated some of the gazelle's flesh which was promptly devoured by their children.

Another time, when two dogs had apparently lost their prey, they were seen to lower their heads and "call", then they straightened up again and listened. Within a few minutes the rest of the pack came racing over the hill.

Occasionally antelopes which are being hunted by wild dogs will flee in mortal terror right into camps, or to where parties of people are working in the fields. Sometimes the dogs can then be driven off with sticks or stones, but often they will pursue their prey and kill it right in amongst the men.

As soon as one dog has got a grip, the others tear the animal to pieces. While the first dog may still be hanging on to the neck the rest of the pack may already be gobbling up the intestines.

Wild dogs even dared to attack a hippo one day, by jumping at its chest. The giant creature was clearly afraid and only too glad to escape into the water when some human observers diverted the dogs' attention for a moment. Immediately afterwards the same wild dogs encircled two elephants. Even they seemed scared and backed away with their trunks raised. A hunted animal is only safe if it can swim across water, for in that case the dogs will not follow. Perhaps they have an inborn fear of crocodiles.

We saw four or five hundred gazelles peacefully grazing. They seemed unafraid although they could see some wild dogs a quarter of a mile away. Similarly a lion can walk right through a herd of wildebeest, and they will only keep a safe distance without any emotion. A visible lion is no danger to them, for they are faster than the big cat. Matters become much more serious if the lion should suddenly disappear. Then the grazing herd becomes rest-

The black, white, and yellow spotted wild dogs are the fiercest predators in Africa.

less for the lion might now be stalking. The wild dogs, however, can run down any animal they choose, and yet the gazelles did not try to escape. They can probably tell when the predators are hungry and in a hunting mood.

Luckily men do not figure on the menu of wild dogs. I only know of one report to the contrary. In one of his books von Lettow-Vorbeck mentions that he heard of a European in Tanganyika being killed by them. All that was found of the settler was five empty shells, (all the ammunition he had with him), five dead dogs and a few remnants of his corpse. But Lettow had heard this story only from others.

In February 1959 a twelve-year-old boy in Switzerland defended his Alsatian dog against two fierce hounds which had escaped from a neighbouring farm. At first the attackers concentrated on the Alsatian, but when the boy hit out with a stick they turned on him and wounded him to such an extent that he died in hospital the next day, despite blood transfusions.

I have collected and published a number of such cases occurring during the last fifty years, in which house dogs have killed people.

Visitors from another country, in which dogs were unknown, who had read this report, would be justified in reaching for their guns whenever they met a dog in our streets. The wild animals of Africa can be viewed in a similar light. Books and film depict them as bloodthirsty and dangerous monsters, so that the man who ventures among them may appear "heroic".

We once met a pack of wild dogs composed of fourteen adults and nine younger ones. They had just had a meal when the two leading dogs stopped and stared at a herd of wildebeest about half a mile away. They began to run towards the herd at a moderate speed. The rest of the pack followed some distance behind. The remaining adults seemed to be guiding the youngsters.

Suddenly a large hyena appeared two hundred yards away from the leaders. The two dogs wheeled round and pursued the hyena, which tried to escape. It did not stand a chance but was quickly overtaken, gripped by the hind leg and thrown to the ground. The hyena cried out but showed no fight. After biting it a few times the dogs left it in peace and once more ran towards the wildebeest.

When the leaders were about a quarter of a mile from the herd they suddenly quickened their pace. The wildebeest jumped in all directions and for a few moments everything disappeared in a cloud of dust. By now the rest of the pack had also broken into a run and caught up with the leaders.

When the dust settled again we saw to our amazement that the wildebeest had formed four small groups. The adults stood with their heads pointing outwards, protecting the yearlings in the centre. The dogs had also split up, but all their attempts to break the rings of wildebeest failed. They were met by lowered heads and pointed horns. We waited. Suddenly an excited wildebeest calf broke out of the protecting circle. In a flash the calf was torn to bits. When we approached a little later, all trace of the young wildebeest had completely disappeared, the rest of the herd had spread out once more and the wild dogs had gone on their way.

One rarely sees wild dogs in zoos because they look so much like ordinary dogs and do not seem dangerous. To my knowledge young ones have only been reared by bottle or by foster mother. Dr. Sosnowski, the Director of the Moscow Zoo, told me, during his last visit in Frankfurt, that he had been more successful by pure chance. One of his keepers had not followed the tradition of separating the dog from the bitch before the birth of the pups. The Russians were astounded to see the big father take the whole head of each puppy into his huge mouth and regurgitate meat directly into the mouth of each youngster.

These wild murderers are remarkably peaceful towards each other. If two packs should meet they intermingle, sniff at each other and separate again without any sign of animosity. It is even said that the same happened when a pack of hunting dogs belonging to the Trappe family met a troop of wild dogs on Mount Meru.

Wild dogs become quite tame when reared by bottle, but they will kill all the poultry in the neighbourhood and are fond of biting people in the leg. As they grow up, however, they acquire such a strong smell that one is only too glad to part with them. Remember: even a bad smell is a good way to preserve freedom.

A roan antelope slowly choking to death in a wire snare.

CHAPTER 11

The Poachers' Lair

---

*One is almost inclined to say that men are the
devils on earth and the animals the tortured
souls.*

ARTHUR SCHOPENHAUER

ARRIVING BACK in Nairobi from a visit home, I was worried as there
was no sign of Michael at the airport, although he had left Germany
three weeks ahead of me. I did not like him flying around in the
Serengeti while I was in Europe, for I was always afraid that he
might have an accident. I suppose this shows what egotists we
men are, for my wife had to spend the whole time in Frankfurt,
worrying about both of us!

I must plead guilty to a small theft. While I magnanimously
left behind me the various beautiful maps and prospectuses which
are given to each passenger on the large air-liners, I stealthily removed some of the water-tight bags fixed to the back of every seat.
We had not discovered where one could buy these useful objects,
and therefore "acquired" a varied assortment for our little zebra-
striped plane, labelled *K.L.M., Lufthansa, B.O.A.C., Sabena* and
S.A.S. We sometimes carried members of the government, or
transported game wardens from one reserve to another, and the
bags occasionally came in useful. The native boys and the Masai
also felt air-sick sometimes.

At last Michael appeared. He had already acquired a tan, while
I was still white. He was thinner, which was not surprising, for
unless someone kept an eye on him he did not bother to eat. He
was accompanied by Hermann, flaunting a large red beard. All
young men enjoy their first opportunity—a war or an expedition—

to find out how a beard suits them. Michael tried it three years ago in the Congo, and I made my effort during the war. Hermann looked very comical, like a real old Teuton in a sun-helmet. He had to wear the topee because his light skin was sensitive to the sun.

Michael was still inwardly raging as the result of something which had happened while we were away. Our trusted and capable driver, Mgabo, had drunkenly attacked our representative with two knives. The intended victim defended himself by throwing a large stone at Mgabo's face, thereby breaking four front teeth. As this was considered almost sufficient punishment he was only fined £10. Since that time, however, Mgabo had withdrawn to Arusha and had become an anti-European politician. We were sorry, for both of us were fond of him.

To replace Mgabo, Michael hired a city boy from Nairobi, but he proved a total failure, letting the truck founder in the sand and not caring how often the radiator boiled. Michael had flown him back to Nairobi that very morning, only to discover among his baggage cutlery, cups, blankets and pillows, all of which were our property. In Nairobi the boy impertinently demanded two weeks' wages in lieu of notice. Michael in return threatened him with the police because of the theft, but when he charged him the local police declared that the case was outside their jurisdiction since the theft took place in Tanganyika, whereas Nairobi is in Kenya. Michael ground his teeth but had not only to pay the fortnight's wages, but to put up with being loudly abused in public as well.

To make up lost time we separated to buy our provisions. One of us went to the Indian greengrocer, another to the Polish baker and the third to the Italian grocer. We had long since learned the almost lost art of our rural grandmothers, namely how to lay in household goods for weeks at a time. Our system consisted of a large sheet of paper fixed to the tin door of our hut, on which each of us made a note of the articles required whenever a shortage became apparent. All these requirements had to be carried in the belly of our "duck": ten large pineapples, two hands of bananas, a sack of potatoes, macaroni, flour, two hundred eggs, half a hundredweight of meat, sugar, matches, batteries, six crates of mineral water and beer, cabbages, lettuce, toilet paper, four large cartons of tins—not to speak of our three selves.

The steadfast, striped old "duck" droned and lifted the heavy load into the rarefied air. Then homeward, across plains and volcanoes, where our arrival was impatiently awaited by an army of twelve cars.

Something had been brewing up in secret, or to be more honest, we were the ones who had fermented the brew. Not long ago we carried out an aerial war against poachers. To catch them from the ground, however, one has to trust to luck and drive a convoy of cars for two or three days, or even longer. Even then one may end up in a region where there are neither animals nor poachers, for one cannot foretell the movements of the herds. Much time and money can be wasted in this way. The administrators of the National Park and the Game Department have at last persuaded the police to take a hand, but policemen lose interest when they go for days on end without meeting either game or poachers.

Now we were about to join an expedition after poachers which was setting out for the bush north of the National Park. In this area, where we had earlier watched wandering herds from the air, the wilderness is already fringed with new native settlements. In many places the poachers have erected their artificial thorn hedges across the grassland. The region is well suited to poaching, for it is criss-crossed by rivers with wooded banks. Although most of the river beds are dry at this time of the year, the channels are fifteen to twenty feet deep. It is a country not normally accessible to cars and the poachers, knowing this, feel secure.

When Myles Turner was still a professional hunter this used to be his favourite ground. He knew it well, and he also knew how one could take cars and trucks across the river beds despite all difficulties.

No European expeditions had gone to this region since hunting was prohibited there. The native hunters could therefore do what they liked without the authorities being any the wiser. If the prohibited areas are merely marked off a map, the effect can be the reverse of that intended by the government, for the animals may be exterminated. If no game wardens are settled in the regions it is useless to proclaim game reserves, National Parks or protected areas. These look impressive on maps, and the plans and brochures describing them are a splendid sedative for allaying the fears of European and American naturalist organisations. The reserves are well suited to that purpose. Even in the remotest colonies, and in the new independent African states, they shower you with sheaves of official regulations: protective laws, hunting laws, laws of game reserves, etc. The only trouble is that the existence of such laws and reservations is completely unknown inside the territory itself. It is a veritable eye-opener to realise how little attention is paid to these prohibitions, even in such a well-administered colony as Tanganyika.

We drove north via Ikoma, and each car was enveloped by the brown cloud of dust thrown up by the one in front. Inside fifteen minutes I looked as tanned as Michael.

A low-flying eagle disregarded the rising dust and dived into the short grass to capture one of a family of civet cats. The African civet cat is a small, elongated creature similar in appearance to the Indian mongoose. It has transverse stripes, like the zebra, and presents a rather comical appearance.

The eagle carried the screaming civet cat into the nearest tree. The remaining fifteen or twenty civet cats did not run away. On their short legs and with their backs humped the little fellows ran after the bird. They screamed and cried and scolded at the foot of the tree. This strong family feeling paid dividends. The eagle released his prey, and the victim escaped into the brush with his fellows. A remarkable testimony to the power of mere swearing — *if you are united.*

Our cars drove across the country in Indian file; around mountains, over the plains and through woods. We started to make camp before it got dark, and in no time the others' tents were springing up all around us. Camp-beds were unfolded and chairs lifted out of cars. Having come straight from the airport we had no tents with us, and had to borrow one from Myles. We had not even brought mosquito nets. Despite this, however, we slept very well, and in the morning our army split up into three battalions, each following a different route.

A huge eland bull of fifteen hundredweight decided to cross the track in front of us. His dewlap was so enormous that it struck

his forelegs when he ran. He hesitated a moment and then jumped
clean across the track without touching it—a leap of at least twelve
feet, I imagine.

We left the last of the months-old track and drove directly across
the country.

A klipspringer stood on an inselberg, clearly silhouetted against
the deep blue sky. These small, isolated mountains look like piles
of flints seen through an enormously powerful magnifying glass.
The huge blocks of stone have rounded corners. One could see
where the sun had split off slabs of rock, which had then slid downwards. The granite rubble at the bottom suffers greater thermal
and chemical decomposition than that on top, so that the mountains do not have sloping shoulders like those in Europe, but
spring directly upward from the plain. I could only see the rare
little antelope for a few moments before a dust cloud intervened.

We slowed down involuntarily.

As we drove across a plain strewn with half-grown umbrella
acacias we saw the irregular line of a brush fence. It was not very
high, consisting merely of thorny twigs and branches piled up or
stuck into the ground. A hunted animal could easily jump over
it. If a herd is slowly driven towards such a fence, however, the
animals prefer to wander along it until they come to a break where
they can cross safely and easily.

We also followed along the fence and soon spotted an opening.
The eyes of men are much sharper than those of grazing animals—
a fact I have proved experimentally—and so we could see the wire
noose in the gap. It was oval in shape, held open by thin vegetable
fibres, and at just the right height to catch the head of a wildebeest. The other end of the wire was securely wound and knotted
around a nearby sapling.

We took down the murderous trap and threw it into the car.
Two gaps farther on the head of a zebra was hanging in another
wire snare. Only the bones of the skull and a few pieces of skin
remained, but there was no doubt that it was still very fresh. The
animal had choked to death only the night before, but poachers,
hyenas, vultures and jackals had already been at work. The grass
all round was dyed red with fresh blood.

The whole fence, and the area all around it, was thick with

snares. We could only collect those we saw at once, but already we had twenty-four in the car. The wind was constantly bringing us wafts of decaying corpses. We came across a dead zebra, with the skin still stretched across the bare skeleton. The poachers had merely cut off the tail to sell as a fly-swatter, the rest was left to the scavengers. We counted the cadavers of twenty-two wildebeest which had also been killed for their tails alone. What horrible torture, and what a waste of good meat. Even the vultures could not cope with their "harvest"; the sun and bacterial decay had to complete the work.

Through my field-glasses I noticed a rhino which stood undisturbed by the tragedy all around it. It was close to a drinking-hole in which two hippos were visible. Two ox-peckers clambered about the back of the rhino and jabbed at its skin, like woodpeckers at a tree.

I cannot confirm that these red-billed birds act as sentinels for the rhino. I have always noticed that they excitedly fly away on my approach, but that the rhino merely turned his head or ears towards me and did not try to escape.

This time the birds also rose, not to flee, however, but merely to have a drink. It seems that they are not happy unless they have a living skin under their feet, for they did not alight on the ground to drink like other birds. They landed on the back of a hippo instead, and from this living island they quenched their thirst.

We had kept the secret of our expedition most strictly. None of the native boys and guides knew of our destination or even our general direction. To them it was only another journey into the bush. The guides or their relations came from Ikoma and the country around it. Why should they be more discreet than Europeans in similar circumstances? Our former driver, Mgabo, had often told us that he frequently went poaching when he was a young man.

In spite of all our precautions the poachers seemed to have been warned of our arrival. This was not really surprising, for our cloud of dust and the noise of our motors must have been noticeable several miles away. The poachers had only to climb down one dried-up river bank and up the other side to present us with an obstacle which might take us an hour to cross.

We found this zebra throttled to death in a wire snare. The poachers had merely cut off the tail to sell it as a fly-swatter.

We stopped looking for snares and corpses. The three cars fanned out and drove at maximum speed across the plain. Speed was our only hope. If we could catch a poacher out in the open he would have no chance of escape.

We were forced to stop at the edge of the woods because a young zebra was struggling in a noose. The hindquarters were already powerless but it still tried to rise on its front legs. The eyes protruded from their sockets and the blue tongue lolled out of the side of the mouth. The wire had cut deeply into the wind pipe and the neck was badly swollen on either side. Two hyenas were waiting and even stones only made them retreat a few steps.

Since we had no wire-cutters with us, we had to place a rope around the half-strangled animal before undoing the wire at the bottom of the sapling. We had to prevent the frightened animal escaping with the snare still in position. The zebra was too weak to rise, and there was plenty of time to loosen the noose and pull it over its head.

I looked at my watch. It took a full twelve minutes before the animal regained its feet. One should not pity the game killed by lions or wild dogs, for *they* are never so cruel.

Our hunt continued. Hermann touched our driver's shoulder, for he had seen something curious at the edge of the forest. It looked like a child's garden with a miniature fence of little sticks around it. We left the car to take a look.

It was not a garden, but a lion's skin laid on the ground, fur downwards, and stretched with many pointed wooden nails to prevent it from shrinking. The grass all around was trampled down heavily, and a little farther on there were six zebra skins similarly treated. Footsteps led into the bush, and one of the scouts began to follow them.

I shouted, "Take care! Perhaps they'll use poisoned arrows."

This did not deter the boy and he struggled through the bushes while we tried to catch up with him. The narrow strip of trees only covered the banks of the river. After following the trail a little way we stopped, hardly trusting our eyes.

Although the comparison is completely unsuitable, I could not but think of the tale of Hansel and Gretel discovering the house of the witch in a clearing of the forest. There was another type of house here, a straw hut, and the sun seemed to shine into the clearing through a curious red roof. It looked as if someone's washing had been hung up to dry on long, wooden, horizontal poles. But the clothes were meat—flat slices of raw meat, surrounded by a cloud of flies, through which the sun was bloodily shining.

The poachers did not dare to dry their meat out in the open, so they used the little clearing instead. Slanting sticks were placed over the still-glowing embers of the camp-fire, and from them hung chunks of meat intended for smoking or grilling. Poisoned arrows and bows were lying beside the hut. The inhabitants of the camp must have left in a hurry.

I picked up a curious pipe, the mouthpiece of which was still wet with spittle. Beside it lay a rolled leaf containing hashish. It was quite possible that the poachers were still watching us from the surrounding forest, and we could only hope that they would not shoot us with poisoned arrows.

There were also bones lying around. The whole thorax of an antelope hung from a branch. Inside the hut we found half a sack of manioc meal, sharpened European knives (probably used for skinning and cutting up meat), blankets and a pile of wire snares. We pushed back the branches and proudly took our booty out

The poachers dried their meat in this hidden camp before transporting it.

into the open. We called to the others to help us in trying to follow the poachers, but we in turn were hailed by Myles. He had discovered a much larger camp little more than a mile away and captured two of the poachers. Unfortunately the others escaped. One scout nearly grabbed two more, but when he had almost caught up with them at the edge of the forest, they turned, aimed their poisoned arrows at him and said: "One more step and you are a dead man."

Since he had no gun, and they undoubtedly meant business, he had to let them go.

The new place looked like the communal laundry of a whole village community. We stooped and walked past the red "washing", some of which was already shrivelling and turning black. Swarms of flies surrounded us. Parts of zebras and wildebeest lay, half prepared, in stinking piles. Bundles of dried meat were tied together, ready for transport. We had discovered a real factory.

According to the number of beds and lean-to-roofs, about ten or twelve men must have camped here. I found it hard to understand how they could endure to live among the stink and the flies. There was no fence of thorns around the camp, despite the fact that it must have looked inviting to lions and other predators. It is true that one does not have to fear lions when armed with poisoned arrows, but perhaps the real explanation was that there were so many rotting corpses on the plain, so that the lions did not bother to contend with the men for the rest of the meat.

We captured even more booty, and backed the truck as close to the camp as possible in order to load it with provisions, equipment, piles of wire snares—in short with all the poachers' goods and chattels. Anything we could not carry with us, including the meat, we piled into great heaps, soaked them with petrol and set them alight.

The two prisoners were handcuffed. They naturally did not know anything. They had quite accidentally strolled to the spot, and happening to find a dead zebra they had only removed its tail. Just at that moment they were captured by our scouts, that was all.

Year after year tens of thousands of animals are killed by these gruesome methods. Only a tiny portion of the meat is utilised;

most of the victims of the poachers only provide tails, ivory, a few hides and rhino "horn". What is the use of the Serengeti National Park when the protected animals have to leave it every dry season, only to be killed in huge numbers? Inside the borders poaching can be fairly well controlled, but even to-day the boundaries are not large enough to sustain the animals all the year round. The National Park is therefore no guarantee that the last, great, natural wonders of Africa will be preserved.

On top of all that the whole thing is so futile. If grazed by cattle and sheep for even a few decades, the grassland and semi-desert would be destroyed and turned into a real desert, like so many other tropical areas. This can already be seen in large stretches of India, North Africa and northern Kenya. The large herds of game provide more meat per acre than any domesticated animal under the same conditions. The wild animals are resistant to tropical parasites and diseases and are adapted to the local vegetation. The predators living amongst them make sure that the herds stay healthy. With a little bit of common sense, a part of the wild herds — outside the National Park and its surroundings — could well be used to feed men. But of course such a reasonable solution (recommended by all the experts) cannot prevail. Hunters do not want to shoot common beasts — such as zebras, wildebeest and Thomson's gazelles — which stand around like cows in a meadow. They get special licences to pursue the rarer species: roan antelope, rhino, bongo, eland, sable antelope, kudu, and gerenuk. The rarer the animal the more it is prized as a trophy of the chase.

Africa is dying and will continue to die. Old maps and remnants of settlements and animals show that the Sahara has advanced 250 miles northward on a 1,250 mile front during the last three centuries. In that short time 390,000 square miles of good land were lost. In neighbouring Kenya the desert advances six miles against the primeval forest every year. So much of Africa is dead already, must the rest follow? Must *everything* be turned into deserts, farmland, big cities, native settlements and dry brush? One small part of the continent at least should retain its original splendour so that the black and white men who follow us will be able to see it in its awe-filled past glory.

Serengeti, at least, shall not die.

We confiscated thousands of wire snares and masses of poisoned arrows.

A few days later we heaped three trucks with all our loot. Loads of beautifully carved bows and mountains of quivers of poisoned arrows. The arrows were little works of art. The pattern of feathers on the shaft determines the owner, so that there is no quarrelling when they are recovered after the hunt. The iron heads are tediously forged from the large carpenters' nails which can be bought in any Indian store. They are thickly covered with the gummy black poison.

Bows and arrows can be burned, but wire snares, the worst of all the poacher's weapons, are not inflammable. The wire comes from abandoned mines and military camps. Other snares are specially imported and sold at about five shillings each. If we simply dumped them somewhere, they would soon find their way back into the black market. Unfortunately it is not illegal to own such snares.

Myles knew of a place where we could dispose of them once and for all. About twelve miles from Banagi, and outside the borders of Serengeti, lies an old gold mine, called Kilimafeza, which has been abandoned for years. We transported our booty there. All that remained of the mine were some dilapidated sheds, a few ruined buildings and a house of corrugated iron with a roof that was still intact. The house was said to contain old machinery. The whole lot was watched over by an old African caretaker who was considered harmlessly mad.

But there was a shaft! This goes down vertically for more than a thousand feet. It is strange and eerie for there are dead men at the bottom of the shaft. Six years ago a cable broke, and twelve men inside the cage hurtled to their death. There was neither moaning nor answer. The Indian merchant who owned the mine decided to close it and the twelve corpses remained at the bottom.

The end of the broken cable swayed gently in the wind. We threw down nearly 2,000 snares — quite a little fortune at current market prices. One load after another disappeared down the yawning shaft, and the bows and arrows followed. Anything down there will not come up again this side of the last trump. It occurred to me that many missing persons, and perhaps the victims of murderers, may also lie at the bottom. But perhaps I was being fanciful; after all there is little difficulty in disposing of a corpse in Africa — the hyenas make short work of it.

During the last year eighty-eight poachers were caught inside the Park and arraigned before a judge. That may sound quite a lot at first, but during a concerted search in Tsavo National Park in Kenya, close to the borders of Tanganyika, the remains of 1,280 elephants were found. These had been killed by poachers during the last two years. In reality the number probably exceeds 3,000, for no search can be thorough enough to find all the corpses. The government finally provided more money and police aeroplanes in an attempt to stop commercialised poaching and mass murder. During the following fifteen months 25,218 lb. of ivory and 462 lb. of rhino "horn" were confiscated, and 429 poachers arrested and convicted. The authorities concerned believe that, despite these efforts, more than £100,000 worth of ivory and rhino "horn" found its way on to the black market. In one district alone they found hundreds of game pits with thorn fences between them, so that the animals either perished in traps or snares. Nobody suspected that poaching had reached such fantastic proportions.

After reading that evidence, how can one get indignant about the few elephants and rhinos shot by Americans and Europeans with game licences?

Seventy-seven elephants' feet turned into wastepaper baskets for gun-happy tourists.

CHAPTER 12

African Big Game Hunters

Even if the end of the world is coming to-mor-row
To-day I shall plant a young apple-tree.

MARTIN LUTHER

"LET'S ENJOY our hunting during the last few years we have left," said my friend Blues, and stretched his long legs. His feet, like mine, were shod with brown gym shoes, but Blues had cut away half of the upper on one of them so that his big toe stuck out. The toe had been painful for a long time, but he refused to make the effort and spend a week in Mombasa because of it.

"In a few years the Africans will be in control, and they'll kill off everything anyhow. It doesn't matter how many animals we shoot now. You know what will happen when we leave."

Blues was a professional or "white" hunter. He was employed to look after European and American tourists who wanted to shoot elephants or lions, and it was his job to see that not a hair of their heads should be hurt. Most of these white hunters are splendid men who cannot bear to be confined between four walls. I have never met a rich one, for the real money goes to the firms employing them. They love the open life but hate most of the guests to whom they have to be guardian angels and to whom they have to be polite as well. Nearly every one of them would prefer to be a game warden in a National Park at half their present wages, but there are very few jobs of this kind. The Governments in Africa are extremely generous in creating parks and reserves on paper, but they refuse to spend money on people who live there and see to it that the animals remain alive.

Blues had been our voluntary helper for several weeks and had not received a penny for his trouble. He had earned sufficient money for his wife and three children to stay in Arusha for some time, and so now could afford to do something to help animals instead of killing them.

At first Michael and I suspected that Blues had been sent to spy on us. Not long ago a German "big game hunter" who posed in the papers as a fearless gorilla and elephant slayer had sent out a circular to Englishmen in Africa, asking whether they had anything discreditable to report about us, or knew of anything that could cause us trouble. We therefore took Blues on a rather "acrobatic" flight which forced him to use one of our stolen paper bags. He remained steadfast, and we soon discovered that he honestly wanted to help us.

"Anyway, I can't understand why you are so much against hunting," he said and replaced a cigarette stub in his breast pocket.

"Quite the contrary," I replied. "I love animals and have been lucky enough to work with them all my life, but I am not a sentimentalist, I am merely logical. I do not demand, for instance, that animals should not be killed, for I am not a vegetarian. As a scientist I also know that life cannot be maintained without killing other living things. Lions eat zebras, and zebras eat grass."

I went on to explain to him that I am not against animals being used for experimental purposes, I merely wish that these could be more strictly controlled. As long as I am willing to be inoculated against smallpox, take tablets against headaches and submit to necessary surgical operations I cannot oppose vivisection. All these things have been tried on animals first and countless numbers of animals and men are alive to-day because these experiments have been carried out. Animals suffer patiently so that we and other animals should be spared agonising pain and death.

I get no pleasure from killing animals, but I am not a fanatic who wants to convert all others to my point of view. I know full well that roe deer, red deer, wild boars and hares would be extinct in Europe if it had not been for hunters. Our last "wild" animals would have been exterminated as pests if the huntsmen had not paid for damages to crops and even fed the game during hard winters. The actual killing of the game is merely incidental to a good hunter. Nowadays many people proudly come home with photographs instead of trophies, for, as every expert knows, it is much harder to shoot a bull elephant with a camera than with a rifle.

I told Blues, "But I do not like the modern type of 'big game hunter' who comes to East Africa for a few weeks, between business trips, and shoots a few elephants or lions, even if he has never had a rifle in his hands before coming here."

"A few weeks!" growled Blues. "You have no idea! I once spent fourteen days on safari in southern Tanganyika, making a camp and marking out a landing strip. All this work was merely to enable a 'hunter' to come directly from America to win a bet by shooting a lion while remaining in Africa for only twenty-four hours.

"He won his bet because I had 'fed' the lion in the meantime. The gentleman left his 'plane and entered my car. I drove for nearly a mile and then made him walk the regulation two hundred yards to a place where a pride of lions were resting under a bush. I made him step three paces in front of me. I never let excited guests stand behind me for I value my life, and their guns are much more dangerous than lions and buffaloes.

"The hunter shot, and I pulled the trigger of my gun at the same time. The fatal bullet naturally came from his gun—that's service for you. I congratulated the great marksman, we smoked a cigarette to make sure the lion was really dead, and he was then photographed with it for the local paper at home. Immediately after this he flew off to India where a Maharajah had arranged a tiger for him.

"He probably didn't need more than a day for that either."

I showed my friend a newspaper cutting which described how a button manufacturer from Scarsdale, New York, had just returned with his fourteen-year-old son from a hunting expedition in Portuguese West Africa during which, he proudly claimed, the boy bagged three hundred wild animals. From a safe platform in a tree he had shot elephants, rhinos, and four hippos; on another occasion he had "blown a leopard's head off with a single shot."

It is, of course, impossible to shoot so freely in British colonies in East Africa because gun-happy tourists are placed under the supervision of a professional hunter, but there are still many African states and colonies where the authorities are not so strict.

Another American even bet that he could shoot an elephant with a bow and arrow. This heroic achievement was given tremendous publicity.

"I remember," replied Blues. "I saw him. He came to East Africa looking for someone to accompany and protect him. I refused the job, and the others did, too. Any expert would know what to expect. The fellow went over the border and won his bet in the Congo. The fact that he was accompanied and covered by a professional marksman with a gun in his hand was naturally omitted in the press reports."

"They also did not mention that he shot fifteen arrows into his second elephant," I added, "or that he followed the wounded beast for nine hours, until his paid protector could no longer bear it and put the animal out of its misery. I wrote this fact to his home-town papers and they published it."

The only activity in the world by which men can boost their egos with no qualification but money is big game hunting overseas. It need not even take up much time. In the old days it took real courage and endurance to march for months through unknown territories, armed with imperfect weapons, threatened by malaria, sleeping sickness and cannibals. Nowadays rich business men can feed on the fame of the real hunters of the past century or politicians out for cheap publicity can buy a mantle of bravery and daring by going big game hunting. I believe that many of them suffer more often from impotence than is common among ordinary men. They have to compensate for their inferiority complexes by making themselves known as courageous lion killers. These, then, are the people who are killing off our noble animals.

"There are some terrible blokes among them," sighed Blues. "You can't imagine how many crates of whisky I had to cart around sometimes, but on other occasions you meet fine people for whom it is a pleasure to work. When all is said and done they pay their dues and bring money into the country, and we keep a sharp eye on them. The black poachers will kill many more animals than they do."

"Comparatively few tourists come to Africa nowadays to *shoot* animals," I said. "There are already tens of thousands who would rather *see* them in their wild state than in zoos. With the further development of aeronautics you should be able to get to Nairobi from London in a few hours and our children or even we will travel to Central Africa more cheaply and quickly than our parents did to France or Italy.

"Why do these people come here? I love African scenery, but then I am biased. The main attraction of Africa is her primitive black people and her wild animals. The Negroes will soon be differentiated from us only by the colour of their skin. They already use bicycles and cars. If wild animals here grow as scarce as they are elsewhere in Africa, if more species are actually exterminated, I can see no reason why people should visit East Africa in future."

As time passes animals and undisturbed nature will become increasingly important to men. A few years ago I wrote in my book *No Room for Wild Animals* that 80,000 more babies are born into the world every twenty-four hours than die during the same intervals. These figures are no longer correct: the United Nations' calculating machines have worked out that daily births exceed deaths by 171,000 and perhaps even 180,000. The world population will exceed three thousand million this year (1960), not in 1962 as was previously supposed. This number will increase to five thousand million before we reach the year 2000. Two-thirds of the world population are already undernourished, and millions die of plain starvation every year. Every eight years a number equivalent to the population of China is added to the people on earth.

Since the birth of Christ, one hundred and six species of animals have been exterminated—wiped off the face of God's earth. It is fated that beautiful wild animals must make way for starving mankind. All that people like Michael and myself, Colonel Molloy and the game wardens want for them are a few large zoological gardens in their own countries: a few National Parks.

They are virtually living inside such "zoos" already. People in Europe and America are deluded by films and books. Wonderful films about African wild life inside the Queen Elizabeth Park or Parks in the Belgian Congo never mention that these are the only areas where such filming is possible. People believe that Africa is an animal paradise, the only continent where the rest of creation is on an equal footing with mankind.

Some years ago I met a Swiss business man in the Congo, who for three months had been travelling all over Africa, by air, railway and omnibus, by steamer on lakes and rivers, and by car. I asked him whether he had seen many wild animals.

"Of course," he said, "masses of them." He told of elephants, lions and giraffes. On closer questioning I got the answer I expected. He had seen these animals only in National Parks. During his three months' journey he had seen exactly *one* large wild animal, an ostrich, outside the Park borders.

Not long ago Countess Erika Reventlow wrote to me: "Tanganyika and Kenya were my constant home before the war, and I have been there three times since 1951. Despite the good hunting laws, and their enforcement has been most effective since the 'thirties, the number of wild game in East Africa has shrunk to a frightening extent since 1939, excepting perhaps the elephants. The region I know best—the western and northern slopes of Kilimanjaro up to Longido and the Meru Mountain, used to swarm with herds of zebras, wildebeest, kongoni, Thomson's gazelles, Grant's gazelles and impala. There were many gerenuks on the lower plains. Elands were frequent as well as giraffes, and there were even a few oryx.

"Apart from a few isolated steinbuck and bushbuck there are no grazing animals left near Kilimanjaro. Lions and cheetahs are scarce and in the plains between the three mountains one can only see a few Thomson's and Grant's gazelles. It is pitiful. It must have happened during and after the war. To-day you see 'No Shooting' signs everywhere. On the 150-mile stretch of bush between Handoni and Bagamojo—where Hemingway gained the impressions for his book *The Green Hills of Africa*—only the frequent signs 'Sables Protected' indicate that this was once a famous hunting ground. Apart from elephant droppings I saw no other game."

Outside the reserves and National Parks there is not much wild game within easy reach in Kenya to-day, so most hunting expeditions prefer to go to Tanganyika, especially the southern part.

Two of the most beautiful types of zebra have been almost exterminated in Africa. These are Grant's zebras found in Serengeti.

Since they usually start out from Nairobi and not from Arusha or Dar-es-Salaam, they spend most of their money for equipment wages and provisions in Kenya, so that Tanganyika only receives cash for the hunting licences, an infinitesimal portion of the total expenditure of a safari.

Our grandparents had chickens in their farmyards and horses and cattle in their barns. Even in the towns they saw horses in harness. If they took their children for walks they saw storks, foxes, hares, roebuck, badgers, owls, red deer and hawks. Ever since man has been on earth, for about half a million years, he has shared his world with other creatures.

This situation has changed for the first time in our era. Increasing numbers of people know only such animals as cats, dogs and parrakeets—and the creatures in zoos—which is why more and more people visit them. The Frankfurt Zoo had an average annual attendance of 313,000 people in the decade before the last war. By 1959 this number had risen to 1.7 million. The same picture is true in most other zoos, whether in America, Russia or China. People feel that something belonging to their lives has been taken from them, and their souls bear the scars. The unconscious longing for something that is lost is often exaggerated and pathological. If a cat climbs a tree and cannot get down again hundreds of people collect and the fire brigade is called out. When a lion is killed by a tiger because a keeper has opened the wrong door it receives much bigger headlines than six people killed in a car crash.

The remaining animals grow ever more precious and desirable. They have begun a paradoxical journey. They are exterminated in their homeland and transplanted into large cities where a second home with an imitation landscape (and centrally heated houses) is built for them. There are five large zoological gardens in Africa already, which would have seemed ridiculous to our grandparents. Even these zoos are not where the animals are most at home, but in the greatest concentrations of the population: Cairo, Khartoum, Leopoldville, Pretoria and Johannesburg.

Large cities continue to proliferate. In the coming decades and centuries men will not travel to view marvels of engineering, but they will leave the dusty towns in order to behold the last places on earth where God's creatures are peacefully living. Countries which have preserved such places will be envied by other nations and visited by streams of tourists. There is a difference between wild animals living a natural life and famous buildings. Palaces can be rebuilt if they are destroyed in wartime, but once the wild animals of the Serengeti are exterminated no power on earth can bring them back.

Men fight and die to change borders and convert others to their way of life. Michael and I must surely be right to work and risk our lives to save the Serengeti.

Game poachers can be arrested, but that does not solve the problem. Black people have hunted since time immemorial and cannot understand why it should suddenly be forbidden in parts of their own country. Their numbers have trebled, wire snares have made the capture of many types of animal easy, and lorries can transport the meat anywhere. It is difficult for a black villager to realise that this type of hunting would kill off all the animals in a very short time. Why should he be expected to be more foresighted than our ancestors of a few centuries ago?

Poaching can be controlled or even wiped out by police action and campaigns, but we will not achieve a real victory until the natives realise the *reason* behind the preserved areas. The last annual report of the Royal National Parks of Kenya states that

The natives believe that Europeans only protect wild animals so that rich Americans can shoot them and take home trophies of the chase.

natives should realise "that game preservation is a question of proper land usage. This latter is yet to be accepted by the African community, who are so apt wrongly to believe that game is preserved in Kenya for the benefit of the white man and his rich friends from overseas."

How can the natives be expected to understand that they will be justly punished for hunting when they see the cars of wealthy Europeans, filled with trophies, pass through their villages?

The present policy in large parts of Africa aims at self-government for the natives sooner or later. Primitive people tend to behave foolishly, especially after a nationalistic upheaval. The Bedouins in the Libyan Desert celebrated the end of foreign rule by pulling out or topping off millions of trees which the Italians had laboriously planted. These future shade-bearers, intended to improve the climate, were already a symbol of "slavery" to the newly liberated people. Their grandchildren may not think too highly of this exploit.

In one recently independent African state we witnessed the erection of a television transmitter—and this in a country where there are hardly any schools and 90 per cent of the population is illiterate. The expensive television programmes were intended for the three hundred or so most important families.

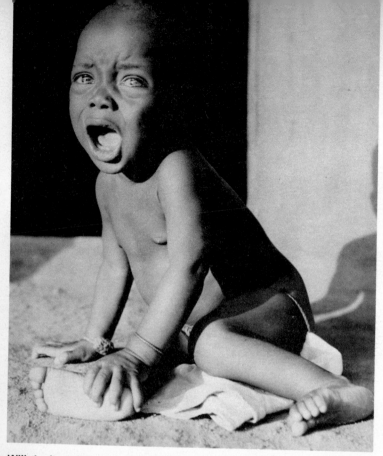

Will the beautiful wild animals still be near his village when this baby has grown up? We hoped to preserve the marvels of nature for him and his black and white brothers.

This particular kind of absurdity is not confined to *coloured* nations, for our European rulers behaved in a similar manner for several centuries. The new African ruling class does exactly the same things that the rich Europeans did in Africa up to the liberation. Our ancestors also imitated their Roman and Greek rulers. Black chieftains who have acquired wealth dress in European clothes, drive large American cars, build pretty villas—and will go elephant shooting, just as they have seen the rich Europeans do.

As long as we have any influence in these countries we should set a different kind of example. We should convince them that wild animals are part of the beauty and wealth of their country and of all mankind, as much as the Acropolis, the Louvre and St. Paul's Cathedral.

No conceivable government in modern Greece would tear down the "useless" Acropolis and replace it with a useful warehouse or a large hotel. Some centuries ago this could still happen. Masterpieces of antiquity were destroyed, Roman temples were wrecked to provide building materials for workers' flats. The whole world would protest and brand any modern government as barbarians if it permitted such vandalism to-day.

It is true that occasionally dams must be built at the expense of an old church or mansion, but it would be an offence against good taste if the *nouveau riche* were permitted to use the old murals and masonry for target practice before they disappeared under the rising water. Such is the case with the last elephants, lions, herds of zebras and rhinos. They will have to give way. A few places should be preserved for them, however, so that their former homeland should not be completely overun by men, black or white. Where the animals have to cede they should be treated with dignity.

To many people this request may appear exaggerated but it will seem commonplace in a hundred years' time. I fear that this may be true even in only twenty years.

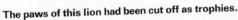

The paws of this lion had been cut off as trophies.

The Masai consider themselves to be "God's chosen people" and feel infinitely superior to Europeans and other African tribes.

CHAPTER 13

The Masai—
"God"s Chosen People"

*Man is an actor. He acts all manner of men,
and each one is a lie. Only the animal in him
is real.*

WILLIAM SAROYAN

I PRESSED my knee against the joy-stick and thirteen yards of striped wing went into a curve. "Those are sheep below us, Michael, there's no doubt about it."

As we approached them the animals ran together from all directions to coalesce into one central bunch. This is typical of all domesticated sheep and goats, and quite contrary to the behaviour of cattle and wild animals.

A few black shepherds were with the herd. They were Masai and had no business to be in this western section of Serengeti.

The Masai were the cause of all our hard work. Because of them we had to learn to fly. They were the reason why we were so far from Frankfurt and why we had been counting, marking and dyeing animals for the past weeks and months. It is to aid the Masai that the area of National Park may be decreased by a third and the highland of the craters cut off from the rest.

A National Park must remain a piece of primordial wilderness to be effective. No men, not even native ones, should live inside the borders. The British colonial administration used to consider that the natives were "a part of nature", but they discovered at some other places that these "children of nature" imported motor-cars into the National Parks and covered their roofs with tin cut from petrol canisters. They refused to hunt with bows and arrows and became modernised. You cannot keep men, even black and brown ones, from multiplying and cannot force them to remain "primitive". It was finally admitted that National Parks should be entirely free of all human beings, whether black or white.

A Masai spits on civilisation, quite literally. He will never wear a European hat or buy a car. On the other hand he can never own enough cattle, and according to Professor Pearsall of London the herds of Masai cattle added to the herds of wildebeest would be more than the Serengeti has room for. During their constant wanderings the Masai cut down the trees to build new huts and to make kraals and thorn shelters for their animals. This means that the shade round the remaining water holes is destroyed and the soil becomes arid. They already keep the wild animals away from the water holes during the dry season. Pastoral people, whether black or white, never consider the soil and its vegetation, they never think of the future. The barren hills of Italy, Spain and Greece, and the new deserts of India, are evidence of this.

Below the equator the land deteriorates more rapidly. The Serengeti cannot support wild animals and domestic cattle at the same time. The wild herds would be the first to disappear, but the Masai's beasts could not long be maintained. For that reason it was intended to keep these nomadic shepherds out of the Park. Things have changed now, and the government wants to segregate that part of the Park in which the black shepherds have grazing rights. This would do no harm in some people's opinion, for they believe that the large herds of wildebeest and zebras from the Serengeti never go there anyhow. The herds which appear in these parts of the plains during the rainy season are said to come from the Ngorongoro Crater.

Be that as it may, it was certain that the Masai and their herds had no right to be in the Western Serengeti. We flew back to our headquarters at Banagi and had a council of war with Myles Turner and Gordon Poolman. The intruders would naturally be fined and forced to leave, but it was considered wiser to take the D.O., or District Officer, as well.

He is the official responsible for all Masai in the region. He looks after them and sees to it that they keep the peace. The officials responsible for wild animals and those who have the interests of the Masai at heart could easily indulge in a little bureaucratic warfare. Next morning Michael and I flew to the headquarters of the D.O. who at once agreed to come with us.

After travelling for two hours in a Land-Rover we arrived at the exact spot we had seen from the air. We found eight hundred sheep and seven Masai, a family elder, four half-grown boys and two warriors with long spears. The warriors had plaited their hair and stuck it together with red clay. The little plaits were tied together at the neck and fastened to a short stick to form a regular pigtail. They only fight with short straight "roman" swords and spears, for they despise poisoned arrows.

The D.O. explained to the elder that he would have to pay a fine. Any other black man would have objected, made denials, pleaded and complained of the drought, as would most white people in a similar situation. We knew that such pleas would have been justified, for that September there had only been one-third of an inch of rain, one-tenth of the rainfall of the previous year. The elder, however, only said: "Yes, you are right, it is forbidden. You have caught me and I must pay."

The fine was thirty sheep and goats and there was no bargaining. The two warriors kept a respectful silence when the elder spoke. They leaned on their spears and looked like young Greek gods. A brownish-red cloth was draped over one shoulder like a toga, leaving the other bare. The Masai are tall and slender and their concept of beauty is close to ours: narrow hips, no corpulent or obese outlines and no exaggerated lumps of muscle.

The sheep were caught and I noticed they were all rams. Their legs were tied together with strips of bark. Perhaps the grazing had been worth the fine, for the Masai shook hands with us as we left and did not seem in the least offended.

"That's just like them," said the D.O. "We have started a cattle market and are slowly teaching them to sell their surplus animals. I provided a hand-bell for the market. One Masai boy seemed fascinated by it. He took it in his hand, played with it and then suddenly ran off, still holding it. We caught him and I asked:

'Which do you prefer? I can either send you to Court, where you will be fined and sent to prison, or you can take a beating here and now.'

"The young Masai looked at the heavy stick in my hand and replied: 'I'd rather go to Court, you'll break my bones with that thing.' His father cut off a pliable switch and gave it to me. The young man bent over and I hit him twelve times across his back as hard as I could. The boy never made a sound. When it was over he gave me his hand—the matter was finished.

"The language is difficult," continued the D.O., "and I still don't know it completely. When I first came here I had to hold Court in Swahili with an interpreter. I made a complete mess of the third case I tried and gave a false judgment, as I later discovered. The man who had been unjustly convicted flew into a rage and threw his spear at me. The long iron tip went through my hat without hurting me. You can still see the hole in my hat after three years. I could not bring myself to punish the would-be assassin, since I had been at fault, and in any case I doubt whether he really meant to kill me."

The Masai are a curious people. Their light-skinned ancestors came from Egypt, where their mummies are still to be found in very ancient graves. When they drove their cattle slowly southward they interbred with the darker people of the Upper Nile.

The Masai greet each other by laying a hand on the head.

In East Africa they took possession of the Great Rift Valley which runs north and south through Kenya and Tanganyika. Although they are so warlike, they never conquered and ruled the other black tribes, as did related tribes of North Africans. The Masai lived a pastoral life and traded their cattle for the fruit and grain of their agricultural neighbours. They cannot have been quite the daring robbers of the travel books or else their neighbours would never have grown so rich and powerful.

The Masai do not like strangers to travel through their country, and this may have saved the peace and lives of the Negro tribes around Lake Victoria, for the Arab slave traders dared not cross Masai territory. The slave caravans from the coast therefore kept south of Masai land and went to Lake Tanganyika. In this locality there was widespread misery and destruction. The first Europeans to meet the Masai and talk peacefully to them were the missionaries Krapf and Rebmann, the explorers with the giant umbrella whom I have previously mentioned.

When the British and German governments drew a straight line across the map of East Africa at the end of the last century, thus creating the German and British colonies of Tanganyika and Kenya, they also cut across the land of the Masai. This territory was 500 miles long and 110 miles wide. The larger portion of it lay in Kenya and the present large city of Nairobi, which is the capital, still bears a Masai name. Nairobi simply means "cold" in their language.

Because the high land around Nairobi has a climate eminently suitable for Europeans, this territory was the first that the Masai had to leave. In 1911 they were even persuaded to give up the whole remaining northern portion of their land, which was then also occupied by Europeans. Thus they had to abandon the best parts of their country, where there was plentiful grazing and water even in the dry season. They drove their herds southward and to-day occupy the high grassy plains in Kenya which border on Tanganyika, as well as their old lands in Tanganyika itself. They number about 140,000 and own more than a million animals. Many families and sub-tribes still have names connected with their former northern home.

The Kilimanjaro and Mount Meru in Tanganyika belong to the

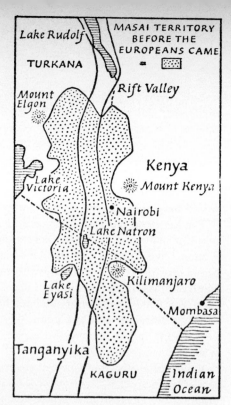

The area where the Masai lived before the Europeans came. The Masai had to cede the northern part of the shaded area to the Europeans. Nowadays the only ones left in Kenya live near the Tanganyika border, the rest live in Tanganyika itself.

Masai, as well as the crater-strewn highland containing Ngorongoro and an adjoining piece of the free Serengeti plains.

The Masai consider themselves God's chosen people, which explains their incredible condescension towards Europeans and other Africans. God, they believe, created the whole earth merely for the Masai. Non-Masai people have no right to own cattle and it is therefore perfectly justifiable to take away their livestock at any time. When drought and rinderpest killed off their cows, the Masai became the scourge of their neighbours. They simply took whatever they needed. Since they hold that honour, decency and love only apply between Masai, it was perfectly permissible, in their view, to lie to strangers, simulate friendliness and break treaties.

Caravans passing through Masai territory often found "sick"

and "half-starved" tribesmen. After they had been medically treated and fed in the camp, these men took the first opportunity to steal away at night and return with their friends to massacre their rescuers.

Their whole lives revolve around their cattle. This idolatry goes so far that during the dry season herdsmen will carry small calves for hours until they find water. They discovered their own method of inoculation against Lung Plague before the arrival of the Europeans. Not long ago I read a pamphlet which one of the few educated Masai had written about his tribe. Whenever he talks of his people he writes "The Cattle" for in their language Masai and cattle are synonymous, there is only one word for both concepts.

Some time ago a delegation of Masai visited an experimental farm in Tanganyika and were shown some freshly imported European bulls. Beasts of such enormous size had never been seen in East Africa before. The Masai were so moved by their splendour that their eyes filled with tears.

A few days ago Michael and I landed our 'plane on the plains close to a *boma,* not far from a rounded hillock of bare granite. A *boma* is a circular kraal enclosed by a high fence of thorny branches. The huts line the circumference inside the prickly,

Married Masai men cut off their hair. This arrogant, slender, pastoral tribe was once the terror of its neighbors in Tanganyika.

The Masai build a circle of low huts and surround it with a high fence of thorny branches. At night the herds of cattle are driven into the open central space.

protective stockade. From the air the huts look like round cheeses, and in reality they have a very similar aroma. The women build them by forcing branches into the earth which they then bend towards the centre. They are interwoven and the bell-shaped structure plastered over with cow dung, followed by a layer of hides to make the house watertight. The huts are so low that you cannot stand upright inside them.

At night the cattle are driven into the central space between the huts and their dung gradually raises the floor level. If this level rises too high, if the dry season forces them to move towards new water holes or if someone dies inside the *boma*, it is abandoned. The Masai load all their goods on to donkeys and set fire to their former homes. When a new *boma* is built many trees and bushes have to be killed to provide a new thorn fence. From the air you can frequently see the circular traces of old *bomas*.

Our "duck" roared downwards. We expected all the people in the *boma* to come running in order to admire our wondrous striped bird. This was not the case. The men were away herding the animals and the women only said "*Jambo*" and carried on with their work. We found this lack of interest almost insulting.

Later on we discovered why the Masai were so indifferent to our metal *Ndegge* (Swahili for bird, aeroplane), and the reason for their general lack of interest in metal things such as cars and guns.

The smiths who make their beautiful swords, spears and daggers are considered "unclean". They are Masai, but if you shake hands with one you have to oil your hand later. You cannot marry a smith's daughter and if a warrior has intercourse with one he is sure to sicken or to die during the next campaign. All our marvellous new appliances are made of iron and the Masai consider them ugly and unclean.

When we told our Masai that the Americans intended to send people to the moon in a rocket they were not surprised in the least. "Why not," they said. "You already fly about in the sky in your iron birds, why should you not fly to the moon?"

When the men returned to the *boma* we did not know where they had been. They were "elders" and not warriors, for they had shaven heads and did not wear a doubly-hooked clasp of horn on their left upper arms. The whole tone seemed to be set by Owe, an old acquaintance of ours, the man who had recently been fined thirty sheep.

He did not seem to bear any ill-will, however, for his greeting was just as friendly as that of the others. He even spat in his palm before shaking hands, a sign of special friendship.

One woman brought us a gourd full of milk in welcome. Michael only touched it with his lips and pretended to drink, but I was thirsty and took a long swig although I knew that the gourd had been rinsed with cows' urine or something even more unpleasant. The milk tasted smoky. I was now not permitted to eat meat in the presence of the Masai, for the proffered drink was a great confidence. The Masai believe that if someone who has drunk milk eats meat during the same day, the cow that gave the milk will sicken and die. That is why the Masai are loath to drink milk if they expect to eat meat later. If this should occur he will tickle his throat with a blade of grass until he has vomited the milk.

The Masai will only eat the meat of their own cattle, sheep and goats, which is why people who are crazy about wild animals, such as Michael and myself, prefer them to any other native tribes. They abhor the flesh of all wild animals as well as birds and fish. The only game they will hunt are the giant elands and buffaloes, since consider them to be almost cattle. This is the reason why elands and buffaloes are so shy in this region and do not allow you to approach closer than six or seven hundred yards. Zebras, wildebeest and other animals graze peacefully side by side with the domestic cattle. If you must have natives inside the Park, the Masai are the least of all evils.

The Masai also hunt lions. Young warriors who want to marry show their bravery by going out into the plains in groups of ten or twelve to kill lions with their spears. This requires more courage than shooting lions on a properly equipped safari. Now that lion hunting and cattle stealing have been forbidden, it has become very difficult for a young Masai to impress his girl friend by his heroism. Personally I doubt whether the prohibition has stopped lions being hunted. In any case lions themselves seem to know better. I frequently saw them run away when Masai warriors with spears appeared on the horizon, and it really takes something to make a lion run.

When the Masai hear talk about clearing them from the Park or from certain water holes, in order to protect the game, they reply: "If we move out the neighbouring people will come with their poisoned arrows and snares. They dare not enter our land now, for they know that we would chase them off like dogs. We let the wild animals live in peace. Only last week we saw a safari with a car load of antlers and lion skins, yet they forbid us to hunt lions. . . ."

During our flights Michael and I also noted the *bomas* of the Masai and counted their herds. We only found a fraction of the number usually given. Unless their numbers rise and their cattle multiply because of modern protective injections, the Masai might not make such bad neighbours of the Park after all.

The Masai drink blood. A bull must give about a gallon of blood a month and a cow about a pint. Since I am a veterinarian I wanted to see how this was done and our friend Owe obliged— especially as he wanted to take a spin in the aeroplane.

We approached a herd and some youngsters caught a black calf. A thin rope was placed round its neck and then the rope was twisted by means of a little stick pushed through it. The tourniquet tightened until the jugular vein became prominent. The elder took an arrow with a short, broad head and from six feet away shot it into the protruding blood vessel. The resulting jet of blood was caught in a wooden bowl. The elder then spat on his finger and thumb, pushed the spittle on the wound and rubbed dust over it. Since the tourniquet had been removed there was no further bleeding; the little slit was securely closed. The blood was stirred with a small stick and one of the boys drank it.

These boys get a new name every few years, since the Masai have a veritable passion for renaming themselves. This chaos of nomenclature is a great handicap for anyone who wants to count the Masai or collect taxes from them. When a child is born the father must kill an ox for the women and children of the *boma,* and another one, four days later, for the men. This is the ceremony at which the child is named. If the father doubts his offspring's paternity the baby is placed in the centre of the gate into the kraal. If the cattle trample it to death when they are driven in at nightfall, the child was a bastard.

On the right-hand side of the gate, as you go in, stands the hut of the first or main wife. The second builds her house on the left, the third on the right again. In later disputes of inheritance it may matter a lot whether one is born on the "right" or the "left". If a father gives a son a steer called Polpol the son is henceforth named "recipient of Polpol". At the circumcision ceremony the father and son exchange names. If the father was named Senda and the son Nana the father will now be called Menye Nana, or father of Nana, and the son Ole Senda, or son of Senda.

Circumcision turns the son into a warrior, which is the dream of every young man. Four days before the feast the father, who as a married man has shorn off his hair long ago, has to dress as a warrior once more and then ceremonially doff the robes again shortly before the ceremony. As soon as the boy has recovered from the operation he runs about and shoots blunt arrows at the girls.

The circumcision ceremony is held once every three years throughout the Masai country, and all youths of the right age celebrate together. There follows the happiest time of their lives. The young warriors wear coloured necklaces, place bells on their legs, plait their growing hair and carry red and black painted shields. The young men of one region leave their parents' *bomas* and build themselves a *manjata,* a free-lying settlement without a

Young men dancing for the girls, leaping high into the air. The young Masai warriors wear their long hair in braids, while the girls shave their heads. On the right the spears of the warriors can be seen stuck into the ground.

thorn fence. Their mothers and sisters accompany them and the unmarried girls live in a state of free love with the young warriors.

A *moran,* as a warrior is now called, is not allowed to work, drink alcohol, smoke, or eat vegetable food. He must live on milk and blood and all he is allowed to do is dance, love and make war.

Making war is no longer necessary, in fact it is forbidden. The young men are reduced to stealing an occasional cow or small herd. In the south they are also in charge of the subterranean water holes, where the herds are driven thirty feet below the level of the ground. The water is brought up from a still lower level by four *morans* standing one on the shoulders of the other against a flat wall and handing up cowhide buckets. Otherwise there is nothing to do but loving and dancing.

The fathers of the *morans* make an occasional present of an ox. The oxen are slaughtered on the bushes near the *manjata* and eaten at once. The young warriors share everything in a brotherly fashion and sons of poor "elders" eat just as well as those of richer ones. All men who have been circumcised in the same year remain in an age group for the rest of their lives. They help each other and place their wives at the disposal of fraternal comrades. In fact any guest entering a *boma* need only plant his spear in front of a hut and everything inside it, including the wife, is his property for the length of his stay.

I do not know how the official veterinary surgeons dare to show their faces among the young Masai at this particular time. The circumcision ceremony had been overdue for three years. The huts at Moshi and the arena had been built long ago, but every year the vets declared an outbreak of foot and mouth disease at just the wrong time. This meant that the herds were not allowed to move and the Masai cannot hold a feast without their cattle. The young men had run around uncircumcised for three years and were missing the best, most carefree and most glorious years of their lives.

Michael and I had a weakness for the Masai, even if they do feel themselves too superior to work. It is only rarely that one of them will hire himself out as a cowherd, and even then he may only do so in order to gradually exchange the farmer's fat cattle for lean ones of his own. The Masai are decreasing in number, at least as far as the true Masai are concerned. They have fewer children because venereal diseases have become prevalent. Although their own "elders" have imposed a fine of about £100 on anyone who infects another person, it is almost impossible to treat or cure these nomadic people. Since many women remain barren, the Masai adopt children from the surrounding Negro tribes. These youngsters grow up as Masai and remain members of the tribe when they are adult, but the light-brown, thin-lipped faces of the real Masai, which resemble those of Europeans, are becoming rarer.

Michael offered twenty shillings for the ear ornaments of a young woman. They consisted of red, white and blue beads stitched closely together on leather to form coloured patterns. The ear-lobes had holes in them big enough to put a fist through and the lower edge of the holes was merely a thin hem. The Masai are a rich tribe, however, and do not need money. They made us a present of the ornaments, but the ensuing conversation seemed full of the word *Ndegge*. The D.O. had said that neither money nor kind words would ever entice a Masai into our aeroplane, but he was proved to be wrong.

We selected four of the most venerable "elders" and made two round trips. I did not think that they could avoid air-sickness and doubted their willingness to use our paper bags, so we selected large flat pieces of hide and bark with which to cover the floor of

Young Masai warriors wanted to sit inside the aeroplane and, if possible, fly with us.

the cabin. Then the first two of the four guests entered.

They did not have the slightest fear and we could not fly high enough for them. Then they wanted to cross the *boma* at low altitude so that the others could see them. We had hardly touched down when we were surrounded by the whole village. They mobbed the machine because all of them wanted to be taken on the next flight.

They brought many flies with them from the *boma*. Michael and I were constantly fanning our faces and beating our arms and legs to get rid of them, but they did not seem to bother the Masai. Their eyes and nostrils were continuously surrounded by swarms of the grey insects, which they did not even bother to brush away, a fortitude they seem to share with their cattle. This must be the reason for the frequent diseased eyes and blind people one sees among the tribe.

The neighbouring tribes are suspicious about what "God's chosen people" will do when the British leave. They fear that conditions will revert to those which prevailed before the arrival of the Germans. The Germans shot a few hundred robbing and murdering young warriors in all their ostrich-feathered glory in order to teach the others not to regard the Negro tribes as *ol nantinda*, or savages who could be robbed of cattle, wives and children with impunity. The neighbours are afraid that the Masai will revert to the habits of the "good old days".

The missionaries have never had much success among the Masai, who believe in *Engai*, a single, benevolent deity who sends them rain. They do not believe, however, that a man's spirit lives on after his death.

Between 1895 and 1902 Captain Moritz Merker, a German officer stationed at Moshi, at the foot of Kilimanjaro, grew friendly with the Masai and studied their language. He wrote a large book about them, and since his time nobody else has studied these proud, tall warriors with comparable thoroughness. Merker's scientific zeal did him little good. When he went to Germany on leave in 1903 he was honoured on all sides by scientists and high officials, which did not seem to please his military superiors. As soon as he returned to East Africa he was given a post as far from the Masai as possible and sent to the humid coast of Dar-es-Salaam to train recruits. He died of pneumonia in 1908.

His Masai friends repeated to Captain Merker all the stories and legends which grandmothers tell the little boys and girls during the long evenings when they sit outside the huts of the *boma*. According to him the Masai knew the stories of Adam and Eve, Cain and Abel, the great Flood and other tales of the Old Testament (though the characters had different names) long before the arrival of the missionaries. He also discovered the way to make a real peace with the Masai. The proud warriors often offered to cut their arms and mingle their blood with that of the enemy, but this did not always result in peace. If, however, two babies were exchanged between the warring parties and each suckled for a few moments by its temporary foster mother, lasting peace would be assured.

The Masai help each other, however false and deceitful they may be with strangers. When a group of them came to the trade exhibition in Berlin in 1896 they saved all their wages and bought the freedom of some of their fellows who had been sold as slaves during the preceding lean years. They had some curious tales to relate when they returned home. "In Germany the children don't eat with their parents like ours, but are herded together like sheep. There are tables in the streets with plates on them. When a crowd of children arrive they sit at the tables and eat. When they have finished eating they are driven away again." The Masai had seen classes of school children being conducted through the exhibition and eating in restaurants.

It is hard to come to terms with the Masai on such matters as water holes or stretches of plain which they should abandon. They have no chiefs or kings to rule over them. The people regarded as chieftains by the Germans and the British were really patriarchs and medicine men. The latter make rain and prophesy about wars by throwing stones from a horn. Queen Elizabeth, the Queen Mother, gained an unexpected reputation as a rainmaker in February 1958. During a festive occasion in her honour she expressed her good wishes for the desired rain. The medicine men had made unsuccessful attempts at rainmaking for months, but half an hour after the royal wish a large thunderstorm blew up and soaked the parched grassland.

It takes a long time for the Masai to reach a decision. The

Masai rounding up their herds of sheep and goats at nightfall.

"elders" must be called together first, and since the *bomas* lie far apart this may take days or weeks. After that there are long sessions of discussion, just like a European parliament, and the matter is thoroughly thrashed out before a final decision is reached. The trustees of the government are usually Masai who can speak Swahili. They place the wishes of the government before the "council of elders" and bring back the result of their deliberations. Everything is carried out in a highly democratic manner.

There is only one Masai habit which infuriated Michael and myself—their incessant spitting. They were not sick during the aeroplane trips but they constantly spat on the floor. It was just as well that we had carpeted the cabin with hides and bark. If we sat down to eat near the 'plane or beside the car they stood around us and persistently spat on the ground. If you bought something from them, the goods were spat on to seal the bargain.

I had to remind Michael that only a few decades ago Europeans and Americans were quite as spit-happy as the Masai, so that we have little cause to feel superior to them for that reason. We do not have rainmakers either, but we possess astrologers and "miracle" cures. Perhaps we could even learn from the Masai and declare our atomic physicists an "unclean caste", as they do with their smiths.

The hippopotamuses of the Ngorongoro crater only leave their lake at night.

CHAPTER 14

A Night in
the Ngorongoro Crater

*Every man should spend at least one night
a month in the open, so as to shed all vain
airs for a time.*

JOSEPH VON EICHENDORFF

ONE DAY Michael put me down in the Ngorongoro Crater. I had
seen two rhinos among a group of lions and not far from them a
pair of leopards on the hunt. We unloaded the heavy tripod of the
cine-camera and some boxes and chests to lighten the machine.
Michael intended to return in an hour, after taking the two game
wardens and Hermann on a short flight outside the crater. It was
difficult to take off with four people in the aeroplane because of the
thin, high altitude air, and even harder to land.

I took off my shirt, hung my field-glasses around my neck and
went for a walk, clad only in shorts and sandals. The two leopards
had already killed a jackal; they must have been very quick, and
were now playing with the dead animal like cats with a mouse.
One of them picked up the corpse in its jaws and hit it with a paw
so that the body sailed through the air. The other leopard was
crouched in the grass. Now it pounced on the dead jackal and
"caught" it once more.

It was easy to find the two rhinos because of the gleaming, white
ox-peckers on their backs. The lions were invisible, but this was
not surprising because a lion can disappear from sight when the
grass is only a foot high. The behaviour of the rhino bull indicated
that there were predators in the vicinity. He lowered his head and

The king of beasts must yield to a stronger animal.

calmly walked towards a particular spot. A large lion with a fine mane rose from the grass and strolled away only to lie down again thirty yards farther on. The rhino followed and again drove the lion away. The king of beasts seemed to acknowledge a master.

I stayed at a respectful distance from these mighty animals. There is quite a difference between sitting in a car and standing on the flat, open plain with not even a tree or bush for shelter.

I went back to our luggage and lay down. It was so pleasant to sizzle in the equatorial noonday sun that I barely opened my eyes when our "flying zebra" returned. It flew across me as if all set for a landing, but Michael suddenly gave full throttle again and flew off. He must have forgotten something, but I had plenty of time and did not worry.

When I looked at my watch again it was half-past four. I felt a little parched, but luckily I had brought a Thermos flask of tea with me. I had lain for four hours in the full mountain sun, but I had become acclimatised to African conditions and did not feel a trace of sunburn. I thought back to our first African expedition, years before, and all the tales we had heard about sunstroke: "You must always wear a sun helmet," they had told us, and now I was not even wearing an ordinary hat!

It was about time that Michael came to pick me up again. Slowly I strolled towards a herd of wildebeest grazing some distance away. They appeared restless, as if something out of the ordinary had happened. I adjusted my field-glasses as I approached. A light-brown object was lying in the grey-green grass and the surrounding black wildebeest regarded it with obvious interest. One of them went up and prodded the brown heap with its nose. The little lump rose on shaky legs — it was a young wildebeest, probably the first one to be born inside the crater this year.

This first-born was a sensational novelty not only for me but for the whole herd. When the little calf moved it was followed by ten or fifteen fascinated adult wildebeest. When it fell down the cows stood in a circle around it, came closer, sniffed at it and gently butted it with their soft noses. They never prodded with their sharp horns, but one of them occasionally made threatening movements to drive the others away from the calfling. This was probably the mother.

In a few weeks there would be hundreds of these calves, and the adult wildebeest would no longer take any special notice of them. This first-born had little chance of remaining alive. Four hyenas were already watching it with greedy eyes. When one of them came too close, a big wildebeest would make a brief attack, but the hyena retreated only a little way. The *fisis* do not live exclusively on carrion by any means; very many young antelopes and gazelles fall victim to them.

That is life in the raw. Newcomers to Africa would like to kill off the hyenas, but that would upset the balance of nature. For a time the leopard was unprotected in East Africa. This led to an enormous increase of wart-hogs and baboons. They destroyed the natives' fields and created far more damage than the value of the occasional goat which the leopards had killed. Since then leopards have been protected again.

By now it was six o'clock and I grew impatient for Michael to come and fetch me. Since the sun would set at seven he would have to arrive within the next ten minutes. If he did not arrive he must have had an accident. This would mean that I would

Most of the young animals of Serengeti fall victim to the spotted hyena and not to lions.

have to spend the night in the crater. I was a little worried because I had neither a torch nor matches with me, and my wrist-watch indicated that there was a new moon.

Suddenly I heard the drone of an engine. An aeroplane was flying high above the western rim of the crater, but it was not striped. It curved over the Lemagrut volcano. I started to sweat. Had the others crashed, and was this a rescue machine looking for them?

The machine turned towards the crater and came lower. It was obviously looking for me. I waved my shirt and the little Cessna 'plane flew straight at me but did not land. It dropped a brown bag. I ran to pick it up and extracted a piece of paper. It carried a message written in English: "Michael damaged his undercarriage. He has flown to Nairobi. Nobody was hurt. Walk in the direction in which we are flying."

The Cessna banked, came back and flew in a direction at right angles to its original approach. Then it climbed and disappeared over the rim of the crater. The hum of the engine died away.

I sat down on a box to think the matter over. Which direction did they mean, the first or the second? The first one was south-east. This would bring me to the lake inside the crater, and in the woods behind the lake there was said to be a hut with two beds. That was the only roof within the entire hundred square miles of the crater. I would be quite safe inside the hut, if I could force the door. I had never been there, however, and it was a good three hours' walk away. It would be dark in twenty minutes and I knew from previous flights that there were many lions by the lake.

No, thanks! I preferred to stay where I was. No animals grazed on the short dry grass of the plain during the cold night, so presumably there would be no lions to hunt for them. I was quite certain that nothing would happen to me during the night, for I had never heard of anyone being killed by lions or leopards inside the crater. I was equally certain that I would not get much sleep. Luckily the tripod was wrapped in an old, quilted sleeping-bag. I could at least slip into that, but I knew that every little sound would make me think of hyenas and that anything glittering would suggest the eyes of lions. If I were a smoker I would at least have had matches or a lighter with me. There was nothing for it. I pulled out the legs of the tripod to their maximum extent and covered them with a bit of canvas. This looked like a tent and gave some shelter. All around me I laid a circle of chests, tin plates and cutlery. If an animal came sniffing around it might be disturbed by the strange smell—or so I hoped.

I would have given quite a lot to be one day older. I thought of the many evenings spent in a cinema and the nights I had worked at my desk. If you have no illumination you can do nothing but think, worry and count the minutes.

The steep, southern wall of the crater was much closer than the hut in the south-east, and only about an hour's walk away. At the foot of the steep, green slope there seemed to be a few trees with something underneath them. I could not make out through my field-glasses what it was; it was probably a bush, but it might have been a hut. There would be exactly twenty-five minutes' more daylight. If I went towards the trees and could not find my way back I might stray into the undulating ground where beasts of prey lurked in the high grass. The tripod and luggage represented a sort of home, a refuge in the wilderness.

There was little time to be lost and I had to act quickly. I had precisely twelve minutes to walk straight towards the trees before making a decision. If I was certain that there was a hut which I could reach in time I would walk on, if not, I must return to the tripod at once. I unwrapped some tools and tied the old newspaper wrappings to the tripod so that I would not miss the frail structure in the twilight.

Then I started, but turned around once more to get a bearing. If I walked towards a certain rock formation on the northern rim I should be able to reach my makeshift tent again. The trees were much farther away than I had imagined. I carried only the old sleeping-bag and my camera and walked as quickly as I could. When the twelve minutes were up I looked through the field-glasses once more. The trees seemed hardly any closer, for it is easy to misjudge distances in the water-clear mountain air. I was willing to bet that the structure under them was only a bush. Before turning back to the tripod I surveyed the surrounding country again.

There were two figures to the left of me, thin vertical lines which could only be men or zebras seen head-on. I had a short mental struggle, decided that they were men and turned towards them.

A sandy depression opened in front of me, seven or nine feet deep. When I had struggled up the other side I could see three thin lines. I thought it unlikely that there were three zebras all turned exactly towards me. The twilight was getting darker as I walked through the hip-high, reedy grass. The ground underfoot was dry and no longer swampy. Suddenly I saw a faint red glow, a fire, and heaved a sigh of relief. This could only mean natives, probably Masai, but at least I would be among men.

They were Masai, six *morans*, or young warriors, and two eleven-year-old boys. They had herded together six hundred sheep on a large, bare spot, covered a foot high with dry sheep's dung. There was no protective thorny stockade. All eight Masai were busily picking out the lambs and placing them in baskets of woven twigs in the centre of the herd. This protected them against predators at night. An enormously tall fellow came towards me, shook my hand and said: "*Jambo*"—good day.

"*Jambo*", I replied. I could not understand a word he said to me, but I thought that I could follow the gist of his talk. I tried to explain my presence in a mixture of English and Swahili. At last a spark of comprehension lit his eyes—he had understood the word *Ndegge*. Then he had to leave me again to look after the sheep.

Apparently the Masai and their herd came here every night. A sort of wind-breaker of branches had been built in the circle of sheep droppings, with skins tied across them as protection against the rain. A fire burned in front of the open side. I lifted my legs, stork-like, over the resting sheep; there was hardly space enough between them to place my feet, as I crossed the sea of sheep and goat bodies to the central shelter. There were two similar shelters closer to the periphery of the herd.

After stepping over the fire I sat down in the small, half-open hut. Its floor was covered with fleeces and a woven mat. All the eight Masai came to the hut, one by one, and sat around the fire. They asked me many questions, but I could only shrug my shoulders in reply. They probably wanted to give me something to eat for I recognised the Swahili word *shukulla*—meaning food. I shook my head, for I did not want to attempt the delights of the

I had to sleep in a crude Masai windbreak.

Masai cusine. Perhaps they were going to offer me fresh blood or similar delicacies. I showed them the piece of bread I carried in my pocket but could not convince them of my lack of appetite.

At a signal from the tallest warrior the two boys fetched a brown, short-haired sheep. It was placed on its back near the fire and four of them got hold of the legs so that it could not move. They looked at me questioningly. What did they intend? Did they expect me to drink ewes' milk direct from the udder? The tall one placed the tip of his spear directly in the centre of the animal's chest and cut through the skin. Ever deeper went the spear. I thought it a cruel way to kill the poor beast, but noticed almost at once that there was no blood. The Masai had strangled the animal beforehand.

Only the boys did any real work. They skinned the sheep and removed the viscera. Spleen, liver and pieces of meat were strung on twigs, one end of them was pushed into the ground while the other, holding the meat, was bent over the fire. The tall *moran* who had originally met me pulled the omentum from the abdomen, a semi-transparent sheet of tissue streaked with fat. He was doubtless asking me whether it was good to eat. I was horrified at the idea of having to eat this mess, whether fried or stewed, but I was cowardly and nodded my head, "Yes". The warriors laughed but I did not know what I had done wrong.

The leading *moran* gave me the twig with the half-cooked liver on it. I took it in both hands, held it in front of my mouth and tried to bite off a piece. It did not taste too bad. They all laughed again, and it was quite clear that the Masai did not consider it good manners to eat your meat that way. One of them produced a knife from somewhere and handed it to me. I ate very slowly because I was afraid of being offered another tit-bit as soon as I had finished the first.

The *morans* put a large cauldron over the fire and placed the cut up meat from the whole sheep inside it. They ate enormous amounts, but then they had probably worked harder during the day than I had. When I refused the twig containing the half-cooked heart, a warrior wedged it between the branches of the shelter, directly over my head. I promised myself that I would not eat it all the same.

The tall warrior lay down beside me, his feet towards the fire, and wrapped himself in the old woollen blanket which he had worn, toga fashion, over one shoulder during the day. He even covered his face and head. I crept into my sleeping-bag and placed the camera case under my head. One of the boys cut off the sheep's feet at the joint and held them over the flames. The wool and skin were singed and scorched. This must have been a special delicacy, for the Masai chewed them with the delight with which we eat sweets and chocolates. One of them started to sing. Each verse in a high falsetto was followed by two bass notes. I naturally did not understand the lyrics, but I had heard of their satirical songs. They laughed frequently and I could hear the word *ndegge*.

The wrapped-up warrior beside me snored, as did two or three of the sheep. I had never known that sheep could snore. A young dog, who had previously been driven away by the Masai, finally managed to snuggle himself into the shelter and lay down on my legs. All the better—he provided extra warmth.

I slept from ten until a quarter to four, then I watched the stars for two hours. I imagined Michael comfortably asleep in the New Stanley Hotel in Nairobi after soaking in a beautifully tiled bathroom. I would not have exchanged places with him. He would be furious that the 'plane was out of action but the main thing was that he and his passengers were unharmed. We were due to return to Europe within a few days anyhow, and by the time we came back the machine would have been repaired in Nairobi. It was a good thing that he had managed to fly it directly to the repair shop.

At half-past seven it grew light. I clambered over the sleeping sheep to take a walk in the plain, but this infuriated the lean dog, and I found myself having to stay with the herd. A real sheep dog cannot bear to see an animal by itself, so I appreciated his point of view.

Two large pied crows with white collars and light tips on their strong, curved beaks walked among the sheep. A ewe stamped at them, but they merely retreated a little way and only flew away when the ewe attacked once more.

When the herd had been started on its way the first *moran* came to show me the way to the "campi" or camp behind the little forest. He could not understand why I insisted on setting off in the opposite direction, but accompanied me nevertheless. The rock formation which I had noted the night before gave me the correct bearing and within forty-five minutes we found my luggage and the tripod. One of my suitcases was a flesh-coloured pink and when the Masai saw it from a distance he grabbed my arm in fear and said *"kufa?"*

which means dead. I reassured him. None of the luggage had been touched. My friends were sure to send a vehicle from the crater's rim during the course of the day in order to fetch me. The Masai would not tolerate this. He rammed the iron tip of his spear into the ground and ran off with his toga flapping behind him. He had gone to fetch donkeys.

More than an hour passed and I grew apprehensive. He had however left his spear as a pledge. What could he be thinking of? He was truly frightened when he believed that there had been a fatal accident. Moritz Merker in his study of the Masai, to which I have already referred, discusses their religious beliefs, and says they pray three times daily with arms raised to the sun. Each Masai has a Guardian Angel who leads him to Paradise after death. In this heaven he is only allowed one wife and all other despised "savages" or Negro tribes are banned.

Though no one else has studied the Masai as intensively as Merker, present-day authorities dismiss these tales as being too much like Christianity. In any case the Masai do not believe in the evil spirits and gods which have been given power over man by a superior god above the clouds, as do the other black tribes. Our God is sufficient for these great warriors of the plains, and He is hardly concerned with the fate of men. The only volcano in this region which is still active now and then is called Oldonio L'Engai by the Masai, the mountain of God. Nor do they believe in life after death, a theology that consoles most men and reconciles them to their fate. At least that is what they told us.

A few weeks ago the D.O. found a young Masai warrior who had been dreadfully gored by a buffalo. His bones were broken, his abdomen pierced and there were deep wounds in his body. The D.O. took the young man to the hospital in Arusha in his badly sprung little van. The vibrations must have hurt the badly wounded Masai dreadfully, for the Englishman could see the contortions of his youthful ebony face. But not a sound passed the sick man's lips, there was no groaning. He died soon after arriving in the hospital. They are a brave people.

If a Masai is dying in his hut, the relatives surreptitiously try to take off his arm bands, ear decorations and necklaces while he is still alive. If he died before they are removed, nobody else may wear them, but otherwise every wife, child and friend gets a memento of the deceased. Children and guests who fall sick in a *boma* are removed to a hut specially built outside the kraal when they near their end. Should they die inside the *boma*, all huts must be burned and the whole large family has to migrate and build another *boma*. The relatives of the dead guest have to pay for the new *boma* and the Masai try to save them that expense.

As soon as a Masai has died, his brothers and wives kill an ox on the plains, preferably under a tree. The flesh is eaten, but the bones and blood remain where they are. The corpse is anointed with fat from the sacrificial beast and then laid in the shade. The face is turned to the East, the legs are drawn up, the left hand is placed under the cheek and the right hand, bearing a tuft of grass, is put in front of the chest. New sandals are bound on his feet. Grass in the hand is a sign of peaceful intentions among the Masai, and the sandals are provided for the long journey ahead. Perhaps they do believe in personal survival after all.

The corpse is nearly always eaten by hyenas and jackals during the first night. If the scavengers do not touch it, this is considered a bad sign. Great medicine men and chiefs are sometimes buried in the ground. In that case every passer-by places a stone on the grave, so that after a time a small hill appears on the landscape.

All the dead man's relatives shave their heads, and he is never mentioned again. If he had a name which occurs in the ordinary language, as for instance "Ol-Onana"—the noble one—his family eschews the word noble, and substitutes another one instead, such as *polpol*, although strictly speaking that means "soft".

The warrior who had left his spear behind him returned with two others. I could see them in the distance driving three donkeys in front of them. The donkeys belong to the women, and only have to work every six months or so, when the tribe moves from one *boma* to another.

On the donkeys' backs were great panniers of untanned leather. These were so hard that we had to stretch them open in order to insert all my luggage. The straps cut deeply into the donkeys' backs, resting on thick horny pads of tissue created by previous loads. One of the donkeys had a ring through his nose.

We walked straight across the plain of the crater towards a dis-

tant forest. I counted seventeen hyenas in a small region, although there was not a sign of a cadaver. Lions resting in the reed-like were doubtless looking for me, they did not come any closer.
were unmistakably afraid of the warriors, and even the donkeys beside the slender figures could not tempt them. My companions took my arm and showed me two clouds of dust in the distance. Two cars were driving about a few miles away. Although they were doubtless looking for me, they did not come any closer.

We walked for three hours. The sun burned on my skull, for I did not have a mane of hair like Michael. When I tried to jump across some swampy ground I landed short and went ankle-deep into the grey-white, viscous, salty mud.

Finally one of the cars came up and I was recognised. At first they had taken me for a Masai. My rescuers offered us food, which we refused, but I drank nearly half a gallon of water, and the Masai did, too. The leading *moran* and I got into the car and led the way, while the other two followed with the donkeys. The driver offered us cigarettes, which I refused, but the Masai took a fistful of six or eight and I later smuggled them into my pocket. We felt like real confederates. I tried to persuade him to have one, but he did not know how to set about it. He held the match to one end, but forgot to put the other in his mouth. Then I remembered that Masai warriors are not allowed to smoke; they only start after they have become "elders".

The Masai was just as interested in the Europeans in the car as they were in him. An elderly lady was sitting in the front seat and he took one of her grey locks and rubbed it between his fingers. He did the same thing to the blond hair of a child. The hairs on my arms also seemed to fascinate him. He pulled at them and then "combed" them with his fingers. His own fine black skin was completely smooth.

I soon discovered what had happened to Michael and the aeroplane. The machine had lurched while starting, and one wheel had hit a hillock. There was only a short jerk, but the leg had broken off, remaining attached to the body at a backward angle.

Michael only noticed that the door jerked open and that it took him all his strength to hold it shut. When he looked down he could see the ground through a large hole through which the wind was whistling.

At the same time the 'plane climbed steeply and lost a lot of momentum. Unless he could increase the speed at once it would stall and crash. Neither the rudder nor the elevators would function, and Michael had to work feverishly.

During such moments one has no time to be afraid, there is too much to do. Only the three passengers, who could do nothing, saw death staring them in the face. Before they had fully realised what had happened the critical moment had passed—at least for the time being.

Michael had restored the equilibrium of the "duck" by trimming it and using the flaps. He had also gained speed. His forehead was streaming with sweat, but he had time to take a deep breath and consider the situation.

Landing on one leg is a matter of life and death. No kind of help could be expected in the open Serengeti plains. If the machine burst into flames on landing there would be no chance of extinguishing the fire, nor was there a hospital or doctor in case anyone was injured. Even if no one was hurt, the repairs would take weeks or even months. It might mean taking the 'plane to pieces and transporting it to the nearest workshop. For the time being the tanks were full and the 'plane was airworthy, although it only flew very slowly.

Michael therefore decided to go on to Nairobi, but first he flew over me and dropped a note. I was half asleep in the sun and did not even notice the broken leg.

The engine used up a lot of petrol, but when they reached Wilson Airport the tanks were still half full. Michael feared that a crash-landing would set the fuel alight and circled for half an hour to use it up. When he looked round at his passengers their faces were pale and serious. Below them people were playing tennis and water-skiing on the lake. How nice it would be to walk on the ground, not having to face a landing on one wheel. Hermann remembered the large battery of the cine-camera. It was filled with sulphuric acid and he threw it overboard in case it splashed over the passengers.

The half hour of circling seemed to last for ages. Michael had announced his arrival by radio and explained his difficulties. Ambulances, a couple of red fire-engines, and newspaper-men were waiting below.

The petrol was used up at last. Michael approached, glided across the tarmac and tilted the machine slightly to the right, the side with the unbroken leg. Then he rolled for a time, putting more and more weight on to the unbroken wheel. Finally, when the machine was moving very slowly, it slewed round and tilted over. The broken leg sheared off completely.

It was a wonderful landing.

The second leg remained whole and the wing was not even buckled. The fire-engines roared up and covered the whole "duck" with foam, despite Michael's protests.

Only afterwards did he and his passengers discover how much they had been affected. When interrogated by journalists, they found that they could not speak.

"Did you notice those four fresh graves in the cemetery while we were circling the aerodrome?" Michael asked them later.

They had all seen them, but no one had mentioned it.

Tsetse flies do not lay eggs but give birth to living larvae, which pupate soon afterwards.

A young tsetse fly emerging from the chrysalis.

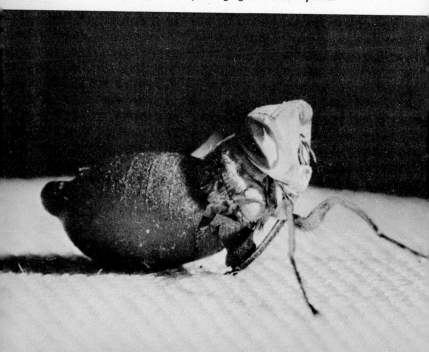

CHAPTER 15

Great Herds
on the Move

*A man who does not love nature is a disap-
pointment to me, I am liable to mistrust him.*
OTTO VON BISMARCK

I HAVE described running races with antelopes and how we played
with rhinos. I have introduced you to roaring ostriches and amo-
rous zebras, but so far I have not mentioned one of the most important creatures in the Serengeti. Its name is well known, I might
almost say notorious, but very few books about Africa describe it
in any detail. It is the only true friend the elephants and zebras
have left, for it makes their homeland uninhabitable for men.

I am referring to the tsetse fly.

It carries sleeping-sickness and the *nagana* disease of cattle.
The "corridor" in western Serengeti, where the large herds live
during the dry season, is infested by tsetse flies. If that were not
the case the area would be settled by natives or white farmers, or
the Masai would be grazing large herds of domestic cattle there.

Michael maintained that I had the skin of an elephant. When I
sat, shirtless, on the bonnet of the moving car he could often see
ten or fifteen bloodsucking tsetse flies on my back. I simply did
not notice them and never even suffered from itching bumps, so
completely used to them had I become.

If we drove through bushes or a river bed the inside of the car
was instantly filled with tsetse flies. They do not seem to hunt
their victim by smell, but will, I believe, attack any moving object
of appreciable size. This would explain their assault on the car.

Sometimes they surrounded us in swarms of over a hundred and fifty and they followed the car in droves.   If I walked twenty yards behind the car when it was moving they took no notice of me, as the vehicle looked larger and more promising.   They even went for the wheels as long as they were moving.

The tsetse fly is no larger than the European house fly, just as African mosquitoes are no bigger than those at home.   There are twenty different species of tsetse fly in Africa, and they occur nowhere else in the world.   They can easily be distinguished from all other flies.   Ordinary flies, including European house flies, point their wings diagonally outward in a slightly fan-shaped form when running or sitting.   A tsetse fly folds one wing over the other, like the blades of a pair of scissors.   You cannot mistake them for anything else.

If you have good eyesight, or use a magnifying glass, you can also see the butcher's cleaver on the wing of every tsetse fly.   It is formed by the veins of the wing, with the blade pointing to the leading edge.   The tsetse fly also has featherlike hairs on its antennae—but there is no need to grow more technical.   These flies are true Africans and do not feel at home anywhere else.   Twenty million years ago they also lived in America, but if any of them have been accidentally transported to Brazil by aeroplane they do not yet seem to have settled there.

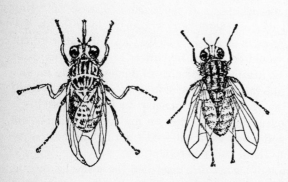

Tsetse fly   **House fly**   The cleaver on the wing of the tsetse fly.

When a swarm of these buzzing bloodsuckers entered the car, it was by no means easy to deal with them, for they are swift and persistent as well as tough. If they are merely swatted, like house flies, they may momentarily give up the fight because of broken legs or bent wings, but they will soon pull themselves together and start biting again. They must be properly caught and squashed between the forefinger and thumb till they crack. Mgabo, our driver, always insisted that they are not really dead until you have pulled their heads off.

Tsetse flies are not only far more bloodthirsty than lions and wild dogs, they are also more successful. Wild animals have to give way to men whenever settlers want to evict them from their homeland. It is easy enough to exterminate leopards, elephants, buffaloes and antelopes. But the tsetse fly does not surrender so easily. To wipe out this insect takes a great deal of intelligence and money.

With mosquitoes and most other flies only the females drink blood. The males live on fruit juice and other innocuous liquids. Both male and female tsetse flies drink blood, however, and have never been observed feeding on anything else. Small cutting teeth on the proboscis quickly penetrate the skin and soon pierce a minute blood vessel. This causes a small lake of blood to form just below the skin. The fly squirts saliva into it to prevent the blood from clotting. Then it begins to suck up the blood, and its shrunken stomach becomes visibly fuller and redder.

Many people do not know that a fly can be pregnant. Ordinary flies, and most other insects, lay large numbers of eggs which hatch out into larvae. Most of these die. The tsetse fly has a different method. After the male and female have paired, which may take up to five hours, the female is fertilised for the rest of her life. If a fertilised fly should stray into a region where there are no others she will still continue to produce fertile eggs for the remaining two hundred days of her life.

She produces eggs but does not lay them. A female tsetse fly will hatch out a single egg inside her own body and feed the larva through special glands, similar in function to the uterus in mammals. The young larva will then shed its skin three times inside the "womb" just as ordinary insect larvae do outside the bodies of their mothers.   Then the single larva is born as a whitish maggot, two-fifths of an inch long.

During the last few days before the birth the mother can no longer suck blood because there simply is no room for a meal.   She chooses shady, loose soil as a nursery and uses her own legs to act as midwife.   The larva burrows from sight within twenty minutes. Once inside the ground, the skin of the larva hardens into a brown pupa, and within thirty-five days the maggot inside the chrysalis changes into an adult fly.   When it is ready, the young fly opens the chrysalis by pushing at the lid with its head.   It even has a special blister on its forehead specifically for this purpose.   Once the young fly is free the blister disappears, probably because the air inside it helps to inflate the crumpled new wings.   A fertilised female can bear two or three children a month.

Nobody would make a fuss about the tsetse fly if nine species of it did not carry a dangerous disease.   Its swift flight and high-pitched buzz have meant death for untold numbers of men and animals.   When travel in Africa became easier at the end of the last century, the tsetse fly was transported into new regions.   Its bite transfers trypanosomes into the blood of its victim, little protozoons one five-hundredth of an inch long, which are the cause of sleeping-sickness.   Anyone stricken by the disease first suffers from a pain in the neck, followed by a fever and a swelling of the glands in the neck.   Finally the victim's brain is affected, his body wastes away and he dies of gradual mental degeneration.   Large areas of Africa were depopulated by this scourge, though now, thanks to modern drugs, it is no longer important in Africa.

The tsetse fly also transfers various trypanosomes to giraffes, antelopes, buffaloes, wart-hogs, hyenas and, indeed, to most other animals in Africa.   Wild animals are acclimatised to these trypanosomes and rarely die because of them, but European domestic animals such as cattle, horses, pigs and sheep quickly succumb to the *nagana* disease.   Many regions infested by the tsetse fly are therefore unsuitable for animal husbandry, and consequently for agriculture, since there is no manure to fertilise the soil.

These facts led to horribly drastic counter measures in Southern Rhodesia.   In the belief that it was too complicated and expensive to exterminate the tsetse flies by the methods successfully em-

The reedbuck lives in pairs in the bush and does not venture into the open plain.

ployed in other parts of Africa, and that if all wild animals were killed off the tsetse flies would die out with them, guns were distributed to the natives. Premiums were given for every dead animal, and all game in the area was systematically exterminated.

Since 1932 no less than 550,594 wild animals have been killed in this manner, excluding the many beasts wounded but not killed outright by inexperienced marksmen. Most of these animals also died but were not claimed for purposes of a reward. The last animal report I saw proudly announced that 36,552 animals had been killed; more than in any preceding year. This number included 3,219 baboons, 61 wild dogs, 35 hyenas, 19 leopards, 4 lions, 55 elephants, 8 rhinos, 312 zebras, 950 bush pigs, 4,503 wart-hogs, 377 buffaloes, 50 wildebeest, 301 waterbuck, 777 reedbuck, 1,357 sable antelopes, 306 roan antelopes, 291 elands, 4,937 kudus, 5 of the rare nyalas, 1,788 bushbuck, 2,219 impalas, 12,566 duikers, 1,037 klipspringers, 134 oribi and 1,206 oryx. All that within one year! This mass butchery occurred in a very distant corner of the globe, but when it became known it was greeted with horror and revulsion, not least in Rhodesia.

Those responsible for what was done do not seem to have tried to find out at first whether the tsetse fly could live on the blood of smaller inexterminable animals such as rodents, jackals and foxes once the big animals had been removed.   A large part of the area borders on the Portuguese colony of Mozambique.   Once it is cleared of game animals and tsetse flies, the land is supposed to be restocked with domestic cattle.   These beasts cannot be slaughtered should they be infected by insects from across the border.   Some areas of the Union of South Africa have been successfully cleared of the tsetse fly by aerial spraying with insecticides.   The Union has a splendid and famous Veterinary College and a good veterinary administration.   They suggested that aerial spraying should be tried in Rhodesia, but the experiment was carried out in the wrong season and was abandoned without a serious try.

The black hunters were paid by the head.   They did not waste time on killing the last few animals.   They were only interested in quantity and hunted where the game was relatively plentiful. This method will never clear the area of *all* game.   Nor were the hunters interested in tracking a wounded animal for hours in order to put it out of its misery.   As a result wounded elephants fled for long distances carrying tsetse flies into previously uncontaminated areas.

The scenes enacted were so gruesome that public revulsion against this mass butchery reached a high pitch.   The government of Southern Rhodesia ordered an official commission of inquiry which held open meetings and interrogated many witnesses.   The evidence was fairly and democratically published in a White Paper. This stated that the committee concerned with the fight against the tsetse fly had applied for its name to be changed, since it had acquired such an unfortunate reputation and that honest efforts would be made to fight the tsetse fly by better means.*

---

*The decades of massive slaughter, instigated by Mr. Chorley, had very little scientific justification. This is shown by the recent investigations of Dr. Weitz and Dr. Glasgow into the origin of the blood sucked by the tsetse flies in East Africa. These indicated that wart-hogs and bush pigs supplied up to 88 per cent of the blood. Buffaloes accounted for a further 5 per cent. Roan antelopes, kudus and bushbuck between them yielded another 15 per cent, while domestic cattle, sheep and goats were also bitten regularly. The most common grazing animals, such as hartebeests, topi antelopes, zebras and wildebeest, were not bitten at all and the tsetse flies rarely attacked elands, duikers, waterbuck, impalas, baboons, monkeys, dogs, cats, hyenas and birds. (*Oryx,* London, vol. 5, page 20, 1959.)

I preferred the tsetse flies in Banagi to the mosquitoes.   The flies at least rest at night, while the mosquitoes haunt the dark hours.   One insect inside the mosquito net can keep me awake for hours, because it will accompany its aerial manoeuvres by a high-pitched buzz.   Every third mosquito carries malarial parasites and 95 per cent of experimental animals bitten by an infected mosquito catch the disease.   Only one in twenty tsetse flies carries trypanosomes and an infected fly will transmit sleeping-sickness to only 10 per cent of the animals it bites.

The grass had been burning for days.   This is not as dangerous as it sounds, nor as exciting as the scenes shown on the cinema screen. Herds of game did not gallop past us in heedless flight, for the fire advanced slowly and could easily be avoided.   Where the grass was not high the flames could be stopped for two, four or even eight yards by merely trampling on them.   The front, however, was so broad that there was no chance of stopping the whole fire. As soon as the flames were quenched in one place they would spring up in another as the wind sparked off a new tuft of grass. I have never found that animals have an instinctive dread of fire, statements in books notwithstanding.   Lions go quite close to the flames and lie down in the warm ashes.   One night when we were sitting in deck chairs round a large camp fire in Banagi, lions walked past us less than twenty feet away.   They paid no attention either to us or to the flames.   Grass fires are only dangerous to small animals, insects and tortoises.   There are always birds close to the flaming front, catching the fleeing and scorched insects.

We were afraid that the wind might veer during the night and endanger our aeroplane.   We therefore lit the grass in a large circle all round it so that the fire would have no hold.   The thorny stockade we had erected to keep off hyenas and lions also caught fire, unfortunately, and the flames rose to nine or ten feet, fed by the dry branches.   We hurriedly opened the barbed wire gate, Michael jumped into the machine, started the motor and taxied our aeroplane outside.   We had to leave our poor "duck" unprotected in the open country.   When we returned a few hours later a lioness was lying in the shade of one wing.   The next morning we found the anchoring ropes had been chewed through by hyenas.

The hyrax lives on the isolated granite hills in the plains. Although only the size of a rabbit, it is related to the elephant.

Luckily they had left the rubber tyres alone.

Towards evening the fire began to climb up Banagi hill. Throughout the black night a flaming red band advanced across the whole width of it. Dead trees flamed like torches. We stood outside our tin hut and enjoyed a spectacle that the Serengeti stages but once a year. A small gust of wind caused a brighter glow from the burning trees, which looked like bizarre neon-lighted advertisements. No modern thoroughfare could compare in brightness to this burning wilderness.

Spectacular as they are, holocausts of this kind are really disastrous. The trees which they destroy do not grow thickly as in a forest, but are scattered as sparsely as in an orchard. Fire kills many of them each year and also singes the re-growth. The soil needs shade, for the sun sucks up the last traces of moisture during the dry season. It would cause sixty-seven inches of water to evaporate every twelve months, if that much water were present, while the sky provides only thirty-one-and-a-half inches of rain annually. If the rainfall were not concentrated within a few months (November, December and March to June) nothing could grow here at all. If Serengeti were covered by a lake five and a half feet deep the sun would evaporate it inside a year. Where last year's withered grass and the sparse shade of trees is lacking the soil grows increasingly drier with each passing decade.

One thing in our favour was that the burned, black plain enabled us to catch zebras by hand. We could see every stone and pothole which would otherwise have endangered our car. We caught wildebeest and tommies with the miracle gun, but zebras were too wary and did not permit us to get close enough. Luckily Gordon Poolman was an expert animal catcher. His experience taught us a lot, and once you knew how, the trick was easy.

As soon as we saw a herd of zebras we drove our car straight at them and split off a small group. These animals we then pursued, picking on one in particular. We overtook it by driving at about thirty miles an hour, not a very sporting effort. The zebra was running for all it was worth. Gordon stepped on the accelerator and within three to five minutes the zebra was growing short of breath, starting to pant and to run more slowly. We tried to get alongside and drive parallel to it.

Sometimes we encountered a very irascible beast which tried to bite the car. Others attempted to escape sideways. Since we could not take sharp bends, we always had two cars, one behind the other. The one in the rear could then head off the zebra and prevent its escape.

After no more than five minutes we would lean out of the car

Who will be the first to grab the tail of the zebra? Michael is in the back seat.

A zebra is provided with a brightly-colored, featherweight, plastic collar.

and catch the zebra by the tail. If this did not succeed or the hunt went on too long, there was a risk that the animal would die of heart failure. Rather than allow this to happen, we would let the zebra escape and chase another instead; there were always plenty of them around.

The animal had to be caught at the right spot first time, close to the root of the tail. If the tail slipped through your fingers the sharp hairs cut the palm. If the zebra had defecated recently it was no use trying, for its tail was too slippery. Once the tail had been gripped the car was slowed down while one or two men inside clung to the zebra until it had to stand still perforce. At that moment the others jumped from the car. One held both ears while another man put an arm round its neck and with his other hand gripped the lower jaw behind the incisors, the spot where animals of the horse family have no teeth at all.

It was nearly always Gordon who performed this trick, for he knew the right grip. Zebras and horses can inflict dreadful bites. Their incisors do not have sharp edges like the teeth of cats and dogs, but flat grinding surfaces. Their teeth bruise and crush bones.

A zebra's teeth are the only dangerous part of it, for luckily it never lashes out with its hooves. Every plough-man and rider learns to beware of both the hind and front legs of horses. They like rearing up on their hind legs and kicking, but our zebras never did, though it is true that they may have been too tired from the chase.

A zebra is released after having a featherweight collar fitted.

Like most of the large antelopes the kongoni, a type of harbebeest, has a maximum speed of barely thirty miles an hour.

A cheetah at full speed. They are believed to be the fastest mammals on earth.

One morning we caught four or five zebras and fitted them with ear-tags and coloured collars. I took the opportunity to look at the speedometer of the car and check the speed of various animals. Zebras gallop at 30 m.p.h. without going full out. A large eland bull ran at 35, a Thomson's gazelle at 37, a hyena at 25, and an ostrich at 29 as did a Grant gazelle, although this animal can also run at 35 for a short period. I could not confirm the alleged high speed of cheetahs. We met one that achieved only 29 m.p.h. and lay down exhausted after a few hundred yards. Cheetahs are reputed to be the fastest animals on earth so I did not pursue it harder in case it was ill.

Another which I met a few days later escaped at only 30 m.p.h. into a small copse by the river bed before I could test it at higher speeds. I do not believe that this can be "top gear" for cheetahs, for their common prey, the Thomson's gazelle, can achieve 37 m.p.h. and perhaps even more when fleeing for its life. If they could not run faster than their prey cheetahs would have a lean existence.

Michael naturally wanted to handle zebras by gripping them round the neck and jaw, too. Equally naturally, I protested.

"Gordon does it splendidly, nobody else could do it so well. Why do you have to try? Didn't you have enough trouble with catching zebras last time?"

I did not enjoy my role of clucking, motherly hen, but this was really nonsense. Michael would be clamouring to train lions next.

Then I remembered that when I was his age I *had* trained tigers and walked the high wire just for fun. Suddenly I was ashamed and felt like a member of the crotchety older generation. I made no further objections and let him have his way.

A fat mare caught his thumb and bit it to the bone.

Michael was so furious that he did not feel any pain at first, while I put sticking-plaster on the wound. After an hour the pain began. Towards evening it grew worse and we bathed the hand in soapy water. I then gave him a penicillin injection and by the next morning the pain had almost gone.

The fat mare remembered the encounter, too. She now had a gleaming yellow collar. After that she and four or five other zebras, possibly relations of hers, started to run if they saw our car more than a mile away.

Gordon helped us a great deal. Some months before we had spent a whole night trying to dazzle gazelles with the headlamps of our car and then catching them by hand. I had rarely been so active in my life. I ran through thorny bushes and over broken ground, taking care not to step on a lion, and bearing in mind that I had to keep near the car so as not to be left behind. The gazelles were only dazzled for a short while and then escaped; we did not catch a single one.

This method should have been practicable, for while we were watching over our narcotised gun all through one night, a number of Thomson's and Grant's gazelles entered the beam of the headlamps almost voluntarily and followed it to the car. Then we remembered that there was a new moon that night and that it had been pitch dark.

We repeated our gazelle hunt during the next new moon. This time we were successful and caught twenty gazelles in a single night. They were ear-tagged and provided with collars.

"There is a best method for catching each type of animal," said Gordon. "The oryx antelopes, for example, try to spit you with their straight needle-sharp horns. If you grip one of the horns in your hand they will suddenly stand stock-still and you can do anything you like with them."

We marked increasing numbers of animals, and our knowledge concerning the migration of the large herds of the Serengeti grew more complete. This knowledge, however, did nothing to lighten our hearts.

The government was determined to cut the National Park through the middle.

This decision was based on the belief, held for decades, that the herds of gazelles, zebras and wildebeest which graze in the narrow, low-lying "corridor" to the east of Lake Victoria only march up to the central line and do not cross to the east of it during the rains (December and January). On either side of the theoretical dividing line lie the large, open, treeless gently undulating plains of Serengeti. They are covered by nothing but grass and during the dry months they are yellow, brown, waterless and deserted.

During a new moon we simply caught Thomson's gazelles by blinding them with a torch.

As soon as the rains start the grassland grows green almost before your eyes. Little ponds collect in shallow depressions and animal flocks concentrate from all directions to these water-holes. At that time the plains are speckled with hundreds of thousands of gazelles, wildebeest and zebras.

It was believed that the herds found on the east side of the demarcation line during the wet season had come from the Ngorongoro crater (cf. illustration on page 240). This opinion was accepted by the government. The herds from the "corridor" and "Ngorongoro" were supposed to meet in the centre of the great open plains.

We made many, many flights. We counted the herds and followed them by 'plane. We looked for zebras and wildebeest with collars and noted where we saw them again. We found that the true facts differed considerably from this theory.

A large part of the herds, more than half perhaps, does move westward into the "corridor" region in June when the rains are over, but others move due north, right outside the borders of the Park, and slightly to the west of the new portion which is to be added to compensate for the loss of the eastern section. Other herds from the "corridor" migrate north of it during the dry season and later return to it.

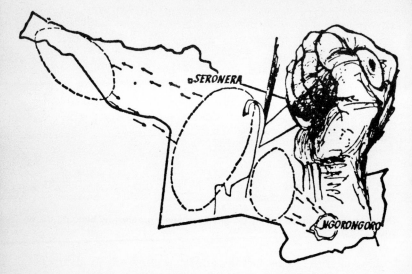

This is how the large herds were supposed to move.

The great rains start in October. They begin in the north and then the cloudbursts move southward at a rate of twelve miles a day. It was Banagi's turn to-day, and by to-morrow afternoon the witches' cauldron would be brewing over Seronera. The black, burned plains greedily sucked up the water and gradually turned green.

Now the armies of animals started to move. They moved eastward, through the valleys between the hills and poured into the open plains. The animals marched in Indian file and did not move haphazardly over the grass. They followed well defined trails, which might almost be mistaken for man-made paths. From the air we could easily recognise the wildebeest as strings of black beads, and the zebras looked much the same. Even when no animals were visible on the plains one could see the persistent trails and deduce the main direction of the migration. All paths from the south, for instance, converged towards the Olduvai Gorge, which runs from east to west across the plains. The trails followed the southern edge and grew denser until they all crossed the gorge at a shallow point. On the northern rim the trails fanned out again across the whole plain. This indicated that the animals always moved up from the south and never in the opposite direction. On the northern edge there was no network of trails because the herds were not looking for a point at which to cross.

Zebras, wildebeest and Thomson's gazelles are grazing animals and have to spend many hours a day feeding. During this time they do not move in Indian file but spread out. Zebras and wildebeest follow the same paths at the same time but rarely intermingle completely. Frequently, but by no means always, we saw a group of zebras at the head of a column of wildebeest. Even when they

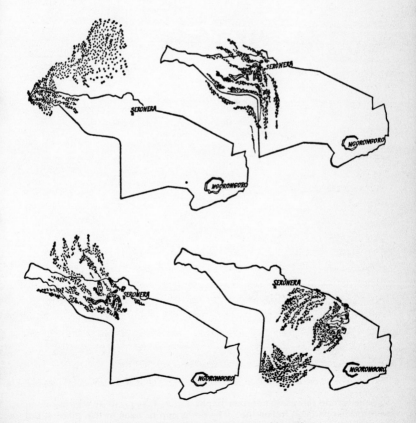

This is how the large herds move in reality.

Wildebeest and zebras do not roam haphazardly; they prefer to migrate along well-trodden paths in Indian file. The paths can be seen in this picture, but the animals are running in all directions because of the aeroplane.

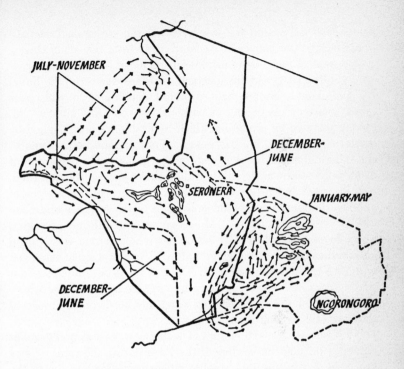

Dotted line: old boundary. Unbroken line: new boundary as of 1959. Arrows: migratory route.

mixed during the actual grazing the zebras remained in distinct groups. They were alert and readier to take flight.

Hyenas, jackals and lions followed the great herds across the plains. When the antelopes and zebras dispersed to graze, the hyenas ran amongst them without causing much excitement. We noticed, and filmed, two hyenas who persistently chased and killed a young wildebeest calf, only a few months old, right among a herd of scattered wildebeest. The big wildebeest hardly noticed the tragedy in their midst.

Towards the end of January we saw a large herd of wildebeest marching past our car. We noticed a plover right in their centre, and saw that the agitated bird was constantly opening and closing its wings. Although surrounded by the big wildebeest and hidden by a cloud of dust, the bird did not take to the air. When all the wildebeest had passed we observed that the plover had successfully diverted the hooves of the herd away from two small chicks.

The sight of those large armies on the move is awe-inspiring.

A hundred years ago this spectacle could be seen on all the broad African plains. Nature had sprinkled millions of animals over them, a vast variety of species with stripes, spots and antlers. Although pursued by predators, killed by pestilence and plagued by decades of drought, life continued. Tens of thousands of moist, shivering babies lay in the fresh, green grass at the beginning of every rainy season and tried their thin, shaky legs for the first time.

A hundred and fifty years ago gigantic herds of other types of animals thundered across the prairies of North America and Canada in similar abundance. Much earlier still Europe presented a similar picture. That was life on earth before man was fruitful and multiplied and "subjugated nature". In the years to come you will have to fly to the Serengeti if you want to see the splendour that was nature, before God gave it to man to keep and cherish.

That will be the only place to watch big herds on the move, *if* they are still moving then.

We observed that the masses of wildebeest, zebras and gazelles circle far outside the borders of the Park during the rains. They graze the newly sprouted grass to an easterly direction, up to the foothills of the Highlands of the Giant Craters. Then they move northwards (constantly outside the planned new borders) before turning south again and returning, partly inside and partly outside the boundaries. In the meantime the grass on which they have grazed has grown once more and they begin the circuit all over again, repeating it several times during a single rainy season.

During several months of the year the new Serengeti Park will therefore contain no zebras and wildebeest and hardly any Thomson's gazelles. The 367,000 animals have to migrate across the borders to graze outside it, yet the whole object of creating the Serengeti National Park was so that the last remaining great herds of grassland animals in Africa should be protected within its borders all the year round.

The most beautiful scenic part of the Park will be taken away, namely the Crater Highlands, with the marvel of Ngorongoro, but also the famous Olduvai Gorge, which harbours the remnants of primeval man.   On top of this despoliation the remaining portion of the Park will not be sufficient to maintain the existing herds.

Our laborious investigation had certainly unearthed a sorry state of affairs.

Migrating wildebeest.

CHAPTER 16

Serengeti
Shall Not Die

*I do not know how God will judge my handi-
work. During the last three weeks I have
written more than fifty pages of the score of
Parsifal and saved three young dogs from
death. We still have to wait and see which
lies heavier in the scales.*

RICHARD WAGNER

WE HAD now established that the huge herds of wildebeest, zebras
and gazelles live outside the new borders of the Serengeti National
Park for a large part of every year. We also knew what paths
they take during their migration, but we did not know *why* they
follow these particular tracks.

Perhaps one day in the future the new Park could be fenced in.
Then the animals would have to remain inside it. They would be
protected from the settlers near the Park and prevented from dying of hunger and thirst when all the timber around their water
holes had been felled and their pastures are over-grazed by native
cattle. But would even that be successful? Do the animals leave
the Park at a mere whim or because of age-old instinct, or do they
migrate because of overwhelming necessity?

The herds do not graze the grass of the plains evenly like a lawn
mower. In some places it remains hip-high and the wildebeest
move through it without tasting it. Elsewhere the grass is as
closely cropped as a carpet while in other areas you find tufts of
long grass left undisturbed in otherwise smoothly cropped pasture.

The grass (Pennistum mezia-num) is not eaten by the animals. It grows almost exclusively inside the new borders of the Park.

Most of the grasses bloom during the rainy season and some of them—*Themeda triandra,* for instance—give the plains a coloured sheen with their countless, brownish flowering stalks. This sheen can only be seen when the observer is close to the ground. Flying over the plain to trace the extent of the flowering area we could see no colours at all. It was all a matter of the angle of vision.

For this reason we flew as close to the ground as possible, only thirty to sixty feet up, and at minimum speed (about thirty-five miles per hour). It was hard work for our trusty "flying zebra", which must have thought we wanted it to walk instead of fly. We would suddenly push the control stick forward at all sorts of possible and impossible places above the plains, point its nose to the ground, and force it to roll over uneven ground, among bumps and grass hummocks, stones and ruts.

As soon as the grass seemed to change colour we landed. It would take months or even years to visit all these spots by car, for the grass only flowers during the rains when the plains are virtually impassable to motorised transport.

Samwel Paulo, the African assistant from the East African Herbarium at Nairobi, accompanied us. After every landing we inspected a circle of about three hundred yards' radius and noted which types of grass were most frequent and which types had been most commonly eaten. We also collected plants and stuck them on blotting-paper. Paulo then placed them in the press which we carried with us in the "duck". Despite the rainy season the sun shone for at least a few hours every day, and during that time the plants were laid out to dry on the granite rocks at Banagi. These rocks absorb heat quickly, so that our material was rapidly dried on both sides.

We were not trying to make a complete collection of all plants to be found in Serengeti. We were only concerned with the grasses and other fodder plants, but even these already numbered more than one hundred and sixty. We also filled small linen bags with local soils and sent them to the Agricultural Institute at Darmstadt. This would tell us the nutrient value of the soil. In addition, we sent samples of hay for investigations of the nutritive value.

All the lists of hundreds of Latin names of plants and grasses clearly showed one thing: the herds migrated to areas where their favourite food was available. The only plants growing in the places which the wildebeest and zebras avoided had little food-value, and the animals refused to touch them. The nutritious plants only grow on special soils, and their protein content is equal to that of average European hay.

Since time immemorial wildebeest and zebras have practised what modern cattle breeders have only learned during the last few decades. Modern textbooks on agriculture stress that the

Michael and a botanist collecting the grasses on which the wild herds feed.

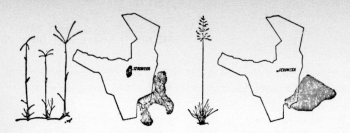

The favourite fodder grasses *Cynodon dactylon* (left) and *Sporobolus marginatus* (right) which flourish mostly outside the new borders. The shaded areas show their distribution.

farmer should not let his grass grow too high. Long grass gives full barns but thin cattle. Tall grass is woody and contains much indigestible fibre, but short grass has a high protein content. An intelligent farmer divides a large pasture into several smaller ones and lets the cattle and horses graze on them in turn. In that way they can eat young, tender grass all the time.

The large herds in the Serengeti behave in precisely this way during the rainy season. As long as the fodder grasses are sprouting they wander along a circular route. As soon as the cropped grass has regrown by one or two inches they return and graze it once more. That is why the zebras always look so round and well fed.

Not all grassy plains are of equal value. You cannot simply cut off a portion of the Serengeti Park and add an equal number of square miles to the north of it. There is a very good reason why

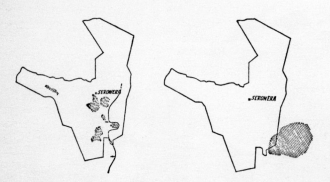

The distribution of the spurned grass *Themeda triandva* (left) and the nourishing sedge *Kyllinga nervosa* (right) inside and outside the new borders of the Serengeti National Park.

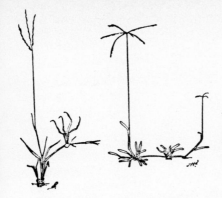

Two other favourite grasses, *Digitaria macroblephara* (left) and *Chloris pycnothrix* (right) which grow predominantly outside the new borders.

the herds prefer the heart of this famous region: they know what is good for them.

While hopping about and collecting plants we once saw a large flock of vultures on a tree-fringed plain. As the aeroplane touched down clouds of these birds took to the air and settled in the trees. They had been feeding on a zebra killed by a poacher's snare. The animal had pulled up the tree to which the snare was anchored, but the wire had cut through its skin, causing the whole neck to suppurate. Poor beast! It had not been dead for long, as the vultures had not even hacked through the stomach wall.

Only a few hundred yards away from where we had just landed, we could see a whole family of lions, one male, five cubs and two or three lionesses, lying in the shady bushes. They were certain to take an interest in the dead zebra. We wanted to film them, together with our aeroplane, so as to convince Doubting Thomases at home how little notice the lions of the Serengeti take of man or his machines. One lioness, a mother with children, approached the carcase first. She hesitated a little on seeing our striped 'plane, but the cubs were greedy and ran up to the dead zebra although it lay practically under one of our wings. After a while, the father followed their example with the remaining children gambolling around him. The other lionesses brought up the rear and the carcase was soon dismembered. The lion tore huge chunks of meat from the hindquarters. Soon all the family had red, blood-smeared faces.

The lions of Serengeti are completely unafraid of cars and aeroplanes.

When we started the engine and the motor sprang to life with a roar, the lions merely retreated a few steps and stared at this thundering interloper. We taxied for fifty yards and then resumed our watch. The paterfamilias was the first to be sated. He went back to the bushes and plopped down in the shade. Soon afterwards the others, including the cubs, followed him. When all the family were resting in the shade the vultures carefully advanced again, and the remnants of the zebra disappeared under a cloud of grey-brown scavengers.

This was too much for one of the lionesses. She trotted from the bushes and the vultures made off. One of them was too slow, however, and received a swipe that filled the air with feathers. Despite this the bird managed to get away. The lions did not seem to object to jackals, on the other hand, because two of them were tugging away at one end of the zebra while the lioness was feeding on the central portion.

We took off and flew towards two curious structures which we had intended to visit for a long time.

These were two greyish-black dunes in the middle of the plain. They were fifteen to twenty feet high and the wind drove the sand up the slope until the grains toppled steeply down the other side after reaching the sharp ridge at the top. These uncanny black sand-dunes move forward about twenty-five yards every year, burying all the small animals on their path. In the full course of time withered giant beetles and desiccated balls of dung containing half-grown dung beetles reappear at the trailing edge. The sun heated the sand to such a temperature that Michael bet me I could not place my palm on it and count to ten. I lost that bet.

If you look down from an aeroplane you can see the tracks which many dozens of these wandering dunes have left in this part of Serengeti. The grass clearly shows the directions in which they moved. The wind moving these dunes changes course when approaching a hill, so the dunes, like a company of soldiers hearing the command "Right wheel!", do likewise and turn.

The Serengeti is so level at this spot that you feel you could close your eyes and walk straight ahead for hours without meeting any obstacle, except perhaps a foxhole or the skull of a wildebeest. In fact if you tried to do anything of the kind, you would suddenly hurtle down three hundred feet within ten minutes of leaving the wandering dunes. A steep gorge suddenly appears, as if cut by scissors in a sheet of paper. It is called the Olduvai Gorge, which in the Masai language means a place where a type of wild sisal grows. This name has hit the headlines of newspapers all over the world.

During a past, wetter era the ground under our feet was covered by a huge lake, which for a few millennia shrank and expanded, according to the rainfalls. Later on surrounding volcanoes sprayed ashes and lava into it and on to its shores. All animal life was asphyxiated. This spewed-up matter settled where it fell and five sharply defined and variously coloured layers were deposited on the basic volcanic rock. You need not dig to observe these layers, since the waters which cut the Olduvai Gorge right down to the bottom exposed them as distinctly as the layers of a Neapolitan ice cream.

During the dry season only a trickle of water flows through the gorge. In 1911, Professor Kattwinkel found fossils of prehistoric mammals there and the Geological Institutes of Berlin and Munich co-operated two years later to send Dr. Hans Reck with a party of fifty bearers and workers to make further investigations. It took him some time to find the place in the almost uncharted wilderness where his predecessor had worked, and then, for weeks, his African helpers scraped through the soil. Gigántic and brittle bones were unearthed, fixed with resin and linen strips, and carefully packed.

Millions of years ago Serengeti was inhabited by many curious creatures. Giraffes with antlers, elephants with downward-pointing tusks in their lower jaws, a small horse that had three toes instead of the single toe of present-day zebras, and a hippopotamus with eyes so high above its head that they seemed to be mounted on telescopes.

"What fate and what events could have assembled the remains of so many animals in one spot?" wrote Dr. Reck at the time. "It cannot have been a herd, for almost every skull belongs to a different type of animal, and yet a great number of animals found death here together."

I discovered one of the answers to his question. A year ago Gordon Harvey and Myles Turner found more than fifty wildebeest with broken legs in the branches of the trees at the escarpment of the cliffs of Olduvai Gorge. A tremendous cloud-burst had flooded the plains and swept a whole herd over the edge. I would not like to have been camping down below at that moment.

One evening Dr. Reck's black assistant, Manjonga, came to his tent and said: "*Bwana,* we have found something which we have not seen before. I believe it is an Arab. He lies there on his side, sleeping. A little piece of bone showed above the surface by the bushes of that slope over there. When I scratched with my knife other pieces appeared until it began to look like a head. Then

Bakari and I uncovered the bones, until we noticed that it was not an animal. The skull is just like that of a man. We left it there and built a hut above it so that the rain should not spoil the bones."

Dr. Reck hurried to the spot in excited anticipation. They had really found a man.

"It is impossible to describe my feelings at this sight," recalled Dr. Reck. "They were a wild mixture of joy, hope, scepticism, caution and eagerness.

"One thing was immediately apparent: if this skeleton was contemporary with the extinct animal world of Olduvai, this find was of tremendous importance to anthropologists. It would not only be the oldest man in Africa, but one of the oldest in the whole world. Nebulous possibilities about the cradle of mankind rose before me."

Fully conscious of his enormous scientific responsibility, Reck preserved the skeleton and the whole block of earth in which it was lying, and took it to Berlin. When the find was shown at a scientific demonstration open to the public it aroused great excitement, and not in the scientific world alone.

The skeleton had been found in the same layer which contained fossil bones of animals long extinct. It was that of a proper man, not of a hominoid or a man with apelike characteristics, such as were later discovered elsewhere in Africa. Nobody had suspected that real men lived at such an early time. The prehistoric man of the Olduvai Gorge was therefore regarded as anti-evolutionary evidence, although all previous finds and excavations had confirmed Darwin's theory.

It took a long time for this riddle to be solved. During his second expedition to East Africa Dr. Reck was called to the colours and became a prisoner of war in Egypt. Seventeen years later an outstanding British anthropologist again tackled the riddle of Olduvai Gorge. This was Dr. L. S. B. Leakey, Curator of the Coryndon Memorial Museum at Nairobi. Justly and fairly he invited Dr. Reck to be joint leader of the expedition at British expense. The truth was discovered. The skeleton had slipped down into an older, lower layer and was of much more recent date than the prehistoric animal bones. At the same time they found stone tools, fashioned by human hands, throughout all the strata.   There were primitive hand axes in the lowest layer and proper knives and axes in the upper one.   Nowadays the Olduvai Gorge is considered the best place to study the gradual development of human skills in Africa, Southern Europe, and parts of Asia throughout the tens of thousands of years of the Stone Age.   On the 17th July 1959, Leakey at last found the relics of a "Nutcracker-man", 600,000 years old, with unusually strong teeth, who comes between the South African ape man and modern man.

The Olduvai Gorge, like the Ngorongoro crater, is, according to present decisions, no longer under the protection of the Serengeti National Park in future.

We packed a sled into our "duck" and flew towards Lake Natron. Our direction was straight towards L'Engai, the "mountain of God", which loomed threateningly above us.   L'Engai, with its tremendously steep sides, is a young volcano shaped like a sugar loaf. During the past few decades there have been some eruptions and there are large white areas round the apex.   These are not due to snow, as on Kilimanjaro, but are caused by the spewed-up salt slurry.

Our aeroplane climbed higher, until we were over the open crater on top.   I wanted to take some photographs.   The walls are so steep that they seemed unscalable, but in 1906–7 Professor Fritz Jaeger made a descent into the crater.   This excellent geographer covered all this region of the giant craters on foot and made a map of it which has hardly been excelled to this day.   The professor now lives in Zurich and it was he who had asked me for photographs.

We flew straight across the crater and even a little downward into it.   There was no smoke, but the small, central hole was bubbling and heaving.   From the outside of the crater vitrified streams of lava swept steeply downwards for 4,000 feet into Lake Natron. This lake was our target, an enormous basin coloured pink and blue, forty miles long and thirteen miles wide.   The red was due to solid salt crusts and the blue was caused by the reflection of the sky in the two lagoons of open water.

Last January we counted the flamingoes on the lake, for it is one of the few large breeding places in the world.   We could not count them in the same way as we did the quadrupeds, for they took to the air when the aeroplane was still five hundred yards away. They evaded us sideways and showed such aerobatic skill that we could not get nearer than three hundred feet at either maximum or minimum air speed. We also avoided worrying them unduly, for if they are repeatedly disturbed during the nesting time the entire season's brood may be spoiled.

To avoid this we placed an aerial camera taking an eighteen centimetre (7 inch) film into our "duck". A hole had been made in the floor and I straddled this to remove the covering lid. I could then see the ground 3,000 feet below between my legs— a sensation which takes some getting used to. The hefty camera

We could not count the flamingoes on Lake Natron directly. We had to take a series of large photographs.

was placed over the opening and then automatically took a series of one hundred and twenty large photographs. Each photograph slightly overlapped the next, so that they could be pieced together later to give an overall picture. The aeroplane had to be kept on a dead level and straight course during all this time.

We flew at 2,600 feet. The camera did not fit perfectly into the hole, which was situated behind the exhaust. This meant that the cabin became filled with fumes and I had to resort to a paper bag. Since exhaust gases can cause serious poisoning we landed quickly and adjusted the camera so that it made an air-tight joint. After that we took a full series of pictures in thirty-five minutes.

We spent many days in Frankfurt counting the birds on the photographs, helped by graticules and magnifying glasses. We pinned the whole series of pictures on the wall until we could see a miniature reproduction of the lake. The overall picture showed 163,679 birds.

We had flown across Lake Natron from time to time throughout the year. During March and April the bird population was only one-twentieth of what it had been in January. Later in the year the number increased again, but the flocks were always greatest in winter. Flamingoes are great travellers. They visit all types of salt lakes when the worms, bacterial sludge and algae are at their maximum. These splendid, pink birds are said to go as far afield as India, but nobody knows a great deal about their migrations. It is hardly possible to ring these birds, and to recover the rings when they are dead. The flat, salty shores have no cover, such as trees or bushes, and when you approach the conical clay nests the adults fly off when you are still a thousand yards away and the chicks take to the open water.

Despite this we wanted some shots of flamingoes for the film which Michael and I were, incidentally, making of the wild life in the Serengeti. The slender, pale-pink birds with their black wings stood out against the deep blue water of the lake. Michael and I had worked out a plan of campaign to get these photographs. We landed our 'plane on a flat, white salt-bed at the edge of the lake. Through field-glasses we could see the far, far distant mirror of water, and somewhere in front of it some indistinct birds on very long legs. Michael wanted to take our heavy camera equipment, including the cine-camera with a tele-photo lens, blankets and provisions, over to where open water began, and to spend the night out there, starting to film the birds next morning. We had had an aluminium sled specially made for us in Nairobi, but this load was too much for the thin runners, which sank through the salty crust into the sludge underneath.

I went out first to look for a trail. To do this I took a bearing on a mountain opposite and walked straight towards the centre of the lake. I crossed some buffalo tracks, so I knew that the ground was solid enough to bear my weight. At certain spots the water had not evaporated completely, so that the subsoil was still soft, and I sank in up to my ankles. I nearly lost my shoes. This could have been dangerous, for if the salty slurry is allowed to dry it corrodes the skin, and there was no fresh water anywhere near with which to wash it off.

I marched on. The line of birds on stilt-like legs turned out to be buffalo tracks. Each footprint looked like the body of a bird at a distance and the legs below it were created by a mirage. When I turned around I could see a similar line of "birds" behind me.

After walking for exactly one hour, or about four miles, the water seemed no nearer than when I had started, which was also due to a mirage. From the aeroplane the distance had seemed much shorter.

I turned around and retraced my steps. The aeroplane on the shore was no longer recognisable and the heat was oppressive. The lake lies only 2,000 feet above sea-level and is surrounded by high mountains. I was wearing a hat for once, but the white sheets of salt reflected the sunlight at me from below. I felt myself being sunburned under my chin and on my face despite the hat. When I regained the shore I felt parched and limp.

In the meantime three Masai had arrived, and Michael was already negotiating with them. They did not want cigarettes but drank large quantities of water from the tank we carried on special occasions. Our aeroplane seemed to interest them, for they asked where the eyes and ears of our bird were situated. They told us that a Masai lad had been attacked and killed by a buffalo the day before. I never believe such tales unless I see the corpse.

Buffaloes and elands are the only wild animals that the Masai will kill and eat. Since buffaloes were protected in this region the tale of the accident may have been an excuse in case we discovered that they had killed one.

Michael and I suggested to the Masai that they should transport our luggage farther into the lake on donkeys. The debate that followed laster over two-and-a-half hours and we had to counter the following arguments: If the donkeys were fetched to-day the Masai could not return to their *boma* that night since they might meet lions in the darkness. If they stayed with us over night the women and children would be alone and unprotected. The donkeys were not accustomed to walking on salt, their legs might get inflamed and they might die. If they died each one would cost two hundred shillings and we would also have to pay that price if one fell ill. They were prepared to fetch the donkeys if we would fly them back to the *boma* before nightfall, in which case we would not have to pay anything at all. Our luggage might be too heavy for the donkeys so they would have to open all the boxes and inspect them. If they stayed the night they would not have enough to eat, and so on and so on.

The three warriors, who were no longer allowed to make war or go on cattle raids, were delighted to have found some diversion. They enjoyed their conversation with Europeans and prolonged it endlessly to get its full flavour. When one excuse after another had been countered they would go back to the first one all over again. I told Michael in German not to continue the argument. We no longer answered them but talked to each other in our own language.

Our refusal to answer paid dividends. The three *morans* rose, shook our hands, picked up their long spears and departed. After an hour they were back with three donkeys, packed our belongings on to two beasts, loaded the rest on the sled which was pulled by the third donkey and set off across the salt.

After travelling for only fifty yards one of the donkeys decided to return to the *boma* and trotted away. The second, which was harnessed to the sled, galloped after it. Within seconds all our property was scattered about on the salt plain and our precious telephoto-lens had fallen from its case into the saline mud.

The donkeys of the Masai bucked and threw off all our equipment.   Little did we know that before sunrise we would gladly have kissed their tails.

The sun was already low over the horizon and Michael decided to camp at the edge of the dried-out portion of the lake and not in the centre.   We cursed the donkeys for their bad behaviour, little knowing that we would willingly have kissed their tails before the next sunrise.

Leaving our "flying zebra" where it was, we spread our only mosquito net over the camera tripod and put our heads in the centre and stretched out, my legs pointing to the south and Michael's to the north.   Our heads, chests and arms were under the tripod, with the rest of our bodies and our legs protected by blankets.   I felt very proud of my ingenuity.

By half-past eight it was completely dark. The wind had died down, the air grew close and the mosquitoes decided on a mass attack. One or two of them always managed to slip under the edge of the net, and when we hunted for them the whole precarious structure shook. After half an hour of this Michael cursed and retired into the aeroplane where he closed all the windows. This was too hot for me and I remained where I was, lying on my back, looking at the stars.

I do not know much about astronomy and could not find the famous Southern Cross, mentioned in all books about the tropics. In the distance summer lightning was playing near L'Engai, but I did not worry because we were in the dry season after all. The sputnik was circling the sky above the equator and was said to be visible to the naked eye.

Clouds drifted across the sky. A hyena howled quite close to us and a lion roared. Although everything seemed deserted during the daytime, there were animals in the vicinity. It seemed as if the roaring lion was only a hundred feet away, but I knew that this was only an illusion caused by darkness and loneliness.

Soon the sky was two-thirds overcast and only in the north were the stars still visible. The summer lightning had changed to real lightning and thunder. A strong wind had sprung up and blown away all the mosquitoes. I began to get worried. If it rained, the dried-out lake bed beneath us would turn into a quagmire and our aeroplane would sink into it, perhaps irretrievably. I ran to the 'plane and woke up Michael, who grasped the situation at once.

He started the engine but found it impossible to turn the machine. The wind had grown stronger and the first rain-drops began to fall. He could taxi the 'plane into the wind when on full throttle, but as soon as he pointed the nose towards the gently-sloping shore the raging gale caught the tailplane and whipped it back.

In the meantime a cloudburst had started and we realised our danger. I groped my way along the body of the 'plane, helped by occasional flashes of blinding lightning, found the rudder and leaned against it with all my might. The ground had become slippery, my sandals were lost in the salty mud and I gripped the ground with my bare toes as best I could. The 250 horse-power engine pulled the tail over me so that I landed flat on my face in the doughy soil. I clung to the tail and pulled myself upright again. Finally the almost water-logged machine was slowly turned in the right direction, climbed up the slight incline and finally came to rest on sandy soil sparsely covered by tufts of grass.

Michael switched on the cabin lights and the spotlight on the right wing, which unfortunately pointed forwards. In the pitch darkness we groped our way back to our equipment and loaded it on to the 'plane, pitching it in through the windows. We were soaked to the skin, but luckily this washed off the salty crust left on me by my fall in the mud.

The thunderstorm and downpour grew so fierce that we had to abandon the rest of our belongings, which were thoroughly soaked by this time in any case. We crept into the cabin and sat in the pilots' seats.

Our clothes were dripping, and as it had grown noticeably cooler we took off our shirts and trousers, preferring to sit there naked. The storm raged outside, and I noticed that the wind tried to lift the machine by its wings. Luckily it did not succeed. The wheels were locked and we had placed chests behind them to act as chocks.

We donned our half-wet sheepskin jackets and waited. The rain seeped through the roof and I put on my old hat. Outside, one streak of lightning followed another. Our aeroplane stood on the slightly raised shore beside the broad, flat lake, the only metal object far and near.

"According to all the rules we *must* be struck by lightning," I told Michael, "and I would not be surprised if it should happen at any moment." "So what?" he replied. "There's nothing we can do about it but wait." He was quite right.

It was a beautiful thunderstorm. I counted the seconds between lightning and thunder and found that they were increasing. The centre of the storm had passed, but the rain still poured down in buckets. The flashes of lightning showed that the whole lake had filled with water. I shuddered as I thought of our fate if the donkeys had not obstinately made tracks for home. We would now have been sitting six miles inside the lake with all our luggage, with the salty water rising to our waists. There would have been little hope of reaching the shore across the muddy bottom.

Donkeys must be very sagacious animals.

"When we get home in ten days' time people will say: 'How was it, did you have a nice holiday?'" said Michael. "Incidentally, all our sweated labour would come to nothing if we should both kick the bucket now," he added, "for nobody else will finish our job. That would be a tactical error; one of us has to survive."

The storm had started shortly before midnight, and by two o'clock the weather had begun to ease off. Michael had fallen asleep leaning against me, with his head on my shoulder. His hair had fallen forward and was tickling my neck. It was thick and unruly and tended to fall over his eyes. Would it ever become as thin and sparse as mine? His naked thighs glowed in the dark; they were still slender and youthful.

He looked young and handsome. It seemed a pity that he would have to grow older and more wrinkled year by year, until he resembled me. All human life is a gradual decay once you have passed twenty, but you only begin to realise this when you yourself are over forty. What would Michael look like when he reached my age? One thing was certain: he would never grow fat, for he was far too active and ate too little.

My own father died when I was three years old. Our mother told us that he never really knew how to treat small children. Sometimes he was envious of men who had grown-up sons with whom they could hold intelligent discussions. I possessed such sons and realised how lucky I was to have one of them sharing my work. I felt like placing one of his cool hands on my knee and covering it with my own. This might have woken him up, however, and in any case men are not expected to stroke their children's hands—only mothers do that.

Michael understood his own small son Stephan much better than I ever did my children twenty years ago when they were the same age. Stephan was allowed to wake his father early and share his bath. Before our last trip the little fellow had noticed for the first time that his father was leaving him. He screamed when we reached the airport, clung to Michael and would not let go.

In twenty years' time Michael would sit beside Stephan, just as we two were sitting now! My parents did not reach an old age, so it was unlikely that I myself would live much longer, but Michael would have more memories of me than I had of my father, and our work would continue.

If we had died that night nobody could have made sense out of our many notes on the life of the herds of animals in Serengeti. Nobody else could have edited and cut the seventy thousand feet of coloured film intended to produce *the* film of our dreams. The chances of survival of the Serengeti inhabitants would have been lessened.

This probably seems unimportant to most people, to the people who would say: "Those two didn't deserve any better. Why did they risk their necks for zebras and lions?" Men have other ideals for which they are willing to die: freedom, glory, politics, religion, the rulership of their class, or the expansion of national borders. But in the long run Michael and I will be proved right.

Millions feared Hitler and millions were enthralled by him. Millions laid down their lives for him and other millions died fighting against him. To-day, when German schoolchildren are asked questions about Hitler, most of them know very little about him and cannot even name his henchmen.

The same applies to Napoleon, to the Anabaptists, the Hussites, and the protagonists of the first World War.

Men are easily inspired by human ideas, but they forget them again just as quickly. Only Nature is eternal, unless we senselessly destroy it. In fifty years' time nobody will be interested in the results of the conferences which fill today's headlines.

But when, fifty years from now, a lion walks into the red dawn and roars resoundingly, it will mean something to people and quicken their hearts whether they are bolshevists or democrats, or whether they speak English, German, Russian or Swahili. They will stand in quiet awe as, for the first time in their lives, they watch twenty thousand zebras wander across the endless plains.

Is it really so stupid to work for the zebras, lions and men who will walk the earth fifty years from now? And for those in a hundred or two hundred years' time . . . ?

I did not sleep much during the night of 9th–10th January, as I was too cold and damp. I half sat and half lay in my seat, changing position from time to time, but taking care not to disturb Michael. What at last the dawn came we wrung out our things and hung them on the aeroplane to dry. Our faithful "duck" looked like a back garden on washing day and I was sorry that I had no camera with me. As soon as the clothes and blankets had begun to dry a little it started to rain again. We bundled everything into the cabin, wet or dry, and I draped a towel round my hips while Michael wrung out a singlet and put it on.

We had made our home in a hut in the Ngorongoro crater for the last few days, so we flew back there and clambered, half-naked, out of the aeroplane. The sun was shining brightly in the crater and one of the boys spread our things on the grass to dry.

You never know your luck, with wild animals. Sometimes you may track elephants for hours, days or even weeks in order to photograph or film them. Just when you have given up in despair one of them will unexpectedly appear, flap his ears, raise his trunk and give a splendidly photogenic display.

This is exactly what happened to us in the case of the flamingoes. During that morning a delegation of four hundred birds settled in the shallow waters of the lake inside the crater and took almost no notice of us. We placed chains on the tyres of our Land-Rover, drove it straight through the mud and into gradually increasing depths of water. We could only drive in a straight line, for as soon as we tried to turn the wheels lost their grip on the slippery bottom.

Finally we dared go no farther, so we stopped the motor, adjusted the telephoto-lens and waited. The flamingoes came closer and closer, poking their heads into the shallow water in their search for food. Our large car did not disturb them in the slightest. We decided four or five times not to waste another foot of our precious film on them, but they came ever closer and loomed ever larger on the ground glass view-finder so that we simply *had* to take another shot. In the end, we had so many pictures that we were almost relieved when they spread their black wings and rose like a pink curtain to fly away.

Since we could not turn the car we reversed until we were on solid ground again. Meanwhile the boy had prepared a mountainous salad of pineapples, apples and bananas. We fried ourselves a steak, and then Michael left. He wanted to fly over L'Engai, Lake Natron and the Salei plain to look for animals which we could film together on the following day.

He asked me not to accompany him as he intended to call at Banagi on the way back in order to collect our two collaborators and bring them to the crater. We had removed one of the back seats to make room for the aerial camera, and there were only three seats left. If we carried four people in the 'plane now the insurance company might raise objections in case of an accident.

I was quite satisfied to remain behind as I had a lot of work to do. I begged Michael to return punctually before half-past six, as having to listen for the sound of the engine during the last half hour of daylight always made me nervous. That is why I preferred to fly myself. Michael thought it might grow too late, so in order not to take any risks he decided to spend the night at Banagi.

We pushed back the car which some Masai children had playfully rolled down the slope into some bushes. I sat down at my work-table and took no notice when Michael left. For a little while I could hear the distant droning of the engine . . .

Postscript

As Dr. Grzimek sat at breakfast in his hut in the Ngorongoro crater the next morning, a black scout reached through the window and placed a sheet of paper on the table. The game warden had written: "I am sorry to tell you that Michael has crashed in the aeroplane and been killed. He is lying at my house."

Quite by chance the 'plane was seen by an Englishman who, with his African assistants, was prospecting for water in the deserted Salei plains. They saw the striped machine flying at about six hundred feet when it suddenly dived. Since the boys insisted that it was not a landing but an accident he sent them after it in the car.

They found the machine smashed to pieces, but it had not caught fire.

Meanwhile it had grown dark. The headlamps of the car did not work, and they dared not light matches because of the strong smell of petrol. They went back for the Englishman who quickly brought a second car and torches. They pulled Michael's body from the wreckage. Despite their fatigue the two black assistants laid it in the car and drove all night to the home of the game warden on the rim of the Ngorongoro crater.

Michael Grzimek had been killed instantly. He was buried the same day in the evergreen landscape, at a place overlooking the floor of the crater, and its herds of animals.

British air officials investigated the cause of the accident. They found that a griffon-vulture had collided with the right wing and *bent it. This had blocked the rudder-cables and the machine had dived downwards in a steep right-hand curve. The official statement confirmed that Michael Grzimek had been an experienced, careful and reliable flier and that the accident had not resulted from negligence on the part of the pilot or shortcomings of the aeroplane. It had been due to one of those external chances to which light aeroplanes are always exposed in these altitudes.*

By this time Michael Grzimek's research work was virtually complete. He and his helpers had also finished the film on which he had been working during the previous months. This was intended to reveal the beauties of the Serengeti to the public throughout the world and to ask them to help preserve these wonders of nature.

In an article published in the East African daily press, the administration of Tanganyika National Parks mourned the death of Michael Grzimek and declared that the cause of Nature Preservation in Africa had lost one of its bravest and most active protagonists. It asked the public to subscribe towards a Michael Grzimek Memorial Fund. From the money which was sent in by black and white people and to which everybody in any country may still contribute, the British administration decided to build a laboratory for scientists in the Serengeti, which will bear Michael Grzimek's name, and to protect wild animals in the Serengeti. The administration erected a memorial stone on Michael's grave at the rim of the Ngorongoro crater, bearing the inscription:

MICHAEL GRZIMEK
12.4.1934–10.1.1959

*He gave all he possessed for the wild
animals of Africa, including his life*

After Some Years . . .

The readers of this and the many previous editions of *Serengeti Shall Not Die* will perhaps be interested to learn what has happened to the Serengeti National Park and to its animals in the five years which have elapsed since the book was first published.

In 1959, soon after Michael Grzimek's tragic death and before the results of his investigations could be made public, the Colonial Government decided to excise from the Serengeti National Park the eastern portion of the plains and the famous Ngorongoro Crater. This excised portion was made into the Ngorongoro Conservation Area, a statutory body set up by the Government and charged with the duty of conserving water supply, forest and pasture in the area—primarily in the interest of man, but with due regard to the preservation of wild animal life. In the words of the Governor, Sir Richard Turnbull, "It is the intention of the Government to develop the Crater in the interests of the people who use it. At the same time the Government intends to protect the game animals of the area; but should there be any conflict between the interests of the game and the human inhabitants, those of the latter must take precedence." Hunting is still strictly prohibited and in general both the Masai and their cattle continue to live in harmony with the wild animals as they had done there since about 1860. Unfortunately, during the first year or so of the new regime, the Masai did spear a considerable number of rhinos and sold their horns to illegal dealers (these events are related in Dr. Grzimek's recent book *Rhinos Belong to Everybody*). The epidemic of rhino spearing was brought under control by Mr. Henry Fosbrooke, the new Conservator of the area and his successor, Mr. G. U. Rugarabamu. They have managed to prevent wide-scale killing of rhinos, both in the Crater itself and in most of the surrounding district. The number of Ngorongoro rhinos has noticeably recovered.

In exchange for the area it had lost — an area unique in its beauty of landscape and of crucial ecological importance to the vast herds during the wet season — the Serengeti National Park obtained extensive new tracts of land lying to the north and southwest of its old boundaries. In general, this land was of much less ecological value to the Park, both in the nature of the pasture and in the use made of it by the migrating herds. The new areas had been little used until then or claimed by the Masai.

"The success of the book *Serengeti Shall Not Die*, which has been published in twenty-four languages, drew the attention of many people in different countries to the Serengeti and its problems. So, also, did the film of the same title which won an American Oscar for the best documentary film of the year. This awakening of interest, both inside Tanzania and in the world at large, has helped the present Director to enlist the help not only of the present newly independent Tanzania Government, but of organisations and individuals in Europe and America," writes Mr. John Owen, the present Director of Tanzania National Parks.

"For I realised that without such help it would not be possible to put in the crash programmes of research and development which were essential if the Serengeti was to be given a good chance of surviving for posterity. Moreover, I immediately set out to acquire a number of light aeroplanes for use in the National Parks system, convinced of their value by the Grzimeks' experience in the Serengeti. The director and a number of other Parks staff learnt to fly and there are now no fewer than five aeroplanes in use in the National Parks. In this we were assisted financially by Professor Grzimek and the Frankfurt Zoological Society. There has resulted a new method of running African National Parks, which is no less than a revolution in their administration, due to the speed, efficiency and economy of light aircraft. These are regarded now as essential tools both in management and research."

In 1961, three years after the Grzimeks' work, another census of the animals of the Serengeti was carried out, partly by the Royal Air Force and partly by a team led by an American biologist, Dr. Lee Talbot. This census covered a larger area and took place later in the year after all the animals had calved and survey produced considerably higher figures than those found by the Grzimeks. Rapid fluctuations in population are well-known features of animal population dynamics and it would appear that in the Serengeti the population cycle is in a phase of increase. Thus in 1963, Mr. Murray Watson, biophylactist who was continuing the work of the Grzimeks, carried out another census which again showed an increase, this time of forty per cent in the number of wildebeest between 1961 and 1963. In 1965, their number had risen to 1,300,000 heads. The realisation that these vast herds have rapidly grown in number over the last few years has focused the attention of the National Parks authorities on the problem of over-grazing and over-stocking. Mr. Owen has succeeded in setting up a small international Research Institute in the Serengeti and in attracting to its work a number of distinguished young scientists. They are engaged in investigating the whole ecology of the area, having special regard to the problem of over-grazing. Their preliminary conclusions tend to show that the dangers of over-stocking may be less than was anticipated, due to the various controlling factors which exist. Should these tentative conclusions be confirmed by further work now being carried out, it will then be possible to follow the classical European concept of National Parks as untouched wilderness areas where human management should only interfere if this can in no other way be avoided.

The group of biophylactists now working at Banagi in the Serengeti, using the "Michael Grzimek Laboratory" which was erected as a result of donations from the people of Tanzania and from readers of the different editions of this book throughout the world, include ecologists, behaviourists, veterinarians and specialists in other branches of biological sciences. These scientists follow the herd in cars or in small planes and are investigating the way in which the many different species of animals, plant, soil and climate each interact on each other and on the general ecology of the area. The results of their work, as they are added to from year to year, will be applicable to large areas of similar habitats in Africa and should help new African States to conserve one of the most important of their natural resources, and to utilise it more effectively.

Mr. Owen has also initiated a very effective drive to awaken African opinion to the value of their National Parks. This campaign includes hostels for African school-children in the National Parks, a series of films in Swahili—the first being *Serengeti Shall Not Die*[1]—posters and brochures; it is directed by a full-time Education Officer. The book, *Serengeti Shall Not Die,* has been translated into Swahili by Mr. G. M. Maina for use in East African schools. In this approach, the National Parks have received most valuable support from the President of Tanzania, Mr. Julius Nyerere, who has publicly stated his determination to ensure the survival of wild life in Tanzania, and has taken a personal and effective interest in the problems of the Serengeti. He has now personally decided that the new wild human settlements adjoining the northern and north-western boundary of the Serengeti Park will be moved so that the annual migration of the big herds shall never be endangered.

His interest, and that of the other leaders of the Government, particularly the Honourable D. N. M. Bryceson, the Minister for Lands, Forests and Wildlife, has resulted in a rapid development of the National Parks system in Tanzania. When the first edition of this book was written, Tanzania had one National Park, the Serengeti, which had just been truncated. Since Independence, four other Parks have been established (Lake Manyara, Ngurdoto Crater, Ruaha and Mikumi Parks) and are developed to a stage where visitors can enjoy them. Furthermore, other new large areas have been set aside as future National Parks and plans are attractively going ahead to have them fully established.

All this, and the fact that the Tanzania Government has doubled its expenditure on National Parks during the last year, is concrete evidence of Tanzania's determination to do its share in the conservation of these unique areas.

[1] It was the first full length evening programme film which has been dubbed in the Swahili language.

But Tanzania is still an undeveloped country; its people badly need more hospitals, more schools, increased communications and all the other things that are necessary to raise the standard of living of its people. The National Parks of Tanzania are a common heritage, not only of the people of Tanzania but of mankind as a whole. Visitors who are coming in increasing numbers from Europe and America, thanks to the decreasing cost of air transport, gain inspiration and pleasure from seeing one of the last remaining corners of paradise in our world. But they must realise that they only pay a small amount of what it costs to keep these Parks going. The bigger part comes from the pocket of needy Africans such as the overseas visitor sees and meets during his visit.

Therefore I venture to ask those who are as concerned as I am to preserve these last wonders of free nature in Africa, to come to the help of the wonderful work now being done in the National Parks of Tanzania by sending contributions to the "Michael Grzimek Memorial Fund," c/o Tanzania National Parks, P.O. Box 3134, Arusha, Tanzania.

Bibliography

Baumann, Oskar, *Durch Massailand zur Nilquelle*, Berlin 1894

Boell, Ludwig, *Die Operationen in Ost-Afrika*, Hamburg 1951

Demoll, Reinhard, *Bandigt den Menschen*, Munich 1954

Geigy, R., *Observations sur les Phacocheres du Tanganyika*, Revue Suisse de Zoologie, Geneva 1955

Geigy, R. u. Herbig, A., *Erreger und Ubertrager tropischer Krankheiten*, Zurich 1955

Gotzen, Graf von, *Duetsch-Ostafrika in Aufstand* 1905/06, Berlin 1909

Grzimek, Bernhard, *Kein Platz fur wilde Tiere*, Munich 1956

Harroy, Jean-Paul, *Afrique qui meurt*, Brussels 1949

Hediger, Heini, *Kleine Tropenzoologie*, Basle 1958

Huntingford, G. W. B., *The southern Nilo-Hamites*, International African Institute, London 1953

Jaeger, Fritz, *Das Hochland der Reisenkrater und die umliegenden Hochlander Duetsch-Ostafrikas*, Berlin 1911

Koenig, O., *The Masai Story*, London 1955

Leakey, L. S. B., *Stone Age Africa*, London 1955

Lettow-Vorbeck, Gerd v., *Am Fusse des Meru*, Hamburg 1957

Lettow-Vorbeck, Paul v., *Heia Safari. Deutschlands Kampf in Ostafrika*, Leipzig 1920

Lindgens, Arthur, *Der grosse Zoo der Erde*, Munich 1958

Marsh, Z. and Kingsnorth, G. W., *An introduction to the history of East Africa*, Cambridge 1957

Merker, Moritz, *Die Masai*, Berlin 1910

Moffett, J. P., *Handbook of Tanganyika*, Dar es Salaam 1958

Molloy, Peter, *The Cry of the Fish Eagle*, London 1957

Moore, Audrey, *Serengeti*, London 1938

Oliver, James A., *Snakes in Fact and Fiction,* New York 1958

Pearsall, W. H., *Report on an Ecological Survey of the Serengeti,* National Park, Tanganyika, Fauna Preservation Society, London 1'57

Reci, Hans, *Oldoway, die Schlucht des Urmenschen,* Leipzig 1933

Richelmann, G., *Mit Wissmann durch Afrika,* Magdeburg 1892

Sanford, G. R., *An Administrative and Political History of the Masai Reserve,* London 1919

Schramm, Percy Ernst, *Deutschland und Ubersee,* G. Westermann, Brunswick 1959

Steere, G. L., *Judgement on German Africa,* London 1939

Stevenson-Hamilton, J., *South African Eden,* London 1937

Thomson, J., *Through Masailand,* London 1887

Tompo ole Mpaayei, John, *Inkuti Pukunot oo Lmaasai,* London 1954

Townsend, Mary Evelyn, *The rise and fall of Germany's colonial empire,* New York 1930

Wichterich, Richard, *Dr. Carl Peters, der Weg eines Patrioten,* Berlin 1934

——*Report of the Commission of Inquiry on Human and Animal Trypanomiasis in Southern Rhodesia,* Salisbury 1955

——*Report of the Serengeti Committee of Enquiry,* 1957, Dar es Salaam 1958

Scientific reports on the authors' work in the Serengeti appear in English in the journals *Wild Life Management, Zeitschrift fur Tierpsychologie* and *Zeitschrift fur Saugetierkunde.*

Index

Once the rainy season has begun ponds form all over Serengeti.

The spearhead of a heard of wildebeest on the march.